In our fast-paced and increasingly complex world, *Hearts in Devotion* brings welcome relief, rest, and renewed inspiration to meet whatever challenges you may be facing in your day-to-day experiences. The theme throughout points to the building of a loving relationship with the Lord; seeking His Kingdom first, surrendering to His will, and allowing Him to work in order to fulfill your deepest desires.

HEARTS

 in

DEVOTION

ORIGINAL SCRIPTURE-BASED
DAILY DEVOTIONALS

Christine Gaeta

Library of Congress Control Number: 2012905452

Printed in the United States of America

DEDICATION

I dedicate this book to Hearts in Devotion everywhere. To my husband Cel, for his love, help, and support throughout the writing of it. To all the original members of Hearts in Devotion, who inspired me over the years to its completion. My Pastor Mark Foreman, whose sermons and spiritual insights, are weaved into many of these daily devotionals; and to Pastor Jim Doyle who gave me the encouragement and support I needed to make H.I.D. possible. Lastly, my faithful and adorable Maltese doggy Amore, who stayed by my side and patiently waited for her afternoon walks. God bless you all . . . .

INTRODUCTION

Daily devotional reading is a powerful tool that can lift our spirits, re-
energize our faith in the Lord, and strengthen our commitment to love,
trust and serve Him day by day. It also helps us to know and to
understand His will and purpose for our lives, individually and
collectively as a church body. Oswald Chamber's: <u>My Utmost For His
Highest,</u> is one of the greatest devotionals of all time. I have read it many
times throughout the years. The book <u>Abiding in Christ</u> by Andrew
Murray is another classic devotional that has influenced and inspired me
greatly. These and many other Christian authors have helped strengthen
my faith, enabling me to experience some of the true riches that are found
only in having a loving relationship with the Lord. The body of Christ is
like a house that is being built, stone upon stone, each member
contributing to its growth, Jesus Himself being the Chief Cornerstone.
Our part is to enter the work that began so long ago and continue to build
upon the house until its completion.

The one thing that I have come to realize in my creative endeavors, such
as in writing or oil painting, is that God is not so much interested in
receiving another book or great masterpiece of art, or any other thing that
we can make or do. His main interest is in having a loving relationship
with us. The Lord uses our creativity and gives inspiration to further His
plans and purposes; creating beauty that draws people closer to Himself.
He is pleased with our efforts, but these are secondary to the main
importance of knowing Him and being known by Him. A book, a poem, a
beautiful song or piece of art serve only as reflections of the Spirit and
become a fruit of our faith. They are like the icing on a cake. The cake
could represent our character which is what God is most interested in
maturing; the cake needs to be baked before the icing can be added. As
we learn to walk in step with the Lord, He will cause the fruits of our faith
to appear effortlessly. I always think of the words of Andrew Murray who
has said "If the Lord has put a desire into your heart, you

can be certain that He will fulfill it." As we give God first priority in our lives every day, the lily, that is your true divine nature, will appear in all its color and beauty in His perfect timing. My prayer and desire is that the book <u>Hearts in Devotion</u> will serve to help bring the readers fresh inspiration and draw them into a deeper and more loving relationship with the Lord.

Yours in His Abiding Love,
Christine Gaeta

THE GOLDEN CAGE

For you died, and your life is now hidden in Christ in God. When Christ,
who is your life appears, then you also will appear with Him in glory.
Colossians 3:3-4

Birds that live in golden cages
Long to soar where the rivers rage.
With eyes so bright, they strain to see
Over the horizon, where it's wild and free.
With hopeful hearts they dream of flying,
With deep yearning and sighing.
All the while safe and cared for, they stare at the door.
Through bars of gold.
Bars of gold hold treasures unknown
Hidden away from sight.
A loving hand will come at last to open the door,
And give the birds sweet flight.
One day a loving hand will come
And open the golden cage.
The birds will spread their wings at last,
And sing a joyful praise.
As time goes by, the birds abide inside the golden cage.
They were meant to fly over the canyons,
To the place where the rivers rage.
There's a hidden secret inside their joyful song,
They know their loving Master though delayed won't be long.
They soar over mountains and rivers of the Kingdom within;
There, the bars of the golden cage cannot hold them in.
Bars of gold hold treasures unknown;
Hidden away from sight.
A loving hand will come at last, to open the door
And give the birds' sweet flight . . .

SEEKING HIM FIRST

Seek first His kingdom and His righteousness, and all these things will be given to you as well. (Matt. 6:33)

Before the new day begins, when we come to seek the Lord with humble and surrendered hearts; His abiding Presence, wisdom, and strength is given to us for the needs of the coming day. Jesus waits and calls for us to seek Him when the morning is new. If you get into the habit of practicing this, you will be putting Him first; making Him your first priority; before any other activity can draw your attention away. God will reward you by overflowing you with His loving Presence. *Know therefore that the Lord your God is God: He is the faithful God, keeping His covenant of love to a thousand generations of those who love Him and keep His commands.* (Dt. 7:9) The Lord has made a covenant of love with you that will last forever. His Kingdom has come into our hearts and fills us each day with newness and fullness of joy. Seeking Him early will bring to your life many blessings; His light will shine bright in you and will continue to grow with ever increasing brightness into that glorious day.

The path of the righteous is like the first gleam of dawn shining ever brighter till the full light of day. (Prov. 4:18) *He who was seated on the throne said, "I am making everything new!" Then He said, "Write this down, for these words are trustworthy and true."* (Rev. 21:5)

LOOKING STRAIGHT AHEAD

Let your eyes look straight ahead, fi x your gaze directly before you. Make level paths for your feet and take only ways that are fi rm. Do not swerve to the right or the left. (Prov. 4:25-27)

It is a discipline to keep your eyes focused upon what is directly before you. We need to make level paths for our feet to travel upon. Straight: is defined in The Strong's Hebrew concordance: *set in order, make erect, honest, and upright.* The Lord has laid out a smooth and well lit place for us to walk in, but sometimes we take the rough, stony, and dark roads for adventure, or because our eyes have drawn us to paths that are not safe. It isn't until we get stuck in a ditch that we finally realize our mistake and get back on track. From the very beginning, God sent John His messenger that went before the Lord crying *"Prepare the way, make straight paths for Him."* (Mk. 1:2-3) Today we are preparing our hearts for His coming again, and it is time to make straight paths for Him; to make our ways honest and upright. We have His Holy Spirit as our guide to show us which way we should go and to keep our eyes fixed firmly upon the Lord and upon His Word.

Whether you turn to the right or to the left, your ears will hear a voice behind you, saying, "This is the way; walk in it." (Isa. 30:21)

NEGATIVE AND POSITIVE CHANGES

For our light and momentary troubles are achieving for us an eternal glory that far outweighs them all. (2 Cor. 4:17)

As we reflect upon the days that have gone past and anticipate the days ahead, we find that there have been lessons learned. Yesterdays are gone and the mistakes we made cannot be changed. Some of the opportunities we did not take will never come to us again, but the Lord can change what Satan may have meant for our harm, into what will turn out to be for our greatest good! I have watched this happen over and over again, both in my own life and in other people's lives too. After the trial is over, and the storm clouds vanish, we become wiser and discerning; ready for whatever the future brings. The Lord uses both the negative and the positive occurrences to change and transform us in order to bring us into spiritual maturity. In Jesus we find the fountain of life; His light banishes the darkness. *For with You is the fountain of life; in Your light, we see light.* (Ps. 36:9) In this New Year, if we give Him the first priority of our day, He will give us understanding about the things He was doing in our past and will shine His light upon our present. We do not know what will happen in the future, but God's Word promises that it will be glorious if we allow Him to make both the negative and positive changes, transforming our lives into an eternal glory.

Christ in you, the hope of glory. (Col. 1:27)

January 4

THE POTTERS WHEEL

This is the Word that came to Jeremiah from the Lord: Go down to the potter's house, and there I will give you my message. So I went down to the potter's house, and I saw him working at the wheel, but the pot he was shaping from the clay was marred in his hands: so the potter formed it into another pot, shaping it as seemed best to him. (Jer. 18:1-4)

Great rest will come to you as a result of submitting to the re-shaping of your life on the Master Potter's wheel. If we are honest with ourselves, we will agree that there have been times that we have jumped off because the changes were too uncomfortable and hard to bear. The Lord is so patient and compassionate with us when we try to take things into our own hands and resist the painful shaping and carving. Eventually we come to know and to trust in His workmanship and understand that it does us no good to fight against Him. There is a bigger design and purpose being formed. Although we do not know what He is aiming at, we learn to submit and to trust God for the desired outcome. Let us yield to the re-shaping, the molding and carving of the Potter's wheel; for the loving hands of the Lord is directing it and knows exactly what needs to be done in order to produce the image of His Son with precision and perfection, *shaping us as it seems best to Him;* for the Lord is the Master Potter and we are all the works of His hand.

Yet, O Lord, You are our Father. We are the clay, You are the potter; we are all the work of Your hand. (Isa.64:8)

A PAINFUL PROCESS

Does the clay say to the potter, "What are you making?" (Isa.4 5:9)

But who are you, O man, to talk back to God? Shall what is formed say to Him who formed it, "Why did you make me like this?" (Rom. 9:19)

I have found myself complaining as well and wondering what is God doing? Questioning God reflects a lack of trust. How much do you trust Him to work in your life? Laying down our hopes, dreams, family, and circumstances and surrendering it all over to God is not an easy thing to do, yet it is what he asks of us. This is also a test of our faith. Here we are at the beginning of another year. Time is a concern for us, but not to God. Let Him take all the time He needs to do His work to its completion. *"Concerning things to come, do you question me about my children, or give me orders about the work of my hands? It is I who made the earth and created mankind upon it. My own hands stretched out the heavens; I marshaled their starry host."* (Isa. 9:11-12) God the Father is making and forming us as He sees best; yielding to the Potter's hand is a painful process but it is where our divine destiny begins, and where it will have its ultimate conclusion and height of perfection: Let His image and purpose be formed and fulfilled in us.

My dear children, for whom I am again in the pains of childbirth until Christ be formed in you. (Gal. 4:19)

GOD SAW THAT IT WAS GOOD

God called the dry ground land and the gathered waters He called seas. And God saw that it was good. (Gen. 1:10)

In the beginning of all creation, *God saw that it was good.* All throughout the first chapter of Genesis, after each of His creations, *God saw that it was good.* Moving forward through the book of Genesis, we see clearly the rise and fall of the good and then throughout the entire Bible we see the good and evil portrayed and lived out in the people's lives. The good is always what triumphs over evil in the end. *For by Him all things were created: things in heaven and on earth, visible and invisible.* (Col.1:16) *For we are God's workmanship, created in Christ Jesus to do good works, which God prepared in advance for us to do.* (Ephes. 2:10) We are His creation, made for good works; the Lord has in His mind the things he has purposed for us to do. The more we draw near to Him, the more we understand what His will and purpose is for us. It is by Jesus Christ that *all things were made* that was made, and all things *God saw that it was good* and that includes you and me.

Through Him all things were made; without Him nothing was made that has been made. (Jn. 1:3)

THE NEW YOU

Put on the new self, created to be like God in true righteousness and holiness. (Ephes. 4:24)

It is hard sometimes for us to understand the way God actually sees us. We have a new nature that has been created in Christ Jesus; made in true righteousness and holiness, yet we continue to wrestle with the things of this world. Our own physical and emotional tendencies often bring discouragement and disappointment. We wonder, what does God see in me? How can He love me so strong and faithfully when I disappoint Him so often? This is because we cannot yet see what we will become. God the Father sees us as fully redeemed in Christ; perfected without spot or wrinkle; Jesus sees us as His treasure and reward. He is the Creator, let Him continually, morning by morning, have the rule over your life, and He will bring that good creation, the "new you" into completion. With eyes of faith, let us acknowledge and receive the fullness of our redemption and move into the future. This is what God says about us; the old has passed away, it is gone! I am brand new each and every morning as I yield my will in order to have His will done in my life. *You are worthy, our Lord and God, to receive glory and honor and power, for You created all things, and by Your will they were created and have their being.* (Rev.4:11) It is time to let go of the past, move forward, and become all that God has purposed for you to be; as you daily surrender your will, you will begin to see what God sees: the new you.

I will give them an undivided heart and put a new spirit in them. (Eze. 11:19)

KINGDOM RESTORED

Let us make man in our image, in our likeness, and let them rule over the fish of the sea and the birds of the air, over the livestock, over all the earth; and over all the creatures that move along the ground. (Gen. 1:26)

It was God's intent from the beginning of the creation of man that he should rule over the creatures and things of the earth. It was a beautiful Kingdom in its original form, mankind having dominion and living in complete freedom and harmony with all of nature. Adam, the first man was truly a son of God, and Eve his wife, a beloved daughter. They were the first children of the Father, made in His image and likeness. We do not know how long that perfect original Kingdom on earth lasted, but sadly the fall of mankind and the entrance of sin into the world made it necessary for the Redeemer to come in order to restore what was lost. Now we, who have received our redemption through Jesus Christ, have been made heirs to a Kingdom restored. We wait in expectation for the completion and full redemption of our bodies and of the whole earth. The catastrophes that happen are like birth pains that will eventually make way for the new creation and kingdom that is still yet to come. God will do this all in His perfect timing.

Now if we are children, then we are heirs—heirs of God and co-heirs with Christ, if indeed we share in His sufferings in order that we may also share in His glory. (Rom. 8:17)

OUR KINGDOM IN CHRIST

We know that the whole creation has been groaning as in the pains of childbirth right up to the present time; we ourselves groan inwardly as we wait eagerly for our adoption as sons the redemption of our bodies. (Rom. 8:22-23)

Although we have been given new spirits that have been made one with Christ, our physical bodies, the earth, and all its creatures are groaning for the time when their full redemption will come. It is so terrible to see suffering, pain, and death in this world. As believers in Christ, we hold within our hearts a great hope for that glorious kingdom that is yet to come. It is *Christ who gives us the strength to stand firm;* (2 Cor. 1:21) we have been given His seal of ownership, and His Spirit as our guarantee. *And you also were included in Christ when you heard the Word of truth, the gospel of your salvation. Having believed, you were marked in Him with a seal, the promised Holy Spirit, who is a deposit guaranteeing our inheritance until the redemption of those who are God's possession—to the praise of His glory.* (Ephes. 1:13-14) The kingdom of Christ presently resides in our hearts, but when our full redemption arrives, we will see His Kingdom come into its fullness in the earth and in our bodies. There will be no more sickness, pain, or death and the earth will be completely restored and made new again.

How great is the love the Father has lavished on us, that we should be called children of God! And that is what we are! (1 Jn. 3:1)

January 10

TRUST

Those who know Your name, will trust in You, for you Lord, have never forsaken those who seek You. (Ps. 9:10)

When we put our trust in someone, it is because we know them. We know that if they say they will do something, they will do it. Time is needed to develop trust. The older we get, the more we learn to trust in what is dependable and in things that have proven to be true. Looking back over my life, I have found the Lord and His Word to be true and trustworthy; even though I may have doubted, He proved His faithfulness to me. When everything in this world falls apart, fades away, withers and dies, God's Word stands true and firm. His Word endures forever and His love is from everlasting to everlasting. Taking the time to know the Lord is the very best investment you could make of your time and energy. He knows all who are His and will never forsake those who put their complete trust in Him. The longer we know the Lord, the more we learn to trust Him because He proves Himself to be faithful to us. We cannot be moved or shaken, but become like strong mountains that will stand and endure forever.

Those who trust in the Lord are like Mount Zion which cannot be shaken but endures forever. (Ps. 125:1)

WHAT IS IN A NAME?

These things have I written unto you that believe on the Name of the Son of God; that you may know that you have eternal life, and that you may believe on the Name of the Son of God. (1 Jn.15:13)

When we think of someone's name, we associate the name with what that person represents to us. The name brings to mind their character and nature, we think of the things they've done and the memories of experiences shared. The longer you know them, the more you grow to love and to trust in him or her all depending upon their character and nature. In the same way, the longer we know the Name of Jesus, who He is to us, what He represents to us, His character and nature; the more we grow to love and to trust Him. In Psalms 124:8 it tells us that *our help is in the name of the Lord who made heaven and earth.* We can call upon the name of the Lord and receive our help when needed. He has given us His most excellent name and now as His representatives we go forth in the power of His name and of His Spirit. Everything that Jesus is, His loving nature, wisdom, strength and power are all encompassed within His wonderful name.

That at the name of Jesus every knee shall bow in heaven and on earth and under the earth. (Phil. 2:10)

THE PRECIOUS NAME OF JESUS

A good name is better than precious ointment. (Eccl. 7:1)

As we give to Him all of ourselves in loving surrender each morning, He in turn gives us all that He is, His name and the use of it. We pray in the name of Jesus. As we seek Him more each day with renewed hope and faith, we receive answers to our prayers in His precious name. What is in a name? Absolutely everything! *God has exalted Him to the highest place and gave Him the name that is above every name.* (Phil. 2:9) We have been called by His name and have been given the privilege to use His name when praying. There is life and power in His name; it is through believing that we may have this life in His name. (Jn. 20:31) The Father wants us to give thanks to Him for everything in Jesus' name. (Ephes. 5:20) What a gift we have in the precious name of Jesus! In every situation, we can call on His name and He will come to help us. It does not matter how far away from the Lord you have drifted or even the worst sinner you can imagine; *whosoever shall call upon the name of the Lord shall be saved!*

Whatsoever you do in word or deed, do all in the name of the Lord Jesus, giving thanks to God and the Father by Him. (Col. 3:17)

THE BRIGHT PATH

The path of the righteous is like the first gleam of dawn, shining ever brighter till the full light of day. (Prov. 4:18)

I love to envision the first gleam of dawn becoming brighter and brighter as the new morning approaches. The Lord has filled us with His glorious light. He is faithful to shine His light upon our pathways as we move on from the dawn of our salvation into the noon day: the full light of maturity. We can begin to understand this as a spiritual journey of growth; from when we first believed, to the final stage of the fullness in Christ. When Jesus walked the earth, the people saw a great light. The light of the Lord dispels all darkness. *The people walking in darkness have seen a great light: on those living in the land of the shadow of death a light has dawned.* (Isa. 9:2) When Jesus spoke again to the people, He said, *I am the light of the world. Whoever follows me will never walk in darkness, but will have the light of life.* (Jn. 8:12)

For we were once darkness, but now are we light in the Lord, we are to live as children of light. (Ephes. 5:8)

LOVING IN THE LIGHT

Love is the fulfillment of the law. Knowing the time, and that now it is high time to awake out of sleep, for now is our salvation nearer than when we believed. The night is far spent, the day is at hand: let us therefore cast off the works of darkness and let us put on the armor of light. (Rom. 13:10-12)

What does it mean to live as children of the light? Showing love to one another is an important part of it. The Lord tells us that we, His followers, are the light of the world. As we daily draw close to the Lord and learn to abide in Him as His followers, the light and love He has given us will shine ever brighter until that perfect day. The Lord will be faithful to bring all of His people into the fullness of His glorious light as we look to Him to make our daily paths bright. The more we learn to love one another as Christ has shown His love for us, the brighter our light in Him will become.

A city that is set on a hill cannot be hid. Let your light so shine before men, that they may see your good works, and glorify your Father which is in heaven. (Matt. 5:14-16)

SEEING THE LORD

In the year King Uzziah died, I saw the Lord seated on a throne, high and exalted, and the train of his robe filled the temple. (Isa. 6:1)

King Uzziah was a high example to Isaiah and when he died, he did not get discouraged or disheartened; He saw the Lord. He had a vision of the LORD. When the Lord takes things away from you, look for a new vision and for a revelation, He is doing it for a reason. He wants all your attention and love and He will take things away in order to bring you a greater reward if you will lay those things down at His feet and re-focus your love and attention back to Him. There will be a time coming when we will see His face; the heavenly vision will appear and we will see the Lord at last. In this world we see only a shadow, a dim reflection of Him. Every day we are being changed to look more and more like Him. Our character is slowly being transformed into His image; God is doing this in each one of His people. One day we will awaken in complete likeness to Him. Allow the Lord to make the necessary changes in you; lay it all down so you may reach to the heights of seeing Him.

The pure in heart shall see God (Matt. 5:8)

In righteousness I will see Your face; when I awake, I will be satisfied with seeing Your likeness. (Ps. 17:15)

THE GIFT OF TIME

What is your life? You are a mist that appears for a little while and then vanishes. (Jas. 4:14)

The time we are given upon the earth from birth to death is a gift from the Lord, though it seems to fly away very quickly. Before you know it, the years have passed by, they are gone and irretrievable. *For a thousand years in Your sight are like a day that has just gone by; or like watch in the night.* (Ps. 90:4) Our whole life span is like a blink of an eye from God's eternal perspective. Let us use our time seeking His wisdom and guidance in all things, making the very most of each opportunity. Dear Lord, Help us to understand the gift of time. The time we have been given is a gift from you. Help us to use it for your honor and glory today, teaching us to walk carefully and with wisdom. Amen . . . .

Teach us to number our days aright, that we may gain a heart of wisdom. (Ps. 90:12) *Be wise in the way you act toward outsiders; make the most of every opportunity.* (Col. 4:5)

LIFE IS SHORT

Show me, O Lord, my life's end and the number of my days; let me know how fleeting my life is. (Ps. 39:4)

We live in very uncertain times. Our lives are but for a brief moment. What will we take with us in death? When we stand before the Father what will we have to give to Him? We came into the world with nothing of our own, and when we leave, there will be nothing that we can take with us. *All men are like grass, and all their glory is like the flowers of the field: the grass withers and the flowers fall, but the Word of the Lord stands forever.* (I Pet. 1:24-25) It is because our time on earth is short that we need to consider our actions carefully; seek His wisdom and guidance, for no one knows what tomorrow may bring. The question I ask is what can I give to Him who has done so much for me? What does the Lord desire to receive from us? He desires to have a strong, loving, and trusting relationship with His people. We know that it is our faith that pleases Him; faith that works by our love for Him and for one another. When we take the time to know Him; you are using your time in the most valuable way possible.

You have made my days a mere handbreadth, the span of my years are as nothing before You Each man's life is but a breath. (Ps. 39:5)

THE GIFT OF GOD

Every good and perfect gift is from above, coming down from the Father of the heavenly lights, who does not change like shifting shadows. (Jas 1:17) *You are always the same, Your years never end. The children of your people will live in security, their children's children will thrive in your presence.* (Ps. 102:27)

If we are trusting and surrendered to the Lord, we are His children. The Lord has always cared for His own and we thrive and abound in His Presence. All throughout the Scripture, God re-affirms His faithfulness to all who put their love and trust in Him. That seems to be the condition needed to be fulfilled in order to obtain the provision and promise. It is encouraging to know that by our act of surrender, God will be everything and provide far above all we could ask or think as we learn to abide *in His presence* daily.

Now to Him who is able to do immeasurably more than all we ask or imagine, according to His power that is at work within us, to Him be glory in the Church and in Christ Jesus throughout all generations, forever and ever! Amen . . . (Ephes. 3:20-21)

MADE FOR ETERNITY

He has made everything beautiful in its time. He has also set eternity in the hearts of men; yet they cannot fathom what God has done from beginning to end. (Eccl. 3:11)

Life is a gift and although our time is limited upon the earth, there is something inside of us that tells us we were meant to last; to go on. It is because God our Creator has set eternity in our hearts. We are eternal beings, immortal. Our actions will determine where we will be for eternity; united to the light and love of God, or separated from the light and in darkness. Tomorrow is not promised, we only have the present. Draw near to Him and seek Him today. Put the Lord first in everything for your life here on this earth is as a vapor that appears for a short while and then vanishes away. God has set eternity in our hearts. We are yearning for our eternal home, looking for the heavenly place that He has prepared for us. So we use the things of the world, but do not allow ourselves to be taken up and carried away by them.

Those who use the things of this world, as if not engrossed in them; for this world in its present form is passing away. So we fi x our eyes not on what is seen, but on what is unseen. For what is seen is temporary, but what is unseen is eternal. (1Cor. 7:31) & (2 Cor. 4:18)

January 20

PROMISED INHERITANCE

For God is not unjust to forget your work and labor of love which you have shown toward His name. And we desire that each one of you show the same diligence to the full assurance of hope until the end, that you do not become sluggish, but imitate those who through faith and patience inherit the promises. (Heb. 6:10-12)

Sometimes we say to ourselves it's just not fair! It seems that your labors are going unrewarded with little appreciation. We can become discouraged and draw back to our old way of thinking and life. It is in those times that we need to remind ourselves that God sees and does not forget our labors of love. The Lord reassures us that the works we do in Him are never in vain and that our reward is certain. Anything in life that is good and worthwhile takes effort and work. Whether you are working on a piece of art, working to sustain your family, attending college or whatever your place in life is. In order to become accomplished in anything, it takes practice and discipline. So it is in spiritual matters. We need to spend the time it takes to build relationship with God, and you will receive blessings beyond what you can imagine!

Therefore, my dear brothers, stand firm. Let nothing move you. Always give yourselves fully to the work of the Lord, because you know that your labor in the Lord is not in vain. (I Cor. 15:58) The Lord is not slow in keeping His promise, as some understand slowness. He's patient with you. (2 Pet. 3:9)

IT TAKES PERSEVERANCE

The one who sows to please the Spirit, from the Spirit will reap eternal life. Let us not become weary in doing well, for at the proper time we will reap a harvest if we do not give up. (Gal. 6:8-9)

It takes perseverance and faithfulness to stay the course, finish the race, and inherit the promises. The key contained in Galatians is *if we do not give up*. Satan wants us to give up and say, "It's too hard, I'll never make it." Don't listen! Resist those thoughts and through faith and perseverance, in the Lord's time, you will reap a harvest. Hold fast, stand firm, and continue your course with faith and perseverance and you will receive the promised inheritance; here in this life, and in the life to come. (Mk.10:31) The Lord also tells us that with the inheritance, you will have persecution. The reason it takes perseverance is because serving the Lord is hard to do at times; people don't understand and you might lose old friends and even your own family. When we keep the end goal in our minds, we must decide that we will not give up no matter how hard it gets. It takes perseverance. Paul the Apostle was encouraging the church of the Thessalonians when he said:

"We continually remember before our God and Father your work produced by faith, your labor prompted by love, and your endurance inspired by hope in our Lord Jesus Christ." (I Thes. 1:3)

NOTHING TO HARD FOR GOD

Ah Lord God, behold, Thou hast made the heaven and the earth by thy great power and stretched out arm, and there is nothing too hard for You. (Jer. 32:17)

There are times we feel as though the Lord is prompting us to do something that is contrary to our common sense. Obedience that is pleasing to the Lord works by our actions of faith. It is in those times that we must look and lean into the everlasting arms of the Father to carry us, and realize that even if what I'm about to do may seem crazy, I'm going to trust that God will make it turn out right. Is anything too hard for God? We have confidence that He will move in our behalf because we were obedient to act according to the leading of the Spirit, and made the decision to trust Him and not to put our confidence in our own way of thinking and strength. It is through Him, we obtain the victory in every situation. Not only will we be victorious, but we shall do valiantly! When all the odds seem stacked against us, and we are fully trusting in God to deliver us, it is in those times that God receives the greatest glory. The Lord will rise up and do the fighting for us. There is nothing too hard for God.

Through our God, we shall do valiantly; it is He who will trend down our enemies. (Ps. 108:13) *The eternal God is your refuge, and underneath are the everlasting arms.* (Dt. 33:27)

HEROIC FAITH

The Lord gave them rest on every side, just as He had sworn to their forefathers. Not one of their enemies withstood them. (Jos. 21:44)

There are so many stories throughout the Bible where God shows Himself strong in behalf of faith filled obedient people. We as believers in Christ, have spiritual battles we're confronted with every day. The Lord will make a way where there seems to be no way. Heroic faith: it takes courage to take a stand in faith and in obedience. When we do, God fulfills His promise to us; He always has and He always will. It is God who made all the heavens and the earth and nothing is impossible with Him. Yes, there will be battles, trials, and sufferings that we will have throughout life, but nothing can move us from the solid rock of God's love and of His Word. The Father watches over every circumstance and event that we go through and has allowed it to further develop our trust and faith in Him. Lean upon Him in those times and do not faint. It takes heroic faith at times but He is faithful who has promised to carry us when we cannot seem to take another step.

"No one will be able to stand up against you all the days of your life. I will never leave you or forsake you. (Jos. 1:5-8) I will never leave you; never will I forsake you." (Heb. 13:5)

January 24

SORROW'S PURPOSE

Sorrow is better than laughter; for by the sadness of the countenance the heart is made better. (Eccl. 7:3)

When we experience sorrow in life, we know that the Lord felt sorrow to a much greater extent. It is an important part of our growing and of our learning. We take comfort in knowing that the Lord understands and is always present to comfort and help get us through it. Sorrow is actually good for our hearts; it enlarges them and increases our sensitivity to others, giving us compassion for those who are suffering. *Sorrow is better than laughter, because a sad face is good for the heart. The heart of the wise is in the house of mourning, but the heart of fools is in the house of pleasure.* (Eccl. 7:2) The best thing is that we know it will not endure for too long. We will find joy awaiting us at the end of the sadness. At that time our capacity for joy will increase as well. The Lord brings rain and sunshine into our lives. Let the rain fall and the winds blow for it is in those times that we are being molded and shaped for His special purposes. The song The Rose by Bette Milder at the end went sometime like this; "just remember in the winter, far beneath the bitter snow, lays a seed that with the sun's love, in the spring becomes a rose."

He was despised and rejected by men, and carried our sorrows. (Is 53:3-4)
Weeping may remain for a night, but joy comes in the morning. (Ps. 30:5)

OVER-COMERS REWARD

He who has an ear, let him hear what the Spirit says to the churches. To him who overcomes, I will give the right to eat from the tree of life, which is the paradise of God. (Rev. 2:7)

There are so many rewards promised to every faithful believer in Christ; to all those who overcome the trials and temptations of this life. Sometimes, we get so caught up in the problems and concerns of living that we forget about the rewards we will receive. We will inherit all the benefits and rewards the Lord has promised; unfortunately, many hear the Lord's call but do not respond, they choose to continue living according to their own ways and wills. They know the truth of God's Word, but refuse to turn around and are not willing to change; they love their darkness more than the light. But to all who *hear* and have given their hearts and lives to God, seeking His will and way, by faith will inherit all the promises. It is our faith that overcomes the world. We have the Spirit of the Lord to give us guidance and all that is needed to bring victory in every circumstance. There is a reward for all who overcome.

For everyone born of God overcomes the world, this is the victory that has overcome the world, even our faith. (1Jn. 5:4)

THE PROMISE

The promise is for you and your children and for all who are far off, for all whom the Lord our God will call. (Ac. 2:39)

The *promise* that Paul is talking about is the greatest of all promises and that is His loving presence forever and ever! We are not that different from the early Christians. They faced the same temptations, trials, and obstacles. The enemy has not changed his tactics; Satan uses his whole arsenal of destructive forces against God's people. The really good news is that the Lord has given us everything we need to defeat him. We were the ones Paul the Apostle was talking about when he said *"all those who are far off."* As we surrender our wills over to God each day, Jesus Christ, through His blood and with the sword of His powerful Word, we can have victory over all darkness and receive the promises for our faithfulness.

I will give some of the hidden manna. I will also give him a white stone with a new name written on it, known only to him who receives it. (Rev. 2:17) Who shall separate us from the love of Christ? Shall trouble or hardship or persecution or famine or nakedness or danger or sword? No in all these things we are more than conquerors through Him who loved us (Rom. 8:35 & 37) I have told you these things, so that in me you may have peace. In this world, you will have trouble, but take heart, I have overcome the world. (Jn. 16:33)

FAITHFUL

Mine eyes shall be upon the faithful of the land that they may dwell with me:

he that walks in a perfect way, he shall serve me. (Ps.101:6) Now it is required

that those who have been given a trust must prove faithful. (1 Cor. 4:2)

When we think of the word *faithful,* what does it bring to our minds? The Webster's Dictionary defines it this way: *Firm or unchanging, adhering firmly to the person, cause, or idea to which one is bound: dutiful and loyal: worthy of trust or credence: consistently reliable: a faithful guide, true, steadfast, constant, devoted.* Faithful in particular, suggests long and undeviating attachment. All of these attributes are what Jesus is to us, He gives us His own example to follow. The Lord is searching out men and women who will be faithful to His cause and to the Kingdom He is establishing upon the earth. We are all partakers in this great work. *Each one of you should use whatever gift he or she has received to serve others, faithfully administering God's grace in its various forms.* (1Pet. 4:10) Whatever we are asked to do, no matter how big or small, faithfulness to do it, consistently, and with our whole hearts, is the greatest way to show our love and devotion to the Lord. The most glorious words we will ever hear will be:

"Well done, good and faithful servant! You have been faithful with a few things: I will put you in charge of many things. Come and share your Master's happiness." (Matt. 25:23)

WHAT ARE SEEDS OF FAITH?

I planted the seed, Apollo's watered it, but God made it grow. So neither he who plants, nor he who waters is anything, but only God, who makes things grow. The man who plants and the man who waters have one purpose, and each will be rewarded according to his own labor. (I Cor. 3:6-8)

All the Words that the Lord has spoken are really seeds of faith. When we share these Words with others, we are planting little seeds of faith. Some take root and grow, others do not. Everyone has been given a garden and some seeds to plant; others come along and water them. Then, God provides the sunlight and rain and makes them grow; He watches over our gardens. What does the water represent?—Love, hope, encouragement, support, strength, and agreement—What about the sunlight? It represents God's light and truth of His Word, shining on, in, around, and through us as we grow in our understanding of His Word. How about the rain? The Holy Spirit that has been given to bring us nourishment that causes our spirits to grow. It is the Lord Himself who makes all things grow and it is God who watches carefully over all of His plantings. We should not hold on to these seeds we've been given, but scatter them around. These little seeds of faith have a large growth potential. They can multiply and grow to be very large trees that produce fruit and many more seeds of faith, exceeding our greatest expectations! When that day comes, the planters, the water bearers, and the gardener can rejoice together and share in a great harvest.

For we are God's fellow workers, you are God's field. (I Cor. 3:9)

GLORY THOUGH SUFFERING

Now if we are children; then we are heirs—heirs of God and co-heirs with Christ, if indeed we share in his sufferings in order that we may also share in His glory. (Rom. 8:17)

God is watching the way we react to our sufferings, and people in the world are watching also. I recently spent time with a dear friend who was stricken with cancer and though she tried different treatments and although so many faith-filled loving friends and ministers prayed for her throughout the whole ordeal, in spite of it all, the Lord took her home to be with Him. It wasn't that her faith or our faith was not strong enough to receive the healing we prayed for, nor was it because of sin in her life or in the others who prayed that prevented the healing from coming. The reason she was not healed, was because it simply was the Lord's timing to take her, and through her sufferings, she glorified God because of her loving heart and courage that so many had witnessed and were inspired by. The Lord uses our suffering and sometimes unanswered prayer for His glory. To bring glory to God is our greatest aim and goal in living examples as Christians. We can take comfort in knowing that the Lord is working strongly throughout our times of suffering and also in our waiting. Our character is what He is interested in forming and it is what will bring Him the greatest glory in the end.

And the God of all grace, who called you to His eternal glory in Christ, after you have suffered a little while, will Himself restore you and make you strong, firm and steadfast. (1 Pet. 5:10)

January 30

READY

At that time the Kingdom of Heaven will be like ten virgins who took their lamps and went out to meet the bridegroom. At midnight the cry rang out, "Here's the bridegroom! Come out to meet Him!" (Matt. 25:1,6)

When I think of meeting the bridegroom, followed by the marriage feast of the Lamb in the marriage union, I get filled with anticipation and wonder! Still the parable of the ten virgins is a sober reminder of the five who were wise and had their oil lamps full and the others who were foolish and did not. The cry came out and was heard, yet five were not ready. To be filled with the oil of the Holy Spirit is something that needs to be replenished every day in order to be wise and not foolish; to be found abiding in Him, full of the light of His Spirit; waiting and watching. The anticipation of the coming of the Lord brings joy and hope in the waiting. The oil could also represent the fruits of the Spirit. The wise virgins were full of the love, joy, peace, faith, patience, and perseverance. There are many other fruits to name but the point is to be found abiding in Him and in having our lamps filled with the oil of His light and full with His love.

The Spirit and the Bride say, "Come! And let him who hears say, Come! Whosoever is thirsty, let him come and whosoever wishes let him take the gift of the water of life." (Rev. 22:17)

NEW MERCIES

Because of the Lord's great love we are not consumed, for His compassions never fail. They are new every morning; great is Your faithfulness. (Lam. 3:22 & 23)

As the sun rises up over the horizon each morning and shines fresh light upon the earth and all of nature; Jesus shines fresh light upon the earth and over all His creation. What happened yesterday is past; there were some good events, and some things may have happened that were not so good. Maybe it was the worst day you can remember for a long while, or it may have been the best day you can recall for a time. We have clear memory of yesterday, but cannot go back and change anything that has already occurred. Each new morning, as we place ourselves and all our concerns into God's loving hands, trusting Him to meet our need for the day, we can actually experience a joy of anticipating what will unfold in the hours to come. Our sins are at once removed and washed away just like a fresh new wave breaking upon the shoreline. His mercies are new every morning.

When we confess our sins and seek forgiveness, He is faithful and just to forgive us all our sins and cleanse us from every unrighteousness. (1Jn 1:9)

I'M YOURS: YOU'RE MINE

"All you have is mine and all I have is yours." (Jn. 17:10)

God is telling us that in Jesus we have been given everything He has, in exchange for everything we have. In the surrendering our lives to Him, He takes all that was broken, sinful, and dark and begins to transform it into something glorious, full of light and wonderful. I can remember a song that you may remember too, it went: "Something beautiful, something good, all my confusion, He understood. All I had to offer Him was brokenness and strife, but He made something beautiful of my life." *He has made everything beautiful in its time.* (Eccl.3:11) Jesus is slowing transforming us and our lives into something that is beautiful and good. *What we will be has not yet been made known. But we know that when He appears, we shall be like Him, for we shall see Him as He is.* (1 Jn. 3:2)

All that belongs to the Father is mine. That is why I said the Spirit will take from what is mine and make it known to you. (Jn. 16:15)

THE FACE OF MY HEART

As a face is reflected in the water, so the heart reflects the person. (Prov. 27:19)

When you look into someone's face, it is the condition of the heart that is reflected in it. If your heart is at peace and is calm, it shows in the facial expression. If in stress or turmoil, anger, or depression, this also shows up. What kind of reflection are we giving to others today? When we have inner joy in Christ; in spite of many trying circumstances and challenges, there is a calm assurance that comes over us. It will be reflected in our eyes and face. If we take some time the first thing in the morning, to get our hearts right with God, we will have a peaceful and calm demeanor that will reflect to others and into the world around us. What is the facial expression of my heart today?

And we, who with unveiled faces all reflecting the Lord's glory, are being transformed into His likeness with ever increasing glory, which comes from the Lord, who is the Spirit. (2 Cor. 3:18)

STRENGTHENED IN THE POWER OF HIS MIGHT

Be strengthened with all power according to His glorious might so that you may have great endurance and patience. (Col. 1:11)

This was Paul's prayer for the Colossian church. It was not something that they could do on their own. They needed the Holy Spirit to help them just as we do today. When you feel oppressed and detached from the Lord; that is the time to call upon Him immediately and seek deliverance. *Be still before the Lord and wait patiently for Him; do not fret when men succeed in their ways, when they carry out their wicked schemes.* (Ps 37:7) When we call upon the Lord to help, He will be faithful to bring the deliverance that is needed. He is compassionate and merciful to all who are sincere in their desire to love and serve Him. Take the time to ask the Lord to fill you with His strength and power; He is willing and always ready to give it. Once again, a renewed determination; a new attitude even towards others who may have offended us in the past will be ours. Learning to look upon others as Jesus does; with compassion, mercy, longsuffering should be our goal. If you find it hard to do, ask the Lord to fill you with His power and love so that you can.

O Lord, be gracious to us; we long for You. Be our strength every morning, our salvation in times of distress. (Isa. 33:2)

DESIRES FULFILLED

Your kingdom is an everlasting kingdom, and Your dominion endures through all generations. The Lord is faithful to all His promises and loving toward all He has made. The Lord upholds all those who fall and lifts up all who are bowed down. The eyes of all look to You, and You give them their food at the proper time. (Ps. 145:13-15)

Over time, the Lord changes our desires and they become His very own. He has placed good and strong desires in our hearts that He promises to fulfill as we give ourselves over to Him and to His will every day. We yearn for this completion in Him. If we are honest, deep down there is a desire, a yearning for goodness and perfection. If we reach out our hands and heart in expectation for the fulfillment of those good desires that God Himself has placed there, they will eventually come into our reality over time, if we do not give up. As we are waiting for His promises to be fulfilled; there is a joy we can have along the way.

You open Your hand and satisfy the desires of every living thing. The Lord is righteous in all His ways and loving toward all He has made. The Lord is near to all who call on Him, an all who call on Him in truth. He fulfills the desires of those who fear Him, He hears their cry and saves them. (Ps. 145:16-19)

JESUS: OUR ETERNAL JOY

I said to the Lord, "You are my Lord; apart from You I have no good thing. You have made known to me the path of life; You will fill me with Joy in Your presence, with eternal pleasures at Your right hand." (Ps. 16:2, 11)

Jesus Himself is our eternal joy. His very presence is our reward and the fulfillment of our every desire. In Him we can begin to understand the gift of life and the joy that can be found in being alive. *With joy you will draw water from the wells of salvation* (Isa. 12:3) Jesus promised that those who drink the water of life that He offers will never thirst again. Joy is like a spring or a fountain of fresh water, bubbling and bursting forth with radiance. It brings light and refreshment continuously. I have experienced this after taking time with the Lord. He gives me gladness, life, energy, hope, and creative ideas. Jesus is the water of life, living and flowing in the heart of every believer. He is our eternal joy.

The ransomed of the Lord will return, they will enter Zion with singing; everlasting joy will crown their heads. Gladness and joy will overtake them and sorrow and sighing will flee away. (Isa. 35:10)

OUR GUIDE

You guide me with Your counsel, and afterward You will take me into glory. (Ps. 73:24)

It seems that as we continue on the path before us, God's light only shines upon our feet and a short distance ahead. As we continue to walk in His light, our shepherd will continually guide our way and point us in the right direction. We are learning to walk by faith and not by what our eyes can see. You will hear His voice speaking softly telling you which way to go; it is our choice to listen and to open our hearts, ears, and eyes to gain the understanding and the wisdom that God wants to impart, or to go the other way. The Lord sees and knows everything concerning you even to the smallest detail. He is constantly watching carefully every move you make; He hears every thought, knows every word even before you speak it. It is with a love that is incomprehensible to us that is constantly prompting us in the way in which we should walk from the time we wake, until we go to sleep. And even in our sleep, He continues to watch and work in us.

For this God is our God forever and ever; He will be our guide even to the end. (Ps. 48:14)

LOVING COMMUNICATION

"Because he loves me," says the Lord, "I will rescue him; I will protect him, for he acknowledges my name. He will call upon me, and I will answer him; I will be with him in trouble, I will deliver him and honor him. With long life will I satisfy him and show him my salvation." (Ps. 91:14-16)

It is because of our love for the Lord that he hears and answers us when we cry out to Him. The more we love Him, the more we desire to please Him by doing His will. In turn, He responds to our prayers and will be faithful to come to our aid; He will rescue, protect, deliver, be with us when we are in trouble. It is because of our loving communication with Him that whenever we call upon Him, He answers. It may not be happening at the present time, but we can be assured that the day is coming that we will be able to walk in close union with the Lord. We love Him because He first loved us; we should always want to grow and to do what is necessary to have this strong and loving communication with God.

I love the Lord, for He heard my voice; He heard my cry for mercy. Because He turned His ear to me, I will call on Him as long as I live. (Ps. 116:1-2)

GOD WILL HEAR AND ANSWER

For the eyes of the Lord are on the righteous and His ears are attentive to their prayer. (1 Pet. 3:12)

When you truly love someone, you desire to please that person. You are willing to sacrifice for them and to show by action that your love is true. In the same way, we show our love for the Lord by following Him in the light of His Word. When we do this, it proves our love to Him and He will always be attentive to our prayers. *This is the assurance we have in approaching God: that if we ask anything according to His will, He hears us. And if we know that He hears us—whatever we ask—we know that we have what we asked of Him.* (1Jn. 5:14-15) This is quite a promise we've been given! The Lord Jesus spoke of the power we have in asking and in the receiving. It is a blessing that God wants to give, although it is dependent upon our doing His will and in our living righteously. Many people may get discouraged when they do not see immediate results; it calls for trust on our part and willingness to wait and to have faith for the promised blessings. As we grow in our love for Him and for His Word, righteous living will follow and answered prayer realized at last. Isaiah speaks of a time when the new kingdom with Christ Jesus as our King comes to the earth and all the people will experience this blessing.

"Before they call I will answer: while they are still speaking I will hear." (Isa. 65:24)

ENOCH WALKED IN TRUTH

When Enoch had lived 65 years he became the father of Methuselah. Enoch walked with God 300 years and had other sons and daughters. Enoch lived 365 years; then he was no more, because God took him away. (Gen. 5:21-25)

We do not hear very much about Enoch's life except to say that *he walked with God* and that because he walked with God so closely and intimately, God took him away. There is no account of him ever dying, just that God took him. It is very interesting to me that people lived to such very great ages. Although not much is known about his life, we are given an account of his lineage. Enoch was the father of Methuselah and the great grandfather of Noah. Enoch was 365 years old when *God took him.* Enoch lived in the time preceding Noah, and the inhabitants of the earth were becoming increasingly evil. I can imagine that Enoch was challenged and opposed by others who were living in corruption and who constantly engaged in evil deeds. Through it all Enoch continued to *walk with God.* He had close communion and loving relationship with his Creator. He walked in obedience to His commands. God's commands have always remained the same throughout time; that we should walk in love and in truth. The apostle John expressed his great joy to find some of the people walking in truth.

"I have no greater joy than to hear that my children are walking in truth". (3 Jn.1 :4)

WALKING WITH JESUS

I am not writing you a new command but one that we had from the beginning. I ask that we love one another, and this is love; that we walk in obedience to His command. (2 Jn. 5-6)

The Lord Jesus desires His people to walk with Him in close union and in love. In spite of the world and all of the corruption that we see around us, we can walk with Him in an intimate and loving union. There will be a day when the people who walk with the Lord will be no more. God will take them just like He took Enoch. When we ask the Lord to teach us His ways; He will help us to walk with Him in this loving way. *Teach me Your way, O Lord, and I will walk in Your truth.* (Ps. 86:11) What is truth? It is the truth of God's Word. When we walk in His truth, we walk in the light of His Word, and in a close loving union with Him. As time goes by, we will experience a deeper love as we walk with Him in this way.

For Your love is ever before me, and I walk continually in Your truth. (Ps. 26:3)

EVERYONE NEEDS TRUE LOVE

Many waters cannot quench love; rivers cannot wash it away. If one were to give all the wealth of his house for love, it would be utterly scorned. (Song 8:7)

Everyone wants and needs to love and to be loved. God created a place in the human heart made and designed to hold and to be filled with divine love. As we grow up our experiences whether good or bad help to form and shape our concepts of what love is and the meaning of it. If we are sincere in our quest to find true love, over time and often through much trial, affliction, and error, we at last find the One True Love that is forever faithful; a love that will *never leave you*. God demonstrated to the whole world through the life and death of His Son what true love is. As humans, our weaknesses, the deceitfulness of riches, the world and the flesh can draw us into a false sense of love. The way we overcome these tendencies, is to call upon the one love that is true; to seek and ask to comprehend this great love that fills the universe and encompasses us. We were made to love God. It is love that drew us and love that sustains us to the very end of time. It is our love for the Lord and for what He did in the act of redemption, and love we have for one another that is the one true love.

Who shall separate us from the love of Christ? Shall trouble or hardship or persecution or famine or nakedness or danger or sword? No, in all these things we are more than conquerors through Him who loved us. For I am convinced that neither death nor life, neither angels nor demons, neither the present nor the future, nor any powers, neither height nor depth, nor anything else in all creation, will be able to separate us from the love of God that is in Christ Jesus our Lord. (Rom.8:35-39)

February 12

THE MYSTERY OF LOVE

All the believers were in one heart and mind. (Ac. 4:32)

The early Christians of course lived in a very different world than what we know of today. Yet in spite of the foreign culture and lifestyle, the one remarkable quality that stands out in Christian faith is the love that is shown one towards another. In our day and age, in spite of the diversities of background, points of views, opinions, etc., the Lord has given us the commandment to love one another that the world may see and know the reality of Christ's love for us; and for them too. We may not agree with each other about many things, but what unites us is the awareness that Christ resides in their hearts and in ours in the same way, making us one with each other and one with Him. It is a great mystery, yet one in which we are discovering more and more about as we grow in love. Jesus said that love is the greatest of all the commandments. *Love the Lord your God with all your heart, with all of your soul, with all of your mind, and with all of your strength. Love your neighbor as yourself. There are no commandments greater than these.* (Mk. 12:30-31)

"That they all may be one, as Thou Father, are in me, and I in you . . . . That they may be one, even as we are one." (Jn. 17:21-22)

DIVINE MYSTERY

My Father will love him, and we will come unto him, and make our abode with him. (Jn. 14:23)

The Lord has given us His Holy Spirit in order that we may live a life of love for Christ and for our fellowmen. Christ gave this great promise to every disciple; in this way the world will be constrained by the love that God's children have for each other and to acknowledge that Christ's words are fulfilled. *That the love wherewith you have loved me may be in them, and I in them.* (Jn.17:23) Let us yield ourselves today to believe the promise of the indwelling Spirit at once and with our whole hearts. This divine love is a great mystery; yet it is what we are all called to demonstrate and to experience. The indwelling Christ in the hearts of you and me and in our fellow believers truly makes us one in Spirit and one in love. This love shown as an example is the great proof and power that can bring others to the knowledge of Christ and of His great salvation. Let us embrace the Spirit and yield to His will with our whole hearts today.

Now to Him who is able to establish you by the gospel and the proclamation of Jesus Christ, according to the revelation of the mystery hidden for long ages past, but now revealed and made known through the prophetic writings by the command of God, so that all nations might believe and obey Him, to the only wise God be glory forever through Jesus Christ. Amen . . . (Rom. 16:25)

ONE TRUE LOVE

If anyone acknowledges that Jesus is the Son of God, God lives in him and he in God. And so we know and rely on the love God has for us. God is love. Whoever lives in love lives in God and God in him. (1 Jn. 4:15-16)

God is Himself love; the one and only true love. Love is the most powerful force in the entire universe. When we were growing up we experienced the love of family and friends; later in life, the love of husband or wife, and then a love of our own children and grandchildren. There is a love we have for nature and the beauty of it, and a love of animal life, including the bird and sea creatures that we admire. In all of these things we observe and learn about love and the nature of it. In other cases, many did not have a positive and loving experience while growing up and found that there was strife, disillusionment, and disappointments throughout. Although our lives shift and change from birth to death, whether positively or negatively, there is one force over all that is never subject to change or variableness; and that is God's love: (Jas.1:17) for He is Love itself in the truest sense of the word. His is the One true love that we can rely on, to seek and desire to know. He will be faithful to meet you right where you are, and reveal to you His love. The one love that is true, that you can rely on and put your whole trust in.

God is Love. (1Jn. 4:8)

February 15

HAND OF BLESSING

"O LORD, the God who saves me, day and night I cry out before You. May my prayer come before You: turn Your ear to my cry. But I cry to You for help, O LORD; in the morning my prayer comes before You." (Ps. 88:1, 2, 13)

The sky was especially beautiful this morning. It was blue with light peach colored steams running softly across. I can picture Jesus passing through the throngs of people on the way to Jerusalem; I can see Him moving; His walk like the beautiful sky, sending out waves of blessing, goodness, love and beauty over the land. This is a picture we can imagine when we think about Jesus. He is always willing to bless, comfort and to heal. As He passes by, let us not pass up the opportunity to receive from His hand the blessings He desires to give us this morning. As we open up our hearts and look to Him, He will fill us with good things that we need for the day.

Morning by morning O Lord, You hear my prayer; Morning by morning I lay my requests before You and wait in expectation. (Ps. 5:3)

IN THE MORNING

The Lord God . . . awaken morning by morning, He awakens my ear to hear as the learned. (Isa. 50:4)

If you determine in your will and in your heart to consistently give the Lord your first waking hour, you will find that the Lord will reward you richly with His presence, strength, provision, and all the help you will need for the day. After awhile you will find how indispensible this is. Your morning time with the Lord will become the most easy and natural, thing to do. Every good habit, takes practice, it does not come easy. This is the one area that Satan does everything he can to distract you. He will put a rush of things and activities in your mind that you could be doing and even make you think that you should be doing them instead of spending time with the Lord and seeking Him. It will take resistance on your part to refuse to get caught up in these activities and to make yourself to sit and rest at the Lord's feet ready and waiting for His direction. If you manage to do this, His blessings, peace and strength will follow you throughout your day.

Cause me to hear Your loving-kindness in the morning, For in You do I trust; cause me to know the way in which I should walk, for I lift up my soul to You. (Ps.143:8)

ACCOUNTABILITY

Nothing in all creation is hidden from God's sight. Everything is uncovered and laid bare before the eyes of Him to who we must give account. (Heb. 4:13)

It is important to understand that there is a time coming when we will give an account for our words and actions. As believers, we have received the light of God's Word into our hearts and have been given a trust. Now that we know the truth of His Word, we must be found faithful and accountable: trustworthy stewards over the mysteries God has revealed. The Lord desires to bless us more than we can even imagine, but in order to obtain the blessings, we have to do our part in being good and faithful caretakers. Even the smallest things matter to the Lord. Remember to do everything, even the most simple and ordinary thing as unto the Lord. Always attempt to do your very best at everything. Just keep doing the very best you can and He will take over. One day you will find the joy in being a servant; one that has been proven to be a faithful caretaker. We are accountable for our actions whether they be good or bad, to God first, and also to one another.

So then, men ought to regard us as servants of Christ and as those entrusted with the secret things of God. Now it is required that those who have been given a trust must prove faithful. (1Cor. 4:1-2)

ENCOURAGEMENT

*For I am the Lord, your God, who takes hold of your right hand and says to you, "Do not fear; I will help you." * (Isa. 41:13)

When I read these words it gives me encouragement and hope to know that it is the Lord who takes hold of my hand and guides me through life's trials and problems. In times of distress or uncertainty, bring to remembrance His promise knowing that He will be faithful to deliver you from every trial. Encouragement is a great virtue and one that we all need to possess. It's a pleasure for me to be around encouraging people who spur me on to do good works of faith and of love. This is a sign of a true friend; one who helps me to see that all things are possible with God; that no matter how high the climb, or how daunting the obstacles may appear, I can always find words of hope and encouragement from these special friends. When you see others, see them in the light of God and the way He sees them. He knows the ultimate outcome and it is determined that He will work those things in you and in your friends, that which we ourselves cannot do. Paul's prayer: *May our Lord Jesus Christ Himself and God our Father, who loved us and by His grace gave us eternal encouragement and good hope, encourage your hearts and strengthen you in every good deed and word.* (2 Thes. 2:17)

*"So do not fear, for I am with you do not be dismayed, for I am your God, I will strengthen you and help you; I will uphold you with my righteous right hand." * (Isa. 41:10)

ENCOURAGE OTHERS

I want you to know how much I am struggling for you and for those at Laodicea, and for all who have not met me personally. My purpose is that they may be encouraged in heart and united in love, so that they may have the full riches of complete understanding, in order that they may know the mystery of God, namely, Christ, in whom are hidden all the treasures of wisdom and knowledge. (Col. 2:2-3)

Paul also recognized that many of the struggles he faced were for the purpose of encouraging others. When people see the trials that you go through and observe the strength of character and faith that you show, it brings encouragement to them. They see firsthand that your faith in God is real and is powerful. The men and women who are the Church, (the Body of Christ on earth), really do need each other to help strengthen and to build one another up with encouraging words. We were designed to be a body of believers that love, pray, and encourage one another throughout our lifetimes. We are eternally united here and in the life to come, so let us lift up one another today with loving words of encouragement and with our prayers. It is the Lord Himself who brings us encouragement when we read His word of promise. He will take hold of our hand; strengthen and help us.

Encourage one another daily, as long as it is called today, so that none of you may be hardened by sin's deceitfulness. We have come to share in Christ if we hold firmly till the end the confidence we had at first. (Heb. 3:13-14)

HOLD ON UNTIL THE END

We are made partaker of Christ, if we hold the beginning of our confidence steadfast unto the end. (Heb. 3:14)

The Webster's Dictionary defines: steadfast: *Fixed or unchanging: steady, firmly loyal and constant; unswerving.* The word: steady: *Having continuous movement, quality or pace, not easily excited or upset: reliable; dependable, temperate, with continuity.* All these words describe the way we are increasingly becoming as we look to the Lord daily for our help and strength. There are many obstacles encountered along the road of faith; like the pilgrim from the book: The Pilgrim's Progress, as we begin to gain some ground and come closer to the finish line, the enemy brings more intense pressures and problems to throw us off course and make us want to abandon ship. This is the time to resist the inclination and hold on to what the Lord directs you to. It is God Himself who will make us firm and steadfast and able to resist. Call upon Him right away in your times of need.

Cast all your anxiety on Him because He cares for you. Be self controlled and alert. Your enemy the devil prowls around like a roaring lion looking for someone to devour. Resist him, standing firm in the faith, because you know that your brothers throughout the world are undergoing the same kind of sufferings. And the God of all grace, who called you to His eternal glory in Christ, after you have suffered a little while, will Himself restore you and make you strong, firm and steadfast. (1 Pet. 5:7-9)

OUR WORK

As long as it is day, I must do the work of Him who sent me. Night is coming where no man can work. While I am in the world, I am the light of the world. (Jn. 9:4-5)

Everything that we do in God's service, with a heart that is motivated by love and faith, is never in vain. A purpose is being served though our work even if no one recognizes it at the time. God sees and will establish us in both our faith and service. We are now the light that is in the world though Christ. As long as we are in the world, we have the victory over the darkness and over Satan himself. As I look around at the times we live, I can't help but to think that we may be nearing the finish line. Today we must hold on and stand firm to the end, it is the last step that wins. God has promised us that He will preserve us to the very end of time. To preserve means also to protect, provide, and to keep, in every way. He cares for the little sparrows and all the little creatures in His grand creation. None who is sincerely seeking, loving, and desiring Him, will be left wanting or in need. He is calling us to believe Him for all of these things. Our real work is to believe upon Him whom God has sent. (Jn. 6:29)

Therefore stand fi rm. Let nothing move you. Always give yourselves fully to the work of the Lord, because you know that your labor in the Lord is not in vain. (1 Cor. 15:58)

THE RIGHTEOUS WILL FLOURISH

The righteous will flourish like a palm tree, they will grow like a cedar of Lebanon; planted in the house of the LORD they will flourish in the courts of our God. They will still bear fruit in old age; they will be fresh and green. (Ps. 92:12-14)

We know that the Lord is building a spiritual house within us that will never perish and that is being renewed daily by His Word and by His Spirit. Our bodies are growing older and we feel the aches and pains that go along with it, although at the same time, there is a child present inside of us that does not grow old, but stays bright and cheerful as we learn to trust in the Father. With new found strength each day, through Christ, we are enabled to go and bear spiritual fruit that will last and keep on producing. The older we get, as the years go by, our spirits are becoming younger and more childlike. We are all like little children unto the Lord. It is because we realize more and more the vastness and magnitude of God, and our smallness before Him.

Therefore we do not lose heart. Though outwardly we are perishing, yet inwardly we are being renewed day by day, for our light and momentary troubles are achieving for us an eternal glory that far out-weighs them all. (2 Cor. 4:16)

FRUIT BEARING

The fruit of the spirit is love, joy, peace, patience, kindness, goodness, faithfulness, gentleness and self-control. Against such things there is no law. (Gal. 5-22-23)

The Lord gives many examples of fruit bearing trees in relation to His people. The Vine and the branches perfectly describe our relationship to Jesus. The Lord brings forth the fruit as we abide in the Vine. He produces the fruit, we only abide. *I am the Vine and you are the branches. If a man remains in me and I in him, he will bear much fruit: apart from me you can do nothing.* (Jn. 15:5) *Fruit trees of all kinds will grow on both banks of the river. Their leaves will not wither, nor will their fruit fail. Every month they will bear, because the water from the sanctuary flows to them. Their fruit will serve for food and their leaves for healing.* (Ez.47:12) We can easily see ourselves described in this scripture: Fruit trees of all kinds: we are all so different and unique, our spirits will not wither but we will be fresh and flourishing, we will bear spiritual fruit as the Holy Spirit flows to us the Living Water from the throne of God. Our fruit will bless and nourish others, and bring healing.

He is like a tree planted by streams of water, which yields its fruit in season and whose leaf does not wither. Whatever he does prospers. (Ps.1: 3)

CHRIST IN YOU THE HOPE OF GLORY

To whom God would make know what are the riches of the glory of this mystery among the Gentiles; which is Christ in you the hope of glory. (Col. 1:27)

God desires to reveal to us the riches of this mystery; *Christ in you, the hope of glory.* As we grow in our faith, slowly we become more aware of the Presence of Christ, His Holy Spirit, living inside of our hearts. Yes, this is a very mysterious work, one that God will reveal to all who trust and believe. It is one that contains great treasure and true riches. Nothing in this world compares to the riches of Christ's own Presence revealed. He Himself is our treasure, the fulfillment of everything we could ever hope for or imagine. It is the Lord's pleasure and desire to reveal these deep truths to His people. Draw near to Him each moment of every day and you will begin to discover the mystery of *Christ in you the hope of glory!*

Wherein He has abounded toward us in all wisdom and prudence; Having made known unto us the mystery of His will, according to His good pleasure which He has purposed in Himself. (Ephes. 1:8-9)

JUSTIFIED BY FAITH AND TRUST

Through Him everyone who believes is justified from everything you could not be justified by the law of Moses. (Rom. 3:28)

The whole life and work of a Christian, (one who professes faith in Jesus) is based upon trust and belief. From the beginning of time, since the fall of Adam and Eve, all of mankind has been held captive in the fear of death, judgment, and condemnation. There was no permanent remedy for sin. Even after and during the giving of the law through Moses and the prophets, the whole world remained in darkness, held prisoners by the grip of Satan. When Jesus was sent into the world, a great light appeared. He was the fulfillment of every Word promised for the deliverance that would come. He proclaimed the Gospel to the world, the Good News that through simple belief and childlike trust we can have eternal and complete forgiveness from all the powers of Satan here and now; in this world and in the world that is to come. He's the only one who is worthy of our trust. Believing and trusting in Jesus is the bridge that all must cross over, that takes us from death and condemnation, to life, justification, and eternal forgiveness.

"I tell you the truth, whoever hears my Word, and believes Him who sent me, has eternal life and will not be condemned, He has crossed from death to life." (Jn. 5:24)

AFFLICTION AND TRIALS

There he proved them. (Ex.15:25) *I have chosen you in the furnace of affliction.* (Is. 48:10)

God allows our trials and sufferings to come in order to test and to prove our faith; that the end result will be to the highest praise, honor and glory when Jesus will be revealed at last. If we keep our eyes on the end result, even though we do not see it right now because of various trials and afflictions, our faith will grow to the praise, honor and glory of the Lord. When you find yourself going through a fiery furnace that the Lord has allowed, let faith have its perfect work and let the refining process do its important work in your life. *I have refined you, though not as silver; I have tested you in the furnace of affliction.* (Is. 48:10)

For our light and momentary troubles are achieving for us an eternal glory that far outweighs them all. (2 Cor. 4:17) *These have come so that your faith, of greater worth than gold which perishes, even though refined by fire, may be proved genuine and may result in praise, glory and honor when Jesus Christ is revealed.* (1 Pet. 4:12)

February 27

PEACE IN HIS PRESENCE

The children of your servants will live in your presence; their descendants will be established before you. (Ps. 102:28)

When we look at the world around us, it appears to be secure and lasting, but the Lord will one day roll it all up like a garment and make all things new. It is common to feel some anxiety about the true state of today's world. The changes that occur on earth are not in our control; what we can control is our wills and our minds. When trusting in the Lord, and praying to Him, we receive a peace and a security that is not dependent upon our physical state of being. God is able to keep our minds in perfect peace when we keep our focus upon Him. Things are not what they may appear to be; God is always moving and changing. It is within our wills to decide to allow God to move and change us. The entire world's ways and all of the natural thinking and wisdom of man, are in direct opposition to God's ways and His wisdom. That is reason why there is persecution and trials for the believing man or woman. We go against the grain of the world and its ways. If we are listening and seeking the Lord's direction, we will have problems, but peace and understanding will prevail. It is supernatural, not comprehended by world opinion.

The Lord is near. Do not be anxious about anything, but in everything, by prayer and petition, with thanksgiving, present your request to God. And the peace of God, which transcends all understanding, will guard your hearts and your minds in Christ Jesus. (Phil. 4: 5-7)

OUR DWELLING PLACE

If you make the Most High your dwelling even the Lord, who is my refuge then no harm will befall you. For He will command His angels concerning you to guard you in all your ways: He will call upon me, and I will answer him: I will be with him in trouble; I will deliver him and honor him. With long life will I satisfy him and show him my salvation. (Ps. 91:9-11, 15, 16)

If we make the Most High our dwelling place, if we dwell; the word "dwell" in the Webster's Dictionary is defined: *To live as a resident; reside. To exist in some place or state; to fasten one's attention; to remain, sojourn, abide.* God is telling us that if we do this; abide, dwell, reside in Him, place ourselves into His hands, trust Him with everything we have, then He will protect and deliver us from every harm, and He will answer when we call upon Him. The Lord will provide and bless us with long and satisfying lives. He is our refuge.

God is our refuge and strength, an ever present help in trouble. Therefore we will not fear, though the earth gives way and the mountains fall into the heart of the sea, though its waters roar and foam and the mountains quake with their surging. There is a river whose streams make glad the city of God. (Ps. 46:1-4) The eternal God is your refuge, and underneath are the everlasting arms. (Deut. 33:27)

: you until I have done what I

OUR REFUGE

For no matter how many promises God has made, they are yes in Christ. And so through Him, the Amen is spoken by us to the glory of God. (2 Cor. 1:20)

There used to be a little gospel track called "The Great Exchange." It describes how God exchanged His royal heavenly life, for an earthly walk as a man with a mission to die a cruel death upon a cross in order that you and I could exchange our sorrowful and sinful lives for an eternal heavenly life of everlasting joy. We are clothed in royal robes of righteousness; if we can abide in Him. There is a choice here, we can choose not to. What a sad mistake if we refuse this offer of exchange. Our loving Heavenly father is waiting to give all goodness, life and blessing to all who choose to make Him their refuge and abiding place. Our part is only to reside, and to take our refuge in Him that we may receive all the promise of blessings from His hand. We have the Word of the Lord when He tells us over and over again in Scripture, that when we come to Him as our refuge and our abiding place, He will fulfill His promises to us.

How great is Your goodness, which You have stored up for those who fear You, which You bestow in the sight of men on those who take refuge in You. (Ps. 31:19) I am with you and will watch over you wherever you go, and I will bring you back to this land. I will not leave you until I have done what I have promised you. (Gen. 28:15)

OBTAINING THE PROMISE

And so, after he had patiently endured, he obtained the promise. (Heb. 6:15)

There are times we find ourselves in the middle of a circumstance or action that we would prefer not to be in, and begin to murmur and complain. Things just aren't going the way we had hoped, planned or prayed for. It is tempting to grumble and lose our faith because it seems God is delaying or is not responding in the way we think He should in answer to our prayers. This is not unnatural for us to react in such a way, but it is an attitude we should resist. We can truly obtain the promises given, if we can resist the temptation to complain and grumble! It is so easy to be negative and so hard to remain in a positive attitude sometimes when everything seems to be going wrong! Once again, these are the times that we must look to the Lord for our strength and help. It is a practice that over time and experience, we will learn if we press on through and not give up. At last we can and will obtain the promise after we have patiently endured.

Do everything without complaining or arguing, so that you may become blameless and pure, children of God without fault in a crooked and depraved generation, in which you shine like stars in the universe. (Phil. 2:14)

PATIENT WAITING WITH EXPECTATION

Godliness with contentment is great gain, for we brought nothing into the world, and we can take nothing out of it. (1 Tim. 6:6)

Patient waiting combined with great expectation will get you through. Financial burdens, health concerns, relational issues, etc. may be problematic in our days, but that's the time to go back to the Word of God which tells us; you will be richly rewarded if you wait with hopeful hearts, while expecting great things. Abraham after enduring a long time received his reward and was satisfied above all he could have ever dreamed possible. We are all naked and completely undone before the LORD God Almighty who made us. We are in poverty both spiritually and materially next to the perfection and riches of the Lord. What will you offer to God when you stand before Him? It will not be anything that is of this world. Only our love and devotion and faithfulness to Him are what God desires and is acceptable. To hear the words *"Enter in my good and faithful servant,"* will be the fulfillment of all our patient waiting and expectations.

Keep yourselves from the love of money and be content with what you have, because God has said, "Never will I leave you: never will I forsake you." (Heb. 13:5)

March 4

THE DIFFICULTY OF REPENTANCE

Then I acknowledge my sin to you and did not cover up my iniquity. I said, I will confess my transgressions to the Lord. (Ps. 32:5)

Daily confession for our sins allows us to receive mercy, cleanses our hearts and gives the assurance that our prayers are being heard. Everyone in the course of a day says or does something that grieves God's Spirit. It may be big, or it may be a small thing. In either case God knows and sees it all. We do not want to be like David who became so anguished with torrents of sorrow because he delayed his repentance. Let's go to God right away and repent. We need cleansing for things that we may not even be aware of but the Lord knows and sees. Allow Him to purge out the old and fill us with the newness of His Spirit every day, and even throughout the day when you commit an offense and become aware of it, ask the Lord for forgiveness at once.

Who is a God like You, who pardons sin and forgives the transgressions of the remnant of His inheritance? You do not stay angry forever but delight to show mercy. (Mic. 7:18)

MERCIFUL LORD

Have mercy on me, O God, according to your unfailing love; according to Your great compassion blot out my transgression, wash away all my iniquity and cleanse me from my sin. Create in me a pure heart, O God, and renew a steadfast spirit within me. (Ps. 51:1-2, 10)

He is always ready to forgive and to be merciful. With each new day we have a fresh opportunity to receive new mercy from His throne of grace. God is merciful and has great compassion upon all of His people. He sees and understands our pain and sorrows. He longs for us to come and receive a fresh washing, a spiritual shower each morning; to renew and revive us daily. We who were once dead in our sins have been made alive by the washing and regeneration of the sacrificed life of Christ. He has shown His love for us and that He is a merciful Lord.

Because of the Lord's great love we are not consumed, for His compassions never fail. They are new every morning, great is Your faithfulness. (Lam. 3:22-23)

HIDING PLACE

You are my hiding place; You will protect me from trouble and surround me with songs of deliverance. (Ps. 32:7)

I love to imagine sitting by a waterfall, or taking a walk by the seaside, or climbing up to a mountain top. It would be great to get away to such a location and find sweet peace and communion with the Lord every day, but instead, we find ourselves in many various locations, and some not so peaceful. Yet, in the very middle of our activities, there is a way to find refuge and calmness, for God Himself is our hiding place. He is our Protector from every storm in life. Jesus spoke of the Kingdom within. It is a beautiful, peaceful place and we can go there at will. There are times when we have to remove ourselves from the chaos and find a place where we can shut out the noise and seek Him. He is there waiting for us to come and to receive the strength for the occasion.

And a Man shall be as a hiding place from the wind and a covert from the tempest. (Isa. 32:2)

SEEK THE QUIET PLACE

Hide thyself by the brook Cherith. (1 Kings 17:3)

If we can't literally go to a quiet shelter to seek the Lord during the day, let's try to find small segments of time to get away in order to replenish our spirits in an undistracted atmosphere; even if it is just for a short while. The more time we can give Him in this way, the more our reservoir of peace by His Spirit will stay full. May the LORD always be our shield and refuge in stressful and uncertain times. Let's seek Him in quiet places as often as possible. He has promised to sustain us and keep us safe. Our only hope is in Him. *For in the day of trouble He will keep me safe in His dwelling: He will hide me in the shelter of His tabernacle and set me high upon a rock.* (Ps. 27:5)

You are my refuge and my shield; I have put my hope in Your Word. Sustain me according to Your promise, and I will live. (Ps. 119:114,116)

March 8

FROM SMALL TO BIG

Whoever can be trusted with very little can also be trusted with much, and whoever is dishonest with very little will also be dishonest with much. (Lk. 16:10)

God starts us out with very small things, and as we prove ourselves faithful, He gives us more, but with more responsibilities. This way of life is reflected in our spiritual and physical conduct, and in the way we honor and perform our commitments both to God and to man. How else will our testimony of faith in Christ stand if we don't follow through with what we said we would do? Before we commit ourselves to do something, consider carefully the cost. (Lk.14:28) Too many times we say yes without thinking it through. Once the decision has been made, do everything possible to fulfill it, otherwise no one will believe the things you say. Over commitment is one thing to guard against because it takes us away from our needed quiet times with the Lord. Try to simplify your life as much as is possible. When you make a commitment, follow through and be on time! If you cannot do it, just say no.

Above all things my brothers, swear not, neither by heaven, neither by the earth, neither by any other oath: but let your yes be yes and your no, no: least you fall into condemnation. (Jas. 5:12)

March 9

HONESTY

You must have accurate and honest weights and measures, so that you may live long in the land the Lord you God is giving you. (Deut. 25:15)

Honesty and accuracy are a few of the qualities that are required of faithful stewards. What the Lord said in the days of old, applies to us today. He requires honesty, and to use just weights and measures in doing the business of life. The Lord said to the faithful servant, *"Well done my good and faithful servant, because you have been trustworthy in a very small matter, take charge over ten cities."* (Lk. 19:17) When I think of what is required to hear the words *"Well done,"* it seems insurmountable. Thank God for the Word of promise that tells me that He will bring this perfection about as I look to, submit, and surrender daily to do His will. It is for this reason that we can be found faithful and honest servants.

May God Himself, the God of peace, sanctify you through and through. May your whole spirit, soul and body be kept blameless at the coming of our Lord Jesus Christ. The one who calls you is faithful and He will do it. (1Thes. 5:23)

THE WORK OF GOD

Jesus answered, "The work of God is this: to believe in the one He has sent." (Jn. 6:29)

The building up of our faith is the work that God expects us to do. How can we cause our faith to grow? It is in the hearing of the Word of God. (Rom. 10:17) There are many ways we can hear the Lord's Word; in our daily reading of the Bible, listening to a radio broadcast, or placing a CD of the Bible in our car or homes as we work or travel. The important thing is to listen and pay attention to the Word that is being read or spoken. The more I do this, the more my faith will grow. It is God's Holy Spirit that brings the Word to life in me and who does the work. As we grow in our faith and keep our eyes fixed upon the source of God's goodness and blessing, we will become like rivers of blessing. Believing does not require physical exertion. It is a state of heart, mind, and spirit. Jesus came to bless us. (Ac. 3:26) We can also bring blessing to the world and to those around us. We, who believe in Jesus, are over-comers in this life. The Lord will help us to overcome every obstacle as we fix our eyes upon the Word which is the source of our faith. This is the work of God.

This is the victory that overcomes the world, even our faith. (1 Jn. 5:4)

March 11

TRUE LOVE

Whosoever shall confess that Jesus is the Son of God, God abides in him, and he in God. And we know and have believed the love which God has in us. God is love; and he that abides in love abides in God and God abides in him. (1 Jn. 4:15-16)

Jesus' life on earth was love in action; a love that the disciples and the people who lived in His time, could observe with their eyes, touch with their hands, and receive with their hearts. *God is love*: His essence, what He is literally made of is true pure love. No one knew, before Jesus came to us for our example, what true love looked or acted like. When the Lord called us to Himself by the Spirit of His great love, true love was birthed inside of us too. We received the gift of that same Great Spirit. True love is powerful, the greatest power there is in existence; there is nothing that is more powerful.

Who shall separate us to from the love of Christ? Shall trouble or hardship or persecution or famine or nakedness or danger or sword? No, in all these things we are more than conquerors through Him who loved us. For I am convinced that neither death nor life, neither angels nor demons, neither the present nor the future, nor any powers, neither height nor depth, nor anything else in all creation, will be able to separate us from the love of God that is in Christ Jesus our Lord. (Rom. 8: 35-39)

LOVE LOOKS LIKE THIS

And now these three remain: faith, hope, and love. But the greatest of these is love. (1 Cor. 13:13)

God commands us to love one another as He has demonstrated to us. For it is by our love for one another that the world will take notice, and it is through our example that people are drawn to understand the source of this love which is God Himself. How can we demonstrate true love? The whole chapter of 1 Corinthians 13 describes what love should look like in the lives of believers. Love helps, nurtures, encourages, protects, promotes, strengthens, always seeks the others greatest good. This is how Jesus shows us how to behave towards one another. We esteem all others above ourselves. Jesus is our teacher as we look to Him to show us how to live a life that reflects true love. *My command is this: Love each other as I have loved you.* (Jn. 15:12) *All men will know that you are my disciples if you love one another.* (Jn. 13:35)

Love always protects, always trusts, always hopes, and always perseveres. Love never fails. (I Cor. 13:7)

WISDOM

Blessed is the man who finds wisdom, the man who gains understanding, for she is more profitable than silver and yields better return than gold. She is more precious than rubies; nothing you desire can compare with her. Long life is in her right hand; in her left hand are riches and honor. Her ways are pleasant ways, and all her paths are peace. She is a tree of life to those who embrace her; those who lay hold of her will be blessed. (Prov. 3:13-18)

Wisdom comes to us when we put God's Word into practice and obey. Jesus is our Wisdom. As we look to Him, and praise Him more, He will by His Spirit guide us into all truth and wisdom. Nothing that you desire can compare to the riches of His wisdom. When we seek Jesus with all of our hearts, we gain wisdom for He is wisdom and He desires to grant to us all the blessings that having wisdom can bring into our lives. This is why it is so important to meditate upon His Word, for therein lies the key to life and to life more abundant and full.

If any of you should lack wisdom, he should ask God, who gives generously to all without finding fault, and it will be given to him. (Jas.1:5) *Therefore everyone who hears these words of mine and puts them into practice is like a wise man, who built his house on the rock.* (Lk. 6:47-49)

JOY IN PRAYER

Why are you so downcast O my soul? Why so disturbed within me? Put your hope in God for I will yet praise Him, my Savior and my God. (Ps. 42:5)

When we take the time to realize and to think upon the Lord's grace and the freedom we have been called into, it will help to lift up, invigorate, and brighten our prayer times. We are not under the law, (the bondage of strict adherence) but under grace whereby we take great joy in the understanding of God's love and in the relationship we are creating. Each day when we come to Him with a true heart of gratitude and praise for His abundant grace and mercy; we receive His joy. Confessing our weaknesses in prayer is the first step to receive the cure. Healing and restoration is a promise we can have when we place ourselves under the great grace of the Lord. Soon our prayer life will become a joyful communication, the way that the Lord desires it to be. *Awake, thou that sleep, and arise from the dead and Christ shall give you light.* (Ephes. 5:14)

By day the Lord directs His love, and by night His song is with me; a prayer to the God of my life. (Ps. 42:8)

GOD WAITS

Be patient then brothers until the Lord's coming. See how the farmer waits for the land to yield its valuable crops and how patient he is for the autumn and spring rains. (Jas. 5:7)

This is a hard lesson to learn; especially in a day and age when we can get what we want almost instantly through the technology and the advancements of our modern time. The Lord has always been long suffering with us. He gives everyone chance after chance for repentance and restoration. He waits because He desires that no one perish. *The Lord is not slow in the keeping of His promise as some understand slowness. He is patient with you not wanting anyone to perish, but everyone to come to repentance.* (2 Pet. 3:9) So it is that we too must wait for God's perfect timing and for the answers to our prayers. There are reasons for delay that we know nothing about, so we must persevere, hold on to the hope until the end. He is working out a greater purpose that will be revealed at long last! If we could remember and learn what Paul the Apostle learned through his trials; if you are waiting on God under a cloud of trial, in time that cloud will turn into showers of blessings!

I have learned the secret of being content in any and every situation, whether well fed or hungry, whether living in plenty or in want. I can do everything through Him who gives me strength. (Phil. 4: 11,13)

March 16

YOUR KINGDOM COME

Your Kingdom come, Your will be done in earth as it is in heaven. (Matt. 6:10)

When we imagine what heaven is like, we think of a place where there is perfect harmony, peace, fullness of joy and love. Everybody is in one accord with everyone else. In Heaven there is no jealousy, greed, strife, evil imaginations, or anything that is left of our old sinful nature. In the earth however, there is a continuous struggle going on between our new and old natures that still exist together in this world. Here in Matthew 6:10, Jesus tells us how we ought to pray and what we should pray for. He says *"Let Your will be done on earth as it is in Heaven."* God's will is for us to live in harmony, peace, joy and love; here, right now. If Jesus said it, it must be possible to do so even while we are still in this fallen state. We know that Jesus by His Spirit within us is continuously working for our good and is in the process of changing and transforming our characters to be more and more like His own. Do not get discouraged if it doesn't seem to be happening fast enough for you. God will enable you to live out His Kingdom here on earth as you daily surrender your will, trusting Him with your life, while you are waiting for His coming Kingdom.

We have not stopped praying for you and asking God to fill you with the knowledge of His will through all spiritual wisdom and understanding. (Col.1:9)

BLESSED ARE THEY WHO MOURN

The lowly He sets on high and those who mourn are lifted to safety. (Job 5:11)

There is much sorrow around us. Many people today are experiencing deep heartache and pain. This may not be the case for you at present, but we should remember those who are in mourning and pray that God would bring comfort and healing in their sufferings. *He has sent me to bind up the brokenhearted.* (Is.61:1) Christ came to heal the wounded and broken hearted. There are many ways that we can be a comfort to those around us that are going through pain and suffering. We might send a card with some encouraging words, or maybe just take some time to just listen and pray with them. When we mourn and cry over our losses, broken relationships, or whatever it is that brings you to tears; God says that you will be blessed. Your heart is soft and tender in His eyes. Some people will not allow themselves to cry and their sorrows get pent up inside; but the Lord says, *"Blessed are they who mourn."* When we can mourn, we are able to receive the divine comfort that the Lord is ready to give us.

Blessed are they who mourn, for they shall be comforted. (Matt. 5:4)

SORROW AND JOY

Rejoice with those who rejoice; mourn with those who mourn. (Rom. 12:15)

When we see someone in deep sorrow, sometimes we need to enter into that place of mourning alongside them and share in their grief. *When Job's three friends heard about all the troubles that had come upon him, they set out from their homes and met together by agreement to go and sympathize with him and comfort him.* (Job 2:11) Mourning is also a sign of brokenness which is precious in the sight of the Lord. *Blessed are those who mourn, for they will be comforted.* (Matt.5:4) David is someone who suffered greatly and found his comfort in the Lord alone. If you are in mourning call upon the Lord, He Himself will comfort you. *My comfort in my suffering is this: Your promise renews my life. May your unfailing love be my comfort, according to Your promise to your servant. Let Your compassion come to me that I may live, for Your law is my delight.* (Ps. 119:50,76) Always and forever we can turn to the promise of God's Word and receive the comfort needed for our moments of pain and suffering.

Praise be to the God and Father of our Lord Jesus Christ, the Father of compassion and the God of all comfort. (2 Cor. 1:3)

SPIRITUAL STONES

For we are God's fellow-workers: you are God's husbandry, God's building. According to the grace of God which was given unto me, as a wise master builder I laid a foundation; and another built thereon. (1 Cor. 3:9-10)

There is much to be learned from the many Godly men and women who have gone before us. Each has given us a special gift so that we who follow after can receive inspiration and continue to build upon the stones that they have laid down for us. *You also, as living stones, are built up a spiritual house, to be a holy priesthood, to offer up spiritual sacrifices, acceptable to God through Jesus Christ.* (1 Pet. 2:5) We are all living stones built upon one another Jesus Himself our Chief Cornerstone. God through His Holy Spirit is willing to reveal to us many mysteries concerning creation, our origin and purpose in His Divine Plan. In studying about the lives and ministries of Christian men and women who have lived and died, we can gain a lot of spiritual insight and understanding. We are all built one upon another from the beginning of the early Church, to the present, one holy spiritual house.

That He might gather together in one all things in Christ, both which are in heaven, and which are on earth. (Ephes. 1:10)

FELLOW CITIZENS IN THE HOUSEHOLD OF GOD

So then ye are no more strangers and sojourners, but ye are fellow-citizens with the saints, and of the household of God, being built upon the foundation of the apostles and prophets, Christ Jesus himself being the chief corner stone; in whom each several buildings, fitly framed together, grows into a holy temple in the Lord; in whom you are also are built together for a habitation of God in the Spirit. (Ephes. 2:19-20)

There will be a day when all the saints of old will be joined together with us and we will all be made perfect in one. The scripture speaks of us being surrounded by a cloud of witnesses. It is a comforting thought to think of all the people who have journeyed though life and finished well. They serve as great examples that go on shining throughout the ages; leaving books and legacies for us to receive so we can gain hope, insight, and wisdom. What kind of legacy will we leave for our children and for the generations to come after? This may be the last one that we are living in, or maybe not. Still the house will go on being built until the very last stone is in place.

And these all, having had witness borne to them through their faith, received not the promise, God having provided some better thing concerning us, that apart from us they should not be made perfect. (Hew. 11: 39-40)

March 21

UNITY

The body is a unit, though it is made up of many parts; and though all its parts are many, they form one body. So it is with Christ; for we were all baptized by one Spirit into one body. (1 Cor. 12:12,13)

The Lord has a unique design for each and every member of His Church. We all have a particular function and specific place that we are destined to fill. Each one is given the fullness of His Spirit and the riches of His Word that assure us of our place and of our work. One great purpose of the Church, is for the edification and building up of one another in love and faith. Encouragement is central in our fellowship with other believers. Everyone can be an encouragement to someone. There have been experiences that you have been through, that when shared, will bring tremendous relief and strength to some heart that is yearning for understanding and compassion.

Just as each of us has one body with many members, and these members do not all have the same function, so in Christ we who are many form one body, and each member belongs to all the others. (Rom. 12:4-10)

UNITY OF FAITH

Until we all attain unto the unity of the faith, and of the knowledge of the Son of God, unto a full-grown man, unto the measure of the stature of the fullness of Christ. (Ephes. 4:13)

Unity and love within the body of Christ helps to bring about this reconciliation to the world. Although we are so different and spread out throughout the earth, we are united by one Spirit. Just as we are loved and have been accepted in Christ, we need to accept and love each other through all of our differences as well. It is God's will for us to live in unity with the Church, and to bring reconciliation of the world back to Christ. The body of Christ, the Church has many operations upon the earth today. One main purpose is to bring delight to the Lord. *Thou art worthy, O Lord, to receive glory and honor and power: for thou hast created all things, and for Your pleasure they are and were created.* (Rev.4:11) Secondly, the church has the all important task of continuing to do the work of reconciliation; reconciling the world back to fellowship with Christ. *And all things are of God, who hath reconciled us to himself by Jesus Christ, and hath given to us the ministry of reconciliation* (2 Cor. 5:18) This is a work that God performs in and through us as we yield ourselves to the power of His Holy Spirit, bringing unity. The Lord uses each member of His body as He wills to accomplish this great commission.

Make every effort to keep the unity of the Spirit through the bond of peace. (Ephes. 4:3)

THE DISCIPLINE OF WISDOM

But it is the spirit in a man, the breath of the Almighty that gives him understanding. (Job 32:8)

The Lord has given us the gift of His Holy Spirit to give us understanding and for us to have and to use as we need it. God's Spirit within us also disciplines and corrects us when we are wrong. When we acknowledge our transgression, we gain understanding. *He who ignores discipline despises himself, but whoever heeds correction gains understanding.* (Prov. 15:32) It is the Lord's will that our lives be blessed. It is a blessing to have understanding and discernment. There are many trials and problems that we continuously face, some may be a discipline from the Lord. Those are the times to seek Him for His wisdom and understanding. He will be faithful to give it when we humble ourselves; if repentance is needed, we should acknowledge our sins and repent. It was Paul's prayer for the church that we be filled with spiritual wisdom and understanding:

For this reason, since the day we heard about you, we have not stopped praying for you and asking God to fill you with the knowledge of his will through all spiritual wisdom and understanding. (Col. 1:9)

PRESERVATION AND OBEDIENCE

Remember Your Word to your servant, for you have given me hope. My comfort in my suffering is this; Your promise preserves my life. (Ps.119: 49)

The Lord has promised to preserve us unto the end of time. He will preserve, protect, and keep us in the shelter of His love to our last breath. I am comforted in the promise that assures me that He will be with me and keep me wholly preserved in Him. *It was good for me to be afflicted, so that I might learn of Your decrees. Your hands have made me and formed me; give me understanding to learn Your commands.* (Ps. 119:71-73) It is through the pain of affliction that we learn and come to understand the Lord's preservation. This promise is for all who follow in the paths of His righteousness. It is through much suffering, trials, and persecutions that we enter into life everlasting. Without this occurring, we would never come to understand the Lord's suffering and sacrifice. Many times the very act of obedience, leads to trials and sufferings. This is something that we must endure in order to receive the promised blessing. The study and meditation for God's Word will lead you to receive what He has promised to fulfill for every believing soul.

I have suffered much; preserve my life O Lord according to Your Word. (Ps. 119:107)

THE SON OBEYED

Although He was a son, He learned obedience from what He suffered and once made perfect, He became the source of eternal salvation for all who obey Him. (Heb. 5:8)

There is also the hope and joy of promised blessing for all those who obey. *Now if you obey me fully and keep my covenant, then out of all nations you will be my treasured possession, although the whole earth is mine.* (Ex. 19:5) It is the Lord's great desire to bless and preserve us to the end; our children, and our children's children, if we would only allow the Lord to work His works in our lives and give our attention to His commandments which are given to protect and preserve us. *Oh that their hearts would be inclined to fear me and keep all my commands always, so that it might go well with them and their children forever!* (Dt. 7:12) *My sons, do not forget my teaching, but keep my commands in your heart, for they will prolong your life many years and bring you prosperity.* (Prov.3:1-2) God Himself will preserve us unto the day of the coming of the Lord. He is faithful and He will do it when we seek to follow in His ways. Just as the Son obeyed the Father, let us follow His example of obedience. Paul's prayer to the Thessalonians was:

May God Himself, the God of peace, sanctify you through and through. May your whole spirit, soul and body be kept blameless at the coming of our Lord Jesus Christ, The one who calls you is faithful and He will do it. (1Thes. 5:23)

LIGHT PROMISED

The path of the righteous is like the first gleam of dawn, shining ever brighter until the full light of day. (Prov. 4:18)

When we find ourselves in darkness, surrounded by unbelief and difficult circumstances, the light of the Lord in the hearts of His believing people shines ever brighter. The darker it gets, the more His Light shines. When Jesus walked upon the earth, the people who were living in darkness, when they saw the Lord, it was as if they'd seen a great light shining. (Matt.4:16) *Your Word is a lamp unto my feet a light unto my path.* (Ps.119:105) It is the light of His Word that brings light into us and gives us wisdom and instruction guiding our steps. This is another great promise we have from the Lord that even in the midst of darkness, light is ever present shining in and through His people, the church. This light shines when we are walking and living in a righteous manner; being gracious and compassionate towards others.

Even in darkness light dawns for the upright, for the gracious and compassionate and righteous man. He will have no fear of bad news; his heart is steadfast, trusting in the Lord. (Ps. 112:4,7)

REFLECTIONS

This is the message we have heard from Him and declare to you: God is light, in Him there is no darkness at all. If we claim to have fellowship with Him yet walk in the darkness, we lie and do not live by the truth. But if we walk in the light, as He is in the light, we have fellowship with one another, and the blood of Jesus, His Son, purifies us from all sin. (1 Jn. 1:5-7)

At the beginning of each new day, it is a good idea to look into the mirror and examine the refection you see. Is your light bright today and getting brighter or is it dim and getting dimmer? God is light and lives inside of you. This light wants to shine into the darkness, casting it out. It is our decision, a choice we make each morning when we get up; are we going to walk in the light and truth of the Lord's Word and His love? Or, are we going to choose to walk away from His light. Every day, as the waves wash over the shoreline cleansing the sand making it new; so the Lord desires to cleanse us daily, washing and cleansing us with the precious blood of Jesus. It is the Lord's will that we let our lights shine. Let us not allow our lights to grow dim. Jesus has told us that:

"You are the light of the world; a city on a hill cannot be hidden. Neither do people light a lamp and put it under a bowl. Instead they put on its stand, and it gives light to everyone in the house. In the same way, let your light shine before men, that they may see your good deeds and praise your Father in heaven." (Matt. 5:14-16)

LOOKING TO GOD

I lift up my eyes to the hills, where does my help come from? My help comes from the Lord, the maker of Heaven and earth. (Ps. 121:1-2)

Lift up your eyes to the Lord to receive the help you need. When we are looking, we are turning our attention to; searching for, anticipating and expecting to see something. We have been given the gift of sight and we know from scripture that God will reveal Himself and we will see Him. We need to be always watching for the Lord, waiting in hopeful expectation, lifting our eyes up to Him from where all our help comes. *But as for me, I watch in hope for the Lord, I wait for God my Savior: my God will hear me. (*Mic.7:7*) I know that my Redeemer lives, and that in the end He will stand upon the earth. And after my skin has been destroyed, yet in my flesh I will see God; I myself will see him with my own eyes—I, and not another. How my heart yearns within me!* (Job 19:25-29) We have this great hope of seeing the Lord at last! We yearn and desire for the time when our bodies will be changed and we will see Him in His full glory. For now we see only dim reflections of His glory.

Now we see but a poor reflection: then we shall see face to face. Now I know in part; then I shall know in full, even as I am fully known. (1 Cor.13:12)

LOOKING FOR THE BLESSED HOPE

Looking for the blessed hope and glorious appearing of our great God and Savior Jesus Christ. (Titus 2:13)

When we train our minds to think upon things that are good and praiseworthy, slowly our eyes will be opened to see the Lord more and more in His holiness *The pure in heart shall see God.* (Matt. 5:8). It is so easy to get distracted away to other things. We must practice fixing our minds and eyes upon Him throughout the day. Your reward will be great! *Looking unto Jesus, the author and finisher of our faith, who for the joy that was set before Him endured the cross, despising the shame, and has sat down at the right hand of the throne of God.* (Heb. 12:2) What a hope we have towards the time when we will see Him and be with Him forever; free from the pain and darkness of this life at last. Let's turn our eyes to Him today looking to Jesus the author and finisher of our faith, who for the joy that was set before Him, endured the pain so that one day we could see and know Him as He truly is. *They will see His face, and His name will be on their foreheads.* (Rev. 22:4)

One thing I ask of the Lord, this is what I seek: that I may dwell in the house of the Lord all the days of my life, to gaze upon the beauty of the Lord and to seek Him in His temple. (Ps.27:4)

March 30

DELIGHTING IN THE WORD

Blessed is the man whose delight is in the law of the Lord and on His law he meditates day and night. He is like a tree planted by streams of water, which yields its fruit in season and whose leaf does not wither, whatever he does prospers. (Ps. 1:2-3)

The first thing about this scripture that draws my attention is the importance of *delighting* in the law of the Lord: Webster's: *To take great pleasure and joy, enjoyment, to allure, entice, afford keen satisfaction greatly pleasing.* When we take the time to mediate upon the Word of God, we receive a refreshing and a replenishing. It is truly the water of life and our roots become securely planted. The more we know by experience that the Words of the Lord are true and were written for our benefit, we can experience life, (not just living), but abundant life; a life that is full, overflowing with fullness. As we read and meditate upon the Word of God, the more we grow to love His Word. *O how I love your law! I meditate upon it all day long.* (Ps. 119:97) Time and time again, God proves His Word is true in all of life's experiences. When I reflect back upon my life, it was the Lord and the promises of His Word that helped me through every trial.

Your Word, O Lord, is eternal: it stands firm in the heavens, Your faithfulness continues through all generations; and it endures. If your law had not been my delight, I would have perished in my affliction. I will never forget your precepts, for by them you have renewed my life. (Ps.119:89-90)

March 31

SEEKING WISDOM

If you accept my words and store up my commands within you, turning your ear to wisdom and applying your heart to understanding, and if you call out for insight and cry aloud for understanding, and if you look for it as for silver and search for it as for hidden treasure, then you will understand the fear of the Lord and find the knowledge of God. (Prov. 2:1-5)

The very first word in the scripture above is "If", suggesting that we have a choice. Should we decide to do these things, we will understand the fear of the Lord and find the knowledge of God. Let us look at these verbs mentioned: *accept* my words, *store up* my commands within you: *turn* your ear to wisdom, *apply* your heart to understanding, *look* for it as for silver, and *search* for it as for treasure: Then, (after you *do* these things) you *will understand* the fear of the Lord and *you will find the knowledge of God.* This is what the Lord promises to fulfill in us. The fear of the Lord is mentioned all throughout the Bible. Fear is defined in the text as reverence (a feeling of profound awe, love, and respect: veneration) It is a reverence, we feel and express to an almighty and all powerful God who holds our lives in His hands. This is the fear that we come to understand as our faith grows in the knowledge of the Lord's goodness and love.

Let all the earth fear the Lord: let all the people of the world revere Him. (Ps.33:8)

BEAUTY UNAWARE

Unless a kernel of wheat falls to the ground and dies, it remains only a
single seed; but if it dies it produces many seeds . . . . John 12:24

Seeds of the flowers sleep long in the earth
Die then awaken when the sun gives them birth.
Flowers grow so slowly as each petal unfolds
With colors so fair.
Seeds that have died in the depth of the earth
Awaken to life, to beauty unaware.
Beauty unaware of the grace that it shows,
Beauty unaware of the blessings it sows,
God's lovely light shines through the eyes of His own
With true beauty unaware.
Although there is pain and sorrow along this road
The Lord helps us bear what we could not do alone.
If we are faithful, and trust in His care,
One day we'll awaken to beauty unaware.
Our trials in this life may be many and long,
Though we are buried in deep, dark despair;
When we cry to the Lord for strength and help,
He hears our prayer.
With our heads lifted up and our hope now alive,
We awaken to life; to beauty unaware.
Beauty unaware of the grace that it shows,
Beauty unaware of the pain it has known,
God's lovely light shines through the eyes of His own,
With true beauty unaware . . .

THE SUMMER WILL COME

Therefore will the Lord wait, that he may be gracious unto you. (Isa. *30:18*)

In the hours during and after the death of Jesus on the cross, I think about how the sun went behind the clouds and all the earth became dark. Many times in life, clouds darken our path. We do not know how to find our way, all is dark. This devotional is a reminder that the joy of Resurrection morning is on its way! No one that has ever lived suffered as much as our Lord did on Calvary. The cruel instrument of the cross that Satan thought would defeat Jesus became the instrument that insured his own destruction and afforded everyone who believes in Jesus, the opportunity to receive healing, forgiveness, and salvation. As we contemplate and remember the Lord's suffering and death, let us ask Him to reveal our own darkness that placed Him there. Let our sin be crucified along with Him and once again renew ourselves to the life we now can live by the power of the resurrected Christ that lives in our hearts today and forevermore. Let hope arise, wait on the Lord and take courage, for He will rise again with brightness and glory! The showers will pass . . . the summer will come.

Since ancient times no one has heard, no ear has perceived, no eye has seen any God besides You who acts on behalf of those who wait for Him. (Isa. 64:4)

PLANTING SEEDS OF FAITH

Let us not be weary in well doing, for in due season we shall reap, if we faint not. As we have therefore opportunity, let us do good unto all men especially unto them who are of the household of faith. (Gal. 6:9-10)

The Lord tells us in John 9:4, "*The night comes when no man can work.*" We must do the work that the Lord has given us to do while there is opportunity, especially for our family in the faith. There are times when we feel tired and weary and wonder how long can I continue to hold on? When will my deliverance come? The Lord will give you the strength you need when you ask for it. It is His strength and power that will rise up in you and get you all the way through to the end. The reward for our perseverance will be in knowing and experiencing His loving presence actively working in our day as we continue to plant the seeds of love and the seeds of His Word in other people's lives. The harvest we shall reap is a harvest of joy, peace, and a love that lifts us up bringing with it the strength to move forward all the way even to the very end of our days. When we finally reach heaven, we will obtain our reward and see the fruit that has come from the seeds of our faith that we planted when upon earth.

Be watchful, and strengthen the things which remain. (Rev.3:2) *Strengthen the weak hands and confirm the feeble knees.* (Isa. 35:3-4)

April 3

TIME TO SEEK THE LORD

It is time to seek the Lord. (Hos. 10:12)

Everyone who seeks the Lord with all their hearts finds Him. I remember when I was young and seeking God but was not looking for Him in the right places! That led to many dead ends. However, because I was truly seeking God, it was the Lord Jesus that revealed Himself as being the one and only true God. There are many gods in the world that Satan to deceive and to distract, but only one that is true. Anyone who is sincerely seeking to find God will discover faith in Christ Jesus. There are times when our faith seems weakened because of things and circumstances in our lives. Springtime reminds us of new birth and the awakening of life in nature. It is a time to renew ourselves to the Lord and once again begin to seek Him with all of our hearts. When we draw near to Him, He will draw near to us and once again our faith will be renewed with the beauty of the springtime.

For everyone that ask receives, and he that seeks finds, and to him that knocks, it shall be opened. (Matt. 7:8)

CREATING A SPIRITUAL ATMOSPHERE

When a man's ways are pleasing to the Lord, He makes even his enemies live at peace with him. (Prov. 16:7)

When we are living our life in ordinary ways, while at the same time focusing out attention upon God and being in union with Him, we are creating a spiritual atmosphere. We are walking in faith believing that all things are possible with God, developing a state of mind and heart that is continuously abiding in Jesus throughout our normal everyday activities. Over time, this will create the fruits of the Spirit manifesting in the form of love, joy, and a peaceful demeanor even when the circumstances may be contrary. We are creating a spiritual atmosphere when we walk in stride with the Lord; not running ahead, nor lagging behind, but step by step, partnering with him; and He with us. Jesus came to do the will of the Father and He had this continuously foremost in His mind. We too can live out the Father's will by putting Him ever before us in our own individual lives and circumstances; acting in a way that pleases Him. We can do this on the inside all the while we are engaged in outside activities, creating a spiritual atmosphere.

And a voice from heaven said, "This is my Son, whom I love, with Him I am well pleased." (Matt.3:17)

ASK AND YOU WILL RECEIVE

Therefore I tell you, whatever you ask for in prayer, believe that you received it and you will have it. (Mk. 11:24)

The Lord came to do the will of the Father and to glorify His name upon the earth. We are here to do the Father's will also, and to bring glory to the Father through Jesus. As the Holy Spirit within us, brings our prayer life into alignment with the Lord's through the surrendering of our wills daily to Him; by faith in His name, we may ask whatsoever we will and it shall be done, that the Father may be glorified in the Son through the lives we lead. As we praise Him and remember His loving kindness and goodness, we know we have been granted our requests, even before we are done speaking. Learning to pray in this manner is a process and a work that God does and desires to do in everyone who is willing and takes the time to seek Him. In my personal life I have found over the years, that the first hour of the day is the best time to pray (talk with God). As you begin to give Him first place in your day, faith will rise and grow; answers to your prayers will come at last and be heard even before you have ceased from speaking.

Before they call I will answer; while they are still speaking will hear. (Isa. 65:24)

BROKENHEARTED

The Lord is close to the broken hearted and saves those who are crushed in spirit. (Ps. 34:18)

When someone or something that we deeply love is suddenly taken from us, by death or separation, maybe under cruel circumstances, we may literally feel the pain of a broken heart, our spirit is crushed! All the questions of why flood our minds. We cry and cry until exhausted, then fall asleep only to awaken to the nightmare staring us in the face once again as the reality of what has just happened sets in and pounds our poor hearts relentlessly once again. The pain continues on as we struggle for sanity and reason. When I read Psalm 34:18 *The Lord is close to the broken hearted,* I can begin to understand how it is that we can draw strength from Him, for He fully understands the pain of a broken heart. His heart was broken and His spirit was crushed. Only He can help to take away the pain. He will heal us as we call to Him.

I have set the Lord always before me. Because He is at my right hand, I will not be shaken. (Ps.16:8)

April 7

WILL TO SUFFER

And yet it pleased the Lord to bruise Him; He hath put Him to grief. (Isa. 53:10)

To think that it is God's will for us to suffer, is an age old wonder and perplexity to our human understanding. Yet we are told over and over in scripture that all our present, past, and future sufferings in this life are allowed and even willed by the Father Himself in order to fulfill a purpose that only He knows. To think that it pleased the Father to bruise His Son and to put Him to grief is a great mystery; and that the Son was willing to do this all because of the great love He had for you and me! God doesn't give us the reason for why, our part is to trust and to commit our lives to a faithful Creator who promises that the suffering we experience, will only last a little while, and tells us we will be made perfect through it and because of it, established, at peace, and settled in the end. When we are feeling pain and suffering, as we turn our attention to God and call upon Him, we receive comfort and compassion. He strengthens us and gets us through.

For just as the sufferings of Christ flow over into our lives, so also through Christ our comfort overflows. (2 Cor. 1:5)

April 8

DESERTED AND ALONE

No one came to my support, but everyone deserted me. But the Lord stood at my side, and gave me strength. (2 Tim. 4:16-17)

Paul the apostle experienced great loneliness and felt deserted many times by his friends. The one thing, that got him through was that he knew the Lord was standing by his side giving him strength. He had the vision and the desire that God had gave him to reach the lost for Christ. This is an example of what many of us feel from time to time. Andrew Murray once stated in his autobiography that the main thought he hung on to in his lonely difficult times was that when the Lord gives you a desire, vision, or dream, He will bring it to pass. If you are feeling lonely and deserted, and you do not see the light at the end of the tunnel; do not despair! Just wait and trust Him. If we are able to release it all to Him, when the time is right, deliverance will come. God is not in any sort of hurry at all. It will take time. Let Him have all the time He needs. Walk with Him, not lagging behind, nor pushing and running ahead. Step in time with the Master and allow Him to unfold the dream as He wills. Paul was alone, he knew the Lord was standing by his side and that is what gave him the strength to continue.

Though the mountains be shaken and the hills removed, yet my unfailing love for you will not be shaken nor my covenant of peace be removed says the Lord who has compassion on you. (Isa. 54:10)

THE LAST TEMPTATION

For in Christ, all the fullness of the Deity lives in bodily form. (Col. 2:9)

Jesus was fully the Son of God and fully the son of man. The last temptation of Jesus in the Garden of Gethsemane was by far His greatest and most severe. The future of all mankind and its redemption was placed upon the body of the Lord Jesus. The reconciliation of the human race to the Father was dependent upon the Lord's strength of purpose and His physical endurance to die the cruel death upon the cross. To make the sacrifice acceptable, He had to totally lay aside His divine nature and become the sacrificial lamb in the form of flesh and blood in order to make the atonement complete and valid. At any time He could have decided it was too much and used His powers to help Him through the process, but He willingly laid His deity down and died the death of a man. He emptied Himself completely and took upon Himself the sins of the whole world. Jesus who never sinned made the perfect sacrifice getting it through to the Father that you and I may also get through to the Father, opening the way for us to enter into life. Jesus' great victory was His death on the cross! He overcame Satan's last temptation and won the victory for us.

Let us fi x our eyes on Jesus, the author and perfecter of our faith who for the joy set before Him endured the cross, scorning its shame, and sat down at the right hand of the Father. (Hew. 12:2)

April 10

LOVING LIKE JESUS

The fruit of the Spirit is love, joy, peace, patience, kindness, goodness, faithfulness, gentleness, and self-control. (Gal. 5:22)

We love Jesus because He first loved us. When we ponder and imagine the love and sacrifice Christ made and demonstrated upon the cross, how can we not love Him in return? God the Father so loved us that He gave us His Son. Jesus agreed to come and suffer because of the nature of love in Him. If Jesus did that for me, that through the sacrifice of His shed blood, I was washed clean from my sins and given new life, meaning and purpose; can He not empower me to love even the most unlovable? Yes, but true love: genuine love must be cultivated, nurtured like you would care for a tender plant: watered, fertilized, and trimmed, given sunshine, fresh air and just the right amount of shade. You don't want to overwater it, or underwater it. God's love is a most precious gift. Our love for Him doesn't always come naturally. It is our nature to be selfish. To understand God's love, we have to develop a relationship with Him and with His Word. To love like Jesus is the opposite of our selfishness. God's love is always giving itself away.

It was just before the Passover Feast. Jesus knew that the time had come for Him to leave this world and go to the Father. Having loved His own who were in the world, He now showed them the full extent of His love. (Jn. 13:1)

April 11

WALK OF FAITH

Let not your heart be troubled: you believe in God believe also in me. In my Father's house are many mansions: if it were not so, I would have told you. I go to prepare a place for you. (Jn. 14:1-2)

The one absolute thing we can depend and safely trust in is God's Word to us. Our walk with the Lord is one of faith and trust. Jesus has proven Himself faithful to us in every way and has given us reason to believe. He will forever protect, lead and provide for all those who put their trust and faith in Him. His voice is full of compassion for us when we hear Him say *"Let not your heart be troubled,"* He asks us to *"Believe in God and believe also in me."* We know that our deliverance will come. We have a home that Jesus has prepared for us. Let your belief in Him and in His Word of promise strengthen you today. The Lord's promises to us are true and they will come to pass if we do not turn back. Keep looking forward and let not your heart be troubled but believe in the one whose love for you is never ending and so much more than what you could know!

For our light and momentary troubles are achieving for us an eternal glory that far outweighs them all. (2 Cor. 4:17)

IT IS AS YOU SAY

The High priest said to Him, I charge you under oath by the Living God: Tell us if you are the Christ, the Son of God. "Yes, it is as you say, "Jesus replied. "But I say to all of you in the future you will see the Son of Man sitting at the right hand of the Mighty One and coming on the clouds of heaven." Then the high priest tore his clothes and said, "He has spoken blasphemy! Why do we need any more witnesses? Look, now you have heard the blasphemy. What do you think?" "He is worthy of death," they answered. (Matt. 26:63-66)

The crime that the leaders of the Sanhedrin and the Chief priests condemned Jesus to death for was blasphemy. The high priest heard these words of Jesus, and he tore his clothes as was the custom when they wanted to demonstrate a great offense, *"He is worthy of death,"* was their reply. This was Jesus' punishment for telling them the truth as to who He was and what was to occur in the future. In spite of, and because of all the many miracles they had heard of and had even seen for themselves, their hearts had been hardened, their eyes blinded with jealously and hatred: condemning Jesus who was all goodness, righteousness and truth. He knew that in speaking this truth it would condemn Him to death.

Greater love has no one than this that one lay down his life for his friends. (Jn.15:13)

April 13

UNWAVERING TRUTH

I am the good shepherd: I lay down my life for the sheep. The reason my Father loves me is that I lay down my life—only to take it up again. No one takes it from me, but I lay it down of my own accord. (Jn. 10:14-15,17-18)

Jesus, when asked the question: *"Are you the Messiah the Christ of God?"* His answer was *"Yes, it is as you say,"* knowing that those words would seal His death; He spoke the truth and never wavered. Jesus laid down His life for us; He made no defense for Himself, just simply spoke the unwavering truth: *"It is as you say."* (Matt. 26:63) Are we speaking the truth of our faith today in the face of unbelief and hardness of hearts? Are we standing in His truth and in His love? Are we willing to make whatever sacrifice necessary in taking the risk of being misunderstood and rejected? Jesus did not waver when asked the question that would determine His fate. He knew it was for this very purpose that He was born. It takes courage to stand up for our faith when in the company of unbelievers and worldly pressure. There are risks that we take in the speaking out of truth. We need to get to that place where we can speak the unwavering truth of our faith no matter what consequences may come as a result.

Let us hold unswervingly to the hope we profess, for He who promised is faithful. (Heb.10:23)

April 14

IT IS FINISHED

When He had received the drink, Jesus said, "It is finished." With that, He bowed His head and gave up his Spirit. (Jn. 19:30)

These were the words that Jesus longed to say at last and that the work the Father had given Him was completed. The time had finally arrived for Him to return to glory and to His rightful authority; offering eternal life to all people from that time forth. Jesus brought glory to the Father throughout His whole life on earth. Every work and miracle that He did gave witness to everyone that He was sent from God and was submitted entirely to the Father. From birth to death all the Holy Scriptures bore witness and fulfilled every prophecy to the highest degree of accuracy. In His own words Jesus prayed this prayer to the Father: *"Father, the time has come, glorify your son, that your son may glorify You. For you granted Him authority over all people that He might give eternal life to all those you have given Him. Now this is eternal life: that they may know you, the only true God, and Jesus Christ, whom you have sent. I have brought you glory on earth by completing the work you gave me to do. And now, Father, glorify me in your presence with the glory I had with you before the world began.* (Jn. 17:1-5) It is in this completed work of Christ that we are all made to be partakers of.

For in Christ all the fullness of the Deity lives in bodily form, and you have been given fullness in Christ, (been made complete in Him), who is the head over every power and authority. (Col. 2:9-10)

April 15

REJOICE

So they went out quickly from the tomb with fear and great joy, and ran to bring His disciples word. And as they went to tell His disciples, behold, Jesus met them, saying, "Rejoice!" So they came and held Him by the feet and worshiped Him. Then Jesus said to them, "Do not be afraid. Go and tell my brethren to go to Galilee, and there they will see me." (Matt. 28:8-10)

The very first word that Jesus spoke after His resurrection to Mary Magdalene and Mary of Bethany was the word "rejoice." Joy and celebration was what the Lord wanted to convey to them at His very first appearance. He had paved the way for all to follow and to obtain everlasting life, victory over death at last! *Christ redeemed us from the curse of the law by becoming a curse for us, for it is written Cursed is everyone who is hung on a tree. He redeemed us in order that the blessing given to Abraham might come to the Gentiles through Christ Jesus, so that by faith we might receive the promise of the Spirit.* (Gal. 3:13-1) This is the reason we rejoice! Easter Day is Resurrection Day the most celebrated of all! We can now be set free from the chains that bound us and receive newness of life and victory over sin and of the world's influences. It is because of our faith in the historical fact of the resurrected Christ, that we have this joy inexpressible: a reason to rejoice, a reason to celebrate. The Lord speaks to us today and tells us to "rejoice!"

Though you have not seen Him, you love Him; and even though you do not see Him now, you believe in Him and are filled with an inexpressible and glorious joy, for you are receiving the goal of your faith, the salvation of your souls. (1 Pet. 1:8-9)

April 16

THE FULLNESS OF CHRIST IN US

And God placed all things under His feet and appointed Him to be head over everything for the Church, which is His body, the fullness of Him who fills everything in every way. (Ephes. 1:18-23)

We have been given this fullness of Christ Himself; the finished work of the cross has been done once and for all time. Paul prayed this prayer for the church: *I pray that the eyes of your heart may be enlightened in order that you may know the hope to which He has called you, the riches of His glorious inheritance in the saints, and His incomparably great power for us who believe. That power is like the working of His mighty strength, which He exerted in Christ when He raised Him from the dead and seated Him at His right hand in the heavenly realms, far above all rule and authority, power and dominion, and every title that can be given, not only in the present age but also in the one to come.* (Ephes. 1:18-21) We are now His fullness expressed on the earth for all to see. It is because of His power that works in us that we are able to do works of faith that bring glory to Him. When Jesus said "It is finished," His sufferings on earth would end, He would return to His rightful place of authority and glory. The Church for all ages would receive the finished work that Christ accomplished in our bodies; *the fullness of Himself which fills all in all.* (Ephes. 1:23) It is because of the completed work of Christ that we now can receive this fullness which is an immeasurable gift that is ours forever!

Christ in you, the hope of glory. (Col.1:27)

April 17

LIVING HOPE

Praise be to the God and Father of our Lord Jesus Christ. In His great mercy He has given us new birth into a living hope through the resurrection of Jesus Christ from the dead. (1 Pet. 1:3)

We have been given a living hope; a hope that is alive and breathing, present in our day by day circumstances and experience. Our spirits were born into a living hope when we first believed. It is the fact of the resurrection of Jesus that brings us into it. When we have living hope in our hearts, we are encouraged. This is something we need every day; to be encouraged in our faith and to have a strong resolution to serve and obey until the end. It gives us optimistic thoughts of better days ahead and of a good future planned as we wait filled with this living hope. In the book of Hebrews, we see that it was God's will to make it clear to the heirs of the promise, (Abraham's seed) which includes you and me) confirming it with an oath in order for us to have this hope, hope that is alive and secured. It is *offered* to us; our part is to take a hold of it. Hope serves to be an anchor for our soul, it tethers us to the Lord. We are grounded and secure in this living hope.

God did this; (made the oath) so that by two unchangeable things in which it is impossible for God to lie, we who have fled to take hold of the hope offered to us may be greatly encouraged. We have this hope as an anchor for the soul, firm and secure. (Heb. 6:18-19)

HOPE IS A SPRING FOR FAITH AND LOVE

The faith and love that spring from the hope that is stored up for you in heaven and that you have already heard about in the Word of truth. (Col. 1:5)

Love and faith also spring up from hope. We all need more faith and more love. Hope is the spring that produces the faith and the love. We have been given the gift of a hope that is alive and active. Whenever we begin to doubt, run to take hold of it once again. It is the anchor of your soul, a firm and secure dwelling place; a promise from God, in which it is impossible for Him to lie. On that first resurrection morning Jesus our Living Hope was born into our hearts. It is because He rose from the dead that this hope remains alive in our hearts today. As a result, more love and faith are produced. It springs up from the hope, that we have been given. In spite of whatever dire circumstances you may find yourself in; hold fast and firm to the hope that is offered in God and be encouraged today.

For everything that was written in the past was written to teach us, so that through the endurance and the encouragement of the Scriptures we might have hope. (Rom. 15:4)

April 19

THE LILY EFFECT

See how the lilies of the field grow. They do not labor or spin. Yet I tell you that Solomon in all his splendor was not dressed as one of these. (Matt. 6:29)

One of the biggest obstacles in our spiritual growth is our own concentrated efforts to be of use. Many times we just get in the way of what the Holy Spirit wishes to accomplish. The principal of the lily effect is to see ourselves as flowers in the process of blooming. The flower is not aware or is conscious of its petals being formed; nor did it decide what color or form it would take. God undertakes the design of it and one day it appears in its full glory. God provides the sunlight and water that the flower needs to grow. Miraculously, overtime, the beautiful flower appears. In the same way, we do not yet know what or how we will appear to be, but the Master does. As we eat and drink in His Word and bask in the sunlight of His love, the Creator God undertakes the design of us and we need not make such a great effort or strain. We are each one to Him more precious that all the flowers of the world put together! Do not worry, He is the one in control, surrender to His will that Christ may be formed in and through you. This is the lily effect.

Therefore I tell you; do not worry about your life, what you will eat or drink; or what you shall wear. See how the lilies of the field grow. (Matt. 6:25, 28)

FOUNTAINS OF LIFE

All my fountains are in You. (Ps. 87:7)

Every good virtue we possess is from Him. Being born again from above is a perpetual and eternal beginning; a freshness all the time in our thinking, talking, and living. It is a continual surprise of the life that God is working in us. It is in the Lord alone that fountains of life and fresh springs of living water can be found. It is from our innermost desires of heart and mind that spring forth fountains of life and new inspiration from God. He is Himself the source and creator of these fresh springs of living water. Sometimes it seems life becomes like a stagnant pool, or a dried up barren desert land. We long for change; for fresh springs to rise up, awakening us so that we might catch a glimpse of some new horizon. It's frustrating at times to go through the day by day routine; having to perform the mundane activities which include all the small details of ordinary living. We want to fly away, but still find ourselves bound to the earth. Ask the Lord to refresh you with these springs of living water that flow from the fountain of life. He will do it!

For with You is the fountain of life. (Ps.36:9)

April 21

THE GARDEN OF YOUR SOUL

The Lord will guide you always; He will satisfy your needs in a sun-scorched land and will strengthen your frame. You will be like a well-watered garden, like a spring whose waters never fail. (Isa. 58:11)

Jesus spoke of this living water flowing out from Him; it is this same water that is freely given to all who seek, believe, and desire it. (Jn.7:37) Our physical circumstances do not necessarily need to hinder this living water from flowing. Though bound in prison, Paul and Silas still praised and worshiped God; the living water was flowing from them in spite of the chains that held them. Let's ask God for these fresh springs of water to flow out from us. Every day brings unique possibilities; we are new creations in Him, old things are passing away, all things are becoming new, like fresh springs of water. Dear Lord, please cause Your fresh springs of living water, and new fountains of life to flow through my desert land today and quench my thirsty lips and heart. Thank You for the gift of Your living waters Amen . . .

For the Lamb at the center of the Throne will be their shepherd He will lead them to springs of living water. (Rev. 7:17)

April 22

RETURN WITH THANKSGIVING

How can I repay the Lord for all His goodness to me? I will lift up the cup of salvation and call on the name of the Lord in the presence of all His people. (Ps. 116:12, 17)

The God we serve desires to be an integral part of all that we do and in how we live. We lift up the cup of salvation and call upon the name of the Lord, for He has done great things for us. We are His people the sheep of His hand. Give Him all praise and honor every day, in all your ways acknowledge Him. He will move, deliver, provide, and restore everything that the enemy has taken from you, just remember to return to give Him thanks! This was Israel's sin and big disappointment to the Lord. They forgot all about the good He had done for them and they went on their way. *Give thanks in all circumstances, for this is God's will for you in Christ Jesus.* (1 Thes.5:18) Dear Lord, thank You for all things, even when I find it hard to understand your workings, I give You praise today and thanksgiving for the gift of my salvation and for the many ways You have shown Your love for me in days gone by and in right now in this present moment. Amen . . .

Let the peace of Christ rule in your hearts, since as member of one body you are called to peace. And be thankful. (Col.3:15)

April 23

ADDING TO FAITH

Make every effort to add to your faith goodness; and to goodness, knowledge; and to knowledge, self-control; and to self-control, perseverance; and perseverance, godliness; and to godliness, brotherly kindness, and to brotherly kindness, love. For if you possess these qualities in increasing measure, they will keep you from being ineffective and unproductive in your knowledge of our Lord Jesus Christ. Be all the more eager to make your calling and election sure. For if you do these things, you will never fall. (2 Pet. 1:5-7,10)

All of the qualities listed in the above scriptures, begin with faith and end with the ultimate and best gift of all which is love. By building up my faith, I can add all of those spiritual gifts to my life increasing them daily; this will cause me to be fruitful and productive in my knowledge of the Lord, and they (the gifts) will keep me from falling and from going backwards. I will never fall or go backwards if I am able to develop these gifts in my character. If the ultimate gift is to love as God loves, and if faith is the key to obtain it, then I want more faith. We are the branches drinking in the Water of Life; (the Living Word of God) This is what we need to do to have more faith.

Faith comes by hearing the message, and the message is heard through the Word of Christ. (Rom. 10:17)

April 24

INCREASE OUR FAITH

Increase our faith! (Lk. 17:5)

The Apostle Luke recognized the importance of building faith and asked the Lord for more faith. Faith produces good fruit in our lives. Faith comes as we gain more knowledge the Lord and of His Word. Knowing His Word brings the faith we need to grow all the good fruits, love being the ultimate one. This implies an action on our part. There is something we must do to secure this life of godliness. How is more faith obtained? The best and most important thing we can do is to continue to hear, read, and meditate upon God's Word. *The only thing that counts is faith expressing itself by love.* (Gal. 5:6) If we are really serious about increasing our faith, then it's time to do the things necessary to really hear and study the Word of the Lord. Just sitting quietly daily reading the Bible is the best; but when I am working around the house or even in the car, I can put in a CD or tape of the New & Old Testament and listen. It is up to us individually to find ways to do the things that build our faith. It is something that needs priority if we are really sincere about wanting to please the Lord and to be fruit bearing branches. To add to my faith, I must seek God's wisdom and knowledge through His Word.

Then they asked Him, "What must we do to do the works God requires?" Jesus answered, "The work of God is this; to believe in the one He has sent." (Jn. 6:28-29)

April 25

HIDDEN TREASURES OF DARKNESS

I will give you the treasures of darkness, riches stored in secret places, so that you may know that I am the Lord, the God of Israel that calls you by name. (Isa. 45:3)

What are treasures of darkness? I think of times when all was very dark in my life. There was no light and I was in the dark. I called upon the Lord and He gave me treasures in my darkness. The Lord does this so often. There are treasures within the dark when we seek Him and call upon Him. The importance of the trial and the benefit of it will be revealed in time. If we have found a treasure, a pearl of great price in Jesus, we must continue to search for and seek out all the riches that reside in Him. Will we gladly give up all we have in order to have more of Him and to know the height and depth of His great love? If you should find yourself lying awake in the night or in the early morning; that is the time to seek and search for Him in that quiet place. The Lord Jesus in the life of a believer is a life that continues to look for opportunities to be alone with Him; there is a yearning and longing for more and more of His Presence, more and more of His love and wisdom. It is this thirst and desire inside of us that can only be filled by Him. He will never abandon anyone who searches for Him. *O God, You are my God, earnestly I seek You.* (Ps 63:1) Continue to seek, search, and draw near, with all your heart. There are inexhaustible treasures in Jesus although sometimes acquired in darkness. It is His desire and joy to reveal and to bless you with these hidden treasures when you have taken the time to search for Him. *I love those who love me, and those who seek me find me.* (Prov. 8:17)

From one man he made every nation of men that they should inhabit the whole earth; and He determined the times set for them and the exact places where they would live. God did this so that men would seek Him and perhaps reach out for Him and find Him, though He is not far from each one of us. (Ac. 17:26-27)

ABOUNDING FRUIT

If you possess these qualities in increasing measure, they will keep you from being ineffective and unproductive in your knowledge of the Lord Jesus Christ. (2 Pet.1:8)

The qualities that Peter was talking about were the fruits of the spirit: faith, goodness, knowledge, self-control, perseverance, godliness, kindness, and love. Our lives need to become one unbroken chain of actions taken, springing out of and from our love for God and others; naturally as a spring of water flows; unconsciously, childlike and simply. Developing good habits of prayer and in the reading of God's Word are important for growing these qualities. At the same time, beware of getting too habitual and in the process, become unable to hear His voice when He leads: even to the changing around of your normal routine. Sometimes we hinder God's designed influence through us by our self conscious effort to be consistent and useful. Our walk with Christ should be spontaneous, ever fresh and new. The Lord says that there is only one way to develop spiritually, and that is by concentration on Him. Pay attention to the source, and out of you will flow living water. You will produce fruit, abounding fruit that will last and last!

You did not choose me, but I chose you to go and bear fruit—fruit that will last. (Jn. 15:16)

DO NOT LOSE HEART

Therefore we do not lose heart. Though outwardly we are wasting away, yet inwardly we are being renewed day by day. (2 Cor. 4:16)

When we feel tired and discouraged and our spirits feel the heaviness of the circumstances, it can be very hard to find strength for even the littlest things. But if we make the decision not to lose heart, and begin doing the smallest things on hand, asking for help from God, He will give you what you need to perform that simple task and the one following will come easier as you lean and learn to depend upon Him for your help. The important thing to remember is to not lose heart and don't give up. Jesus came to set us free from depression, sadness of heart, and to give us the oil of joy for the spirit of heaviness (or depression). This is exactly what Jesus came to do for you and me. Let us take a little step today asking for His strength and help. He will continue to provide you with the next one and the one after that as we lean upon Him for our strength. Don't give up and do not lose heart.

He has sent me to bind up the broken hearted, to proclaim freedom of the captives to comfort all who mourn: to bestow on them a crown of beauty instead of ashes, the oil of gladness instead of mourning, and a garment of praise for a spirit of despair. (Isa. 61:1,3)

GROWTH OF THE KINGDOM

For as the soil makes the sprout come up and a garden causes seeds to grow, so the Sovereign LORD will make righteousness and praise spring up before all nations. (Isa. 61:11)

It is the Lord Himself that will cause righteousness and praise to spring up before all the nations. In Isaiah chapter 61 verse 10, speaks of the state of the Church; *He has clothed me with the garments of salvation and arrayed me in a robe of righteousness.* In the current world events we can see the many peoples of different countries and nations crying out for their freedoms. This cry for liberation seems to be sweeping across the globe. It is a desire being expressed by those who have been suffering under oppressive and cruel governments. This oppression has been going on since the fall of man. Chapter 61 in Isaiah is a description of Jesus' whole purpose for coming, it says: *He came to claim freedom for the captives* (Is 61:1) Freedom to choose and have a free will is a God given right from the beginning of creation. People are willing to die and are dying in order to be free. In Isaiah 61:11, we are given hope to know that God's Word will be fulfilled and that righteousness and praise will spring up before all the nations. The Lord will make this happen; the righteous will one day be victorious in all nations.

He was given authority, glory and sovereign power; all peoples, nations and men of every language worshipped Him. His dominion is an everlasting dominion that will not pass away, and His Kingdom is one that will never be destroyed. (Dan 7:14)

THE LORD WILL REIGN

Of the increase of His government and peace there will be no end. He will reign on David's throne and over his kingdom, establishing righteousness from that time on and forever. The zeal of the LORD Almighty will accomplish this. (Isa. 9:7)

God is coming to establish His Kingdom here on earth and we can see this growth of the Kingdom here and now. We see the Kingdoms of the earth crumbling all around us: in the midst of it all, God is creating a Kingdom that will last forever. This is where we can have great hope for today. Jesus has been given all authority both in earth and in Heaven. His Kingdom is from everlasting to everlasting; today, tomorrow and forever. *Jesus has gone into heaven and is at God's right hand—with angels, authorities and powers in submission to Him.* (1 Pet. 3:22) Dear Lord, let Your Kingdom come into the lives of every soul all over the earth that is crying out for freedom in our day. Please protect and help them in their quest . . . Let Your Kingdom grow and sprout up righteousness before all the nations . . . Amen.

And God placed all things under His feet and appointed Him to be the head over everything for the church. (Ephes. 1:22)

April 30

COME UNTO ME

Come unto me. (Matt. 11:28)

When Jesus calls us to *"Come unto me,"* at the same time, He wants to come unto us. We must get everything, all our pride and hesitations out of the way and embrace Him fully. Come to the foot of the cross and gaze into the suffering Christ. Can you not bring to Him your brokenness and allow your heart to melt before Him? He has purchased us with His own blood, we belong to Him. Give Him everything. He can and desires to hold you when we simply come. We should always keep in our minds the atonement of Christ. We died, (our old sinful nature) with Christ and have been raised to new life. *Offer yourselves to God as those who have been brought from death to life.* (Rom. 6:1) Our obedience will lead into righteousness; so will follow our works of faith because of Christ's completed work upon the cross. I like what Oswald Chambers once said, "The great need is not to do things, but to believe things." More faith is what we all need. Obedience will follow your faith and your works also. Our Salvation in Christ will manifest itself in our everyday lives as we come unto Him daily.

For He has made Him to be sin for us, who knew no sin, that we might be made the righteousness of God in Him. (2 Cor.5:21)

May 1

THE GREATEST TREASURE IS WISDOM

You will understand what is right and just and fair—every good path. For wisdom will enter your heart, and knowledge will be pleasant to your soul: discretion will protect you, and understanding will guard you. (Prov. 2:8-9)

Some of the great results from listening and adhering to the Lord's wisdom through His Word are this: we have discernment and understanding into circumstances, we are saved and protected by using discretion, (prudent cautious reserve) and in so doing, avoid painful mistakes. We also have the assurance of protection and safety. If the wisdom from the Lord is something that we know to be more valuable than gold or any other thing; and if we truly value the Words of the Lord more than any other earthly treasure, then these things meditating on His Word and prayer are not burdensome but become our passion and greatest desire. There is joy and renewal of life as we pursue it. As our love for the Lord grows, our love for His Word grows in proportion, for He is the Word Himself and He is Wisdom itself. (John 1:1-4) The God of all wisdom, is worthy of all our reverent praise and worship. As we practice to seek after His wisdom, we will obtain instruction from the Lord, discretion and understanding through His Word, and it will become more and more pleasant to our souls.

By wisdom the Lord laid the earth's foundations, by understanding He set the heavens in place. (Prov. 3:19)

May 2

THE FLAWLESS WORD OF GOD

As for God, His way is perfect. The Word of the Lord is flawless. He is a shield for all those who take refuge in Him. You give me your shield of victory and your right hand sustains me. (Ps 18:30)

We are shielded from harm and danger when we take our refuge in Him. He gives us a shield of victory over all our enemies and His right hand provides and takes care of us. We have been given the Sword of His Word as our defense; it is pure, flawless, clean, true and perfect, able to give us victory in every situation. *Take the helmet of salvation and the Sword of the Spirit, which is the Word of God.* (Ephes. 6:17) The sword is a defensive weapon that is used for protection and combat. The weapon mentioned here is the Sword of the Spirit which is the Word of God given to us as a means of defense against the spiritual battles we may face from time to time. There are many scriptures that link the Word of God as a means of protection for us to have and to take hold of.

"I will now arise." says the Lord. I will protect them from those who malign them. The Words of the Lord are flawless, like silver refined in a furnace of clay, purified seven times. (Ps.12:5-6)

REJOICING IN PERSECUTIONS

Blessed are you when people insult you, persecute you, and falsely saying all kinds of evil against you because of me. Rejoice and be glad, because great is your reward in heaven. (Matt. 5:11-12)

If you have family and friends who are non-believers, often they will not accept or receive your new found faith with open arms of love and welcome. They may judge or criticize you without cause; this is something that may surprise you but can be expected. When you feel the undercurrents of being wrongly judged or accused, rejoice because the Lord has said it would happen. It is part of what we experience in Christian life. Our responsibility is to pray for them because they probably do not even understand what it is they are doing or why. *Blessed is the man who perseveres under trial, because when he has stood the test, he will receive the crown of life that God has promised to those who love Him.* (Jas. 1:12) *And when the Chief Shepherd appears, you will receive the crown of glory that will never fade away.* (Rev. 2:10) The enemy of our souls, Satan, the liar and accuser wants so badly to take your crown and trample upon it. We must resist the temptation to retaliate and hold on to what we have been given thus far. If we are to be over comers in this life, we must fight the darkness with light; anxiety, fear and unbelief with faith; doubt and depression with hope; strife and anger with peace. The enemy cannot stand or prevail against these things.

I am coming soon. Hold on to what you have, so that no one will take your crown. (Rev. 3:11)

May 4

PEACEMAKERS

I came not to send peace on earth, but a sword. (Mt.10:34)

Christ is the great Peacemaker; but before peace, many times there is war. When the light comes, the darkness resides close by as well. Where there's truth, lies vanish away. If truth abides, there is usually stern conflict; for truth must prevail, and the lie exposed to be done away with. We can be assured that the Christian will have enemies. It is still better to have a brief warfare and an eternal rest, than false peace and everlasting torment. Even though it is inevitable that we will acquire enemies as the result of living our belief, it is the responsibility of Christians to love them and to pray for them *Love your enemies and pray for those who persecute you, that you may be sons (and daughters) of your Father in heaven. He causes His sun to rise on the evil and he good, and sends rain on the righteous and the unrighteous.* (Matt. 5:44-45) Not only do we have enemies within family circles and with people we thought were our friends, but the worst and most painful situations occur right within our own churches. The scripture also talks about the wheat and the tares growing side by side until the harvest. If you cannot find it in yourself to forgive, ask the Lord to give you the forgiveness for those who have hurt you. Over time, it will happen!

Blessed are the peacemakers, for they will be called sons of God. Blessed are those who are persecuted because of righteousness, for theirs is the kingdom of heaven. (Matt. 5:9-10)

May 5

TAKE REFUGE IN HIS PERFECTION

Let all who take refuge in You be glad; let them ever sing for joy. Spread Your protection over them; that those who love Your name may rejoice in You. For surely, O Lord, You bless the righteous; You surround them with Your favor as with a shield. (Ps. 5:11-12)

Take refuge in the Lord and be glad, for surely He surrounds us as with a shield. We have every reason to rejoice, to sing and be glad, for it is His will that we do. The more we practice this, the more favor and blessing we will find. To think that the one thing that you can always depend upon is God's Word; its perfection, without error, and it is ours to have and use when we need it in each and every situation. It is sure to protect and keep us this very day, in and through everything. With this in mind, we gain a renewed sense of appreciation and awe in the reading of it. So many things around us are flawed and imperfect; it is very assuring and comforting to know that the one place we can go and are always welcomed, in our broken and imperfect state, is to the perfect Word of God, accepted into His Presence, there to receive the grace and strength needed for our daily concerns. Every Word of God is flawless; it is perfection. *He is a shield to those who take refuge in Him.* (Isa.30:5)

The Word became flesh and dwelt among us.

(Jn.1:14) *His name is the Word of God.* (Rev.19:13)

May 6

FOUNDATIONS WITH SAPPHIRES

Oh afflicted city lashed by storms and not comforted, I will build you with stones of turquoise, and your foundations with sapphires, great will be your children's peace: in righteousness you will be established. (Isa. 54:11, 13-14)

There are many upheavals and great storms that we go through in life. The Jerusalem here on earth, has been afflicted and lashed by storm after storm throughout the ages. In the end, God will rebuild and establish it with foundations of sapphires, restoring it in righteousness and peace. *The foundations of the city walls were decorated with every kind of precious stone.* (Rev. 21:19) The beautiful and precious foundational stones of the heavenly Jerusalem are representative of the lasting and sure foundation that we have in Christ: precious, enduring and strong. Jesus Himself the Chief Cornerstone and it is Christ who has laid the foundation and is the foundation upon which we stand. *See, I lay a stone in Zion, a tested stone, a precious cornerstone for a sure foundation; the one who trusts in Him, will never be dismayed.* (Isa. 28:16) Zion is a picture of the church; it is Jesus our precious cornerstone that has given us the firm foundation of His Word to stand upon and the precious gift of grace that establishes it and us eternally. *For no one can lay any foundation other than the one already laid, which is Jesus Christ.* (Ephes.2:20) Although the winds of great storms may blow upon us, those who are firmly established in His Word and in His grace will withstand everything that comes. The foundations of our faith may be invisible to the eye, but they are like sparkling sapphires, jewels that shine and radiate eternal in the heavens.

Therefore, everyone who hears these words of mine and puts them into practice is like a wise man who built his house on the rock. (Matt.7:24)

May 7

MOUNTAINS TO ROADS

He who has compassion on them will guide them and lead them beside springs of water. I will turn all my mountains into roads, and my highways will be raised up. (Isa. 49:10-11)

It may appear that there are great mountains and boulders obstructing our paths and making it difficult to move forward. The Lord Almighty God will turn those mountains into a clear highway for us to travel freely upon. The Lord is compassionate and cares when we feel that we are at an impasse in our lives. He is our Great Sheppard that guides and leads us; He is the Sheppard that enters by the gate. *The man who enters by the gate is the shepherd of His sheep. The sheep listen to His voice. He calls His own sheep by name and leads them out. When He has brought out all His own, He goes on ahead of them, and His sheep follow Him because they know His voice.* (Jn.10:3-4) When we look to the Lord, and allow Him to go before us, and open our ears to hear His voice, He will take the lead and make a clear way for us to go. There are many mountains that come up before us in life. God has promised to turn all of our mountains into roads, but we must trust, depend, and look to Him to do this. No matter how difficult and big those mountains appear, He will level them and make a way for you to walk.

I will go before you and will level the mountains; I will breakdown gates of bronze and cut through bars of iron. (Isa. 45:2)

MAKING LEVEL PATHS

Therefore, strengthen your feeble arms and weak knees, Make level paths for your feet. (Heb. 12:12-13)

If we should find ourselves feeling distressed and at a crossroad where we do not know what to do or where to go, we should ask for direction from the Lord. He will be sure to answer and bring us His peace. *This is what the Lord says, " Stand at the crossroads and look; ask where the good way is, and walk in it, and you will find rest for your souls."* (Jer. 6:16) The Lord leaves it up to us to make our paths level, He would not tell us to do this if it were not possible. We cannot do this in our own strength, but we can through Him who strengthens us. (Phil. 4:13) Reach ahead to what and where the Lord is directing you to. The past is gone and cannot be altered or changed, learn from the mistakes made and press on into the future that the Lord our Great Sheppard is gently leading you to. Fix your eyes straight ahead; not veering off to the right or to the left, or over your shoulder and God will surely make your path level. *"Forget the former things; do not dwell on the past. See, I am doing a new thing! Now it springs up; do you not perceive it? I am making a way in the desert and streams in the wasteland."* (Isa. 43:18-19).

Forgetting what is behind and straining toward what is ahead, I press on toward the goal to win the prize for which God has called me heavenward in Christ Jesus. (Phil. 3:13)

May 9

REDEEMING THE TIME

See then that you walk circumspectly, not as fools but as wise, redeeming the time, because the days are evil. (Ephes. 5:15-16)

To walk circumspectly is to walk carefully. We all do foolish things from time to time; the Lord would have us to put away the foolish things of our past and begin to walk with purpose and understanding. It is the will of the Lord that we become mature and no longer tossed and turned back to our previous life and mistakes. Spiritual understanding and maturity is a long process, but there are things we can do that will help us to walk carefully in the wisdom of the Lord. The Redeeming our time is making the most of every opportunity that we have. In our world today, there are a million things that can we can turn our attention to and that does not edify or build up our spirits. The two very best ways we can redeem our time is in the reading of God's Word and in prayer. Let us renew our commitment to do this every day. As time goes by, we will know and understand what the will of the Lord is. There will be new opportunities from God that we will recognize and take hold of. The reason that Paul tells us to walk carefully is because the days are evil; just as it was in their time, so it is today.

Be self controlled and alert. Your enemy the devil prowls around like a roaring lion looking for someone to devour. Resist him, standing firm in the faith. (1 Pet. 5:8-9)

MATURE IN CHRIST

Until we all reach unity in the faith and in the knowledge of the Son of God and become mature attaining to the whole measure of the fullness of Christ. Then we will no longer be infants, tossed back and forth by the waves, and blown here and there by every wind of teaching and by the cunning and craftiness of men in their deceitful scheming. Instead, speaking the truth in love, we will in all things grow up into Him who is the Head that is Christ. From Him the whole body, joined and held together by every supporting ligament, grows and builds itself up in love, as each part does its work. (Ephes. 4:14-16)

This is a great picture of the way the Lord desires to see us. He continues to develop the quality of spiritual maturity in us as we do our part in yielding our wills and hearts over to Him each day. Time is something that we only have so much of and then it will vanish away. When I reflect back over my life, it is hard to imagine all of the years that have come and gone by. It seemed as though they have flown away! Time is the most precious thing I have. When I give my time to the Lord in the studying of His Word, prayer, or in service, it is the greatest way of making the very most of my time and the very best gift I can give to Him. These are acts that show our love, and will teach us the way to walk circumspectly and with wisdom.

When I was a child, I talked like a child, I thought like a child, I reasoned like a child, When I became a man, I put childish ways behind me. Now, we see but a poor reflection; then we shall see face to face. Now I know in part; then I shall know full, even as I am fully known. (1 Cor. 13:11-13)

May 11

LOVE WILL SEEK AND FIND

I love those who love me, and those who seek me find me. (Prov. 8:17)

The word *seek* in the Webster's dictionary is defined as: *To try to locate or discover; search for; to endeavor, to obtain or reach; to move to; go toward; to inquire for, request, to make a search, explore . . .* Sometimes it is not easy in this world of chaos, distraction, trials and perplexities, to make the effort to *seek* and to *know* God through relationship as our top priority. Yet this is what it will require in order to obtain the blessings that are waiting for us when we actually begin to earnestly seek Him. This is a love relationship. We search for Him because we love Him; we are found of Him because He loves us. This is the way the Lord has always meant it to be. Love seeks itself out. The people I love the most are the ones who have shown love and kindness to me; the ones who have encouraged me over the years. You may not have many friends that you love in this way; they are rare treasures. Not only do we seek to find love in people, but most importantly in the one true God who has revealed His great love for us in sending Jesus. It also takes an investment of our time to have long lasting friendships. The promised end result is joy; joy in seeking and knowing His great Love; and in the joy of discovering the love that resides in others!

May all who seek You rejoice and be glad in You; may those who love Your salvation always say, The Lord be exalted! (Ps. 40:16)

May 12

THE LORD OUR STRENGTH

God is our refuge and strength, an ever present help in trouble. Therefore we will not fear, though the earth gives way and the mountains fall into the heart of the sea, though its waters roar and foam and the mountains quake with their surging. (Ps. 46:1-3)

In times of great distress, it is good to remember that God is our strength and help, present in the middle of our troubles. I think of some nations around the world that are at war for their freedom and how difficult it must be for them. It is my prayer that in their times of turmoil and chaos, they will call upon the name of the Lord and begin to serve Him. Although there are terrible wars being fought on other lands, and for the most part, we cannot lend any help in a physical sense other than contributing money for food and medicine; although every Christian believing man or woman should be remembering them in our daily prayers. For the most part, they are the innocent civilians who are caught in the middle of wars and have no real way of defending themselves against oppressive government, military power, and corrupt leaders. We do not understand why, yet we must continue to trust in God who knows all and who will be faithful to help us and them to carry on. Along with growing older, comes a greater awareness of our own frailties and physical weaknesses. It is the Lord who is our strength.

My flesh and my heart may fail, but God is the strength of my heart and my portion forever. (Ps. 73:26)

May 13

THE LORD ARMS US WITH STRENGTH

You descendants of Abraham my friend, I took you from the ends of the earth; from its farthest corners I called you. I said I will strengthen you and help you; I will uphold you with my righteous right hand. Those who oppose you will be as nothing and perish. Though you search for your enemies, you will not find them. For I am the Lord your God who takes hold of your right hand and says to you, "Do not fear; I will help you". (Is. 41:8-10, 12 & 13)

We need strength just to live out our daily lives; just to get up in the morning and perform ordinary activities. Then there are times when we need strength for battle. In David's time, usually there were real life wars and the armies that would go out to fight enemies with weapons and many would die every day. He knew it was the Lord who was his strength and went before him making his victories sure. For the most part, it is spiritual battles we face in our country today; enemies, principalities and powers of Satan that war against your soul and mine. (Ephes. 6:12) In Isaiah, the Lord gives us a clear picture as He refers to this kind of battle when He addresses the descendants of Abraham: (who we are). Whether a physical or spiritual battle, or when we face danger of war and natural disasters, we have a sure promise from the Lord that He will strengthen us, help us, and He tells us over and over again, *"Do not fear."* the Lord God Almighty is the complete and entire source of our strength and help.

It is God who arms me with strength and makes my way perfect. (2 Sam. 22:33)

The Lord is the strength of His people. (Ps. 28:8)

May 14

COVENANT BLESSINGS AND GLORY

This is the sign of the covenant am making between me and you and every living creature with you, a covenant for all generations to come: I have set my rainbow in the clouds, and it will be the sign of the covenant between me and the earth. Whenever I bring clouds over the earth and the rainbow appears in the clouds, I will see it and remember my covenant between you and all living creatures of every kind. (Gen. 9:12-13)

When cloudy days come, rain usually follows. I always look around in the sky for rainbows and when I find one, it is a reminder to me of God's faithfulness to His covenant promise that He made to Noah and to all the future generations to come. Though the waters may rise, they will never again completely cover all the dry land of the earth causing all the living to perish. I am also mindful of the New Covenant we have now in Jesus. The word *covenant* defined in Webster's Dictionary as: *binding agreement between two or more persons, a solemn vow, and contract: Jesus the mediator of a new covenant:* (Heb.12:24) The covenant we have with the Lord is one that brings everything that is good so that we will be well equipped to do His will, and in doing so, have all the fullness of life and blessings. The New Covenant is an everlasting agreement made with the precious blood of Jesus. We do our part; God is faithful to do His, not just for today, but forever and ever.

May the God of peace, who through the blood of the eternal covenant brought back from the dead our Lord Jesus, that great Shepherd of the sheep, equip you with everything good for doing His will, and may He work in us what is pleasing to Him. (Heb. 13:20)

May 15

JESUS IS OUR RAINBOW

Like the appearance of a rainbow in the clouds on a rainy day, so was the radiance around Him. This was the appearance of the likeness of the glory of the Lord. When I saw it, I fell face down. (Ezek. 1:28)

Jesus Himself also has the appearance of a rainbow. It was a rainbow that John saw encircling the throne. *At once I was in the Spirit, and there before me was a throne in heaven with someone sitting on it. And the one who sat there had the appearance of jasper and carnelian. A rainbow, resembling an emerald, encircled the throne.* (Rev. 4:2-3) When you see the dark clouds and the rain that follows, look for the rainbow and remember the everlasting covenant we now have through Christ Jesus. Think of the glory of the Lord in all His beauty and power. The rains will come, but the waters will never cover the earth again. Remember the words of Isaiah in chapter 54, that describes all the covenant blessings. In the end the Lord says *"This is the heritage of the servants of the Lord."* We can have all the covenant blessings and even more through Jesus who is the mediator of a new and better one. (Heb. 12:24)

Though the mountains be shaken and the hills be removed, yet my unfailing love for you will not be shaken nor my covenant of peace be removed, says the Lord, who has compassion on you. (Is. 54:10)

KEEPING PACE AND TIME WITH THE LORD

The Lord is near. Do not be anxious about anything, by prayer and petition, with thanksgiving; present your requests to God. And the peace of God, which transcends all understanding, will guard your hearts and your minds in Christ Jesus. (Phil. 4:4-6)

It may not be so easy to figure out what God is aiming at in the fulfillment of His purposes for you. I think the key to understanding this, is in the time we spend alone with the Lord. The more time we give to Him, the more we are enabled to receive the answers to these important questions. There are times when we find ourselves rushing around. This is not the way we should be living. Jesus walked everywhere He went, and was never in a hurry or anxious about anything. By our learning to abide in Him throughout our days and nights, we become like Him. And the peace of God will rule in our hearts. We have been called to peace, not stress. The more we pray and develop relationship with the Lord, the less we seem to be in a hurry. Prayer and thankfulness go together; the more we know Him, the more thankful we become. Let us walk with the Lord at His pace and in His timing, not with the world and its fast speed, but begin to walk at His pace with peace and thankfulness. Once we get a good sense of what and where the Lord is calling us to, set your heart and mind resolutely to go forward God's way, and in His timing.

Let the peace of the Lord will rule in your hearts, since as members of one body you were called to peace. And be thankful. (Col. 3:15)

PRACTICING GOOD HABITS

Therefore everyone who hears these words of mine and puts them into practice is like wise man who built his house on the rock. (Matt. 7:24)

We know that The Word of God is wisdom itself. It is a guide for us to follow that will take us safely through every possible circumstance that comes our way. Here in this scripture Jesus speaks of the importance of putting into practice the words that He speaks to us. *Practice* defined in Webster's Dictionary: *To perform habitually or customarily, make a habit of, to exercise or perform repeatedly in order to learn or perfect a skill, to carry out an action.* Throughout our lifetimes, we are in the process of forming good or bad habits. These things become second nature to us; we perform them without even thinking. The forming of our new nature in Christ takes a long time. The Lord is building a house that will stand forever; one that nothing can shake or tear down. In Isaiah the Lord says: *"See, I lay a stone in Zion, a tested stone, a precious cornerstone for a sure foundation; the one who trusts will never be dismayed."* (Isa. 28:16) When we discipline ourselves in the good practice of prayer, in the studying of God's Word, and in the doing of His will, we are actually laying up for ourselves treasures both in earth and in heaven.

They will lay up treasures for themselves, as a firm foundation for the coming age, so that they may take hold of the life that is truly life. (1 Tim. 6:19)

May 18

COMPASSION NEW EVERY MORNING

Because of the Lord's great love we are not consumed, for His compassions never fail. They are new every morning; great is Your faithfulness. (Lam. 3:22-23)

The love that God has towards His people is very great. It is so great that our finite minds have a hard time grasping and understanding the full extent of it. There are many questions I have about the past, present, and the future, but as time goes on I begin to realize that there are things that I'm not meant to know, at least for now. It is a great mystery! I'm learning to place all the unanswered questions into His care and keeping, for I know they will be revealed in His way and in His time. One thing that I have come to know and to understand is that God's love, faithfulness, and His compassion never fail; they are always new every morning. When walking along the beach, every now and then I'll find a new and unique looking shell the tide brought in; it reminds me of the Lord's love and compassion that He brings to us new every day. It is like a treasure that we can find and hold on to. *He saved us, not because of righteous things we had done, but because of His mercy.* (Titus 3:5) His compassion for us was the very reason the Lord came and saved us, even while we were still living apart from Him. God's mercy is new every morning.

O Give thanks unto the Lord, for He is good; His mercy endures forever. (Ps. 106:1)

May 19

IN MEMORY OF HERO'S

To everything there is a season, and a time to every purpose under the heaven: A time to be born, and a time to die: a time to plant, and a time to pluck up that which is planted; A time to kill, and a time to heal: a time to break down, and a time to build up: A time to weep, and a time to laugh: a time to mourn, and a time to dance: A time to cast away stones, and a time to gather stones together: a time to embrace, and a time to refrain from embracing: A time to get and a time to lose: a time to keep, and a time to cast away. A time to rend, and a time to sew: a time to keep silence, and a time to speak: A time to love, and a time to hate: a time of war, and a time of peace. (Eccl. 3:1-8)

The providence of God turns the seasons of our lives and as He does this, we see His mighty hand move in all creation. All the times and seasons of our lives are under His control. I remember the ones that I have loved and who are now passed away. I think of the men and women who have served our country and lost their lives or have been physically or emotionally scarred. They gave everything, their life's blood, wholehearted faithfulness to the high call of service and sacrifice for a cause they believed was greater than their very own lives. I am thankful for the memories of the ones who have gone before and have given the ultimate gift of the laying down of their lives for their friends, and for you and me. The Lord's hand moves the seasons of our lives and His providence in all creation is fulfilling its course in its perfect time.

The memory of the righteous will be a blessing. (Prov. 10:7)

THE LORD OUR RIGHTEOUSNESS

The Lord is righteous in all His ways and loving toward all He has made. (Ps. 145:17)

The meaning of righteousness according to Webster's Dictionary is: *meeting the standards of what is right, just, and morally right.* When the Lord God created man and woman in His image, He gave us all a moral compass, a conscience that directs us towards things that are by their very nature good, true and just. It speaks of this in the book of Romans. *For since the creation of the world God's invisible qualities—His eternal power and divine nature have been clearly seen, being understood from what has been made.* (Rom. 1:20) God's righteousness has always been a matter of heart and conscience. On the other side of having a good conscience, when we do wrong, our inner moral compass, brings a guilty feeling, there is a conviction that lets us know right from wrong. *Since they show that the requirements of the law are written on their hearts, their consciences also baring witness.* (Rom.2:15) If we continue to do wrong, our hearts can become hard and no longer feel the conviction sin. Jesus came to show us the righteousness of God and direct us away from this behavior. *Righteousness and justice are the foundation of His throne.* (Ps. 97:2) *This is the name by which He will be called: the Lord Our Righteousness.* (Jer. 23:6)

Sow for yourselves righteousness, reap the fruit of unfailing love, and break up your unplowed ground: for it is time to seek the Lord, until He comes and showers righteousness on you. (Hos. 10:12)

May 21

RIGHTEOUSNESS BY FAITH

I consider everything a loss compared to the surpassing greatness of knowing Christ Jesus my Lord. I consider them rubbish, that I may gain Christ and be found in Him, not having a righteousness of my own that comes from the law, but that which is through faith in Christ, the righteousness that comes from God and is by faith. (Phil. 3:8-9)

It has been forever established in scripture that the Lord our God is righteous in all His ways. It is natural that He would desire His sons and daughters to grow up into His likeness, true to the image we were created in and for. This goal would seem impossible if it were not for the fact that Jesus Christ Himself has been made to be our righteousness: by faith. Paul expressed this when he considered everything that he had given up as nothing compared to the attaining of His righteousness. Just like the Israelites of old times, we seek to establish our own righteousness. Theirs was established by the law. We act like that when we elevate the rules and laws of men over God's. Jesus Christ is the end of the law for all who believe. *Since they did not know the righteousness that comes from God and sought to establish their own, they did not submit to God's righteousness. Christ is the end of the law so that there may be righteousness for everyone who believes.* (Rom. 10:3) Thank goodness that we don't have to perform every expression of the law to know righteousness and to experience the grace of God. It is our work as Christians to believe in the One whom He has sent: righteousness by faith.

For the eyes of the Lord are on the righteous and His ears are attentive to their prayers. (I Pet. 3:12)

RISE UP AND WALK

Jesus said to him, "Will thou be made whole?" The impotent man answered him, "Sir, I have no man to put me into the pool." . . . . Jesus said unto him, "Rise . . . and walk," and immediately the man was made whole and walked. (Jn. 5:6-9)

This story of the lame man being restored to wholeness can be looked at in the light of spiritual wholeness and restoration. The modern day Christian man or woman is asked, *"Will you be made whole?"* Do you want to be made whole and restored to newness of life? Three things come to mind in regard to the parable of the lame man: one is the hope and desire for health and healing, second: the acknowledgment to the Lord of his need to be healed: the third is that he realized his own helplessness and his failure in finding anyone who would put him into the water. Jesus wants us to look up to Him as our only helper. Christ asks him the question, *"Will you be made whole"?* His answer required faith, his surrendering in faith. When Jesus spoke to the lame man, His command had to be obeyed. The man believed that there was truth and power in Christ's Word, in that faith, he arose and walked; by faith he obeyed. When we finally come to realize our own weakness and inability to help ourselves and are fully dependent upon the Lord to answer, then by faith in His Word, we do what He asks of us. This is a big step in bringing a sure and certain hope of deliverance. Listen to the words of the Lord as He offers to restore our spiritual strength and to fit us for walking like healthy, strong men and women in all of His ways. Think about the walk He desires to restore and empower us to have.

Blessed are those who have learned to acclaim You, who walk in the light of Your presence O Lord. (Ps. 89:15)

WALKING IN NEWNESS OF LIFE

That like as Christ was raised up from the dead by the glory of the Father; even so we also should walk in newness of life. (Rom. 6:4)

Can it really happen? Yes it can. He has done it for many; He will do it for you. When the lame man was made whole, he still had to learn how to use his new found strength. Do not expect to be proficient in every aspect of your Christian life immediately, but do expect and be confident that you have trusted yourself to Christ to be your health and strength; He will lead and teach you. Rise and walk each day in a confidence that He is with you and in you. Just accept Jesus Christ the Living One, and trust him to do His work. This is the walk Jesus can make possible and true for His people in greater power than ever before. It is a walk pleasing to Him. Rise and walk in newness of life. It is a walk in heavenly love. *Walk in love, as Christ also has loved us.* (Ephes. 5:2)

That you might walk worthy of the Lord unto all pleasing, being fruitful in every good work. (Col. 1:10)

May 24

OUR INCORRUPTIBLE CROWN

Everyone who competes in the games goes into strict training. They do it to get a crown that will not last; but we do it to get a crown that will last forever. (1 Cor. 9:25)

When the Olympics begin, the world's eyes and attention are fixated upon the games and on the young men and women competing in all the various sports. They have worked endless hours in training and preparation for the moment they will stand against all the best athletes the world has to offer. The winners receive gold, silver and bronze metals, honor, fame and endorsements. On television there are many shows where people are competing with each other; these young and talented ones go before the judges to hear the decisions that could change their lives forever. As I was thinking about these things and remembering the words of scripture that tells me; although there are crowns and metals to be won in the world, there is only one crown that will last eternally and that is the crown of life that the Lord has promised to all those who love Him, (Jas. 1:12) a crown of glory that will never fade away. When an Olympic athlete trains and prepares, or the young performer practices their art, they do it for a corruptible crown and reward. We train and prepare ourselves spiritually for a crown that is incorruptible and one that will never fade away.

When the Chief Shepherd appears, you will receive the crown of glory that will never fade away. (1 Pet. 5:4)

May 25

THE VALUE OF SPIRITUAL EXERCISE

For physical training is of some value, but godliness has value for all things, holding promise for both the present life and the life to come. (1 Tim. 4:8)

There is some value in physical exercise and proper diet to help our bodies stay healthy and functional, but this is only helpful while we are still living. Training ourselves by doing the things that help grow and mature our spirits, all work together to bring us an eternal promise of life in the present and in the world to come. One of the very best ways to develop spiritual strength is to get into the habit of devoting your first waking hour to the Lord; committing the day before you to Him, and in the reading of Scripture. In reality, we as Christians are in a way just like those Olympic athletes. They have their minds and hearts set upon winning that gold metal, we have our hearts and minds set on winning that incorruptible crown. Paul talks about the Christian life as a race. *I press on toward the goal to win the prize for which God has called me heavenward in Christ Jesus.* (Phil. 3:14) Like Paul, it is time to fight the good fight of faith and finish the race all the way to the finish line, and receive our incorruptible crown so we can say: *"I have fought the good fight, I have finished the race, and I have kept the faith."* (2 Tim. 4:7)

Therefore, since we are surrounded by such a great cloud of witnesses, let us throw off everything that hinders and the sin that so easily entangles, and let us run with perseverance the race marked out for us. (Heb. 12:1)

May 26

PERSEVERANCE

Blessed is the man who perseveres under trial, because when he has stood test, he will receive the crown of life that God has promised to those who love Him. (Jas. 1:12)

Perseverance—Webster's Dictionary defines: *the holding to a course of action, belief, or purpose without giving way; steadfastness, persistence, tenacity. Perseverance conveys a sense of endurance in the pursuit of a desired end, continuing strength or patience in dealing with something arduous, unswerving adherence to principals, usually in the face of opposition.* At times we feel just like a salmon swimming upstream against a great current that is pressing against us. There are varying degrees of perseverance that apply to our lives. In some instances it may take a great amount of strength, and in other times, to persevere may be just walking through your day resolving to stay the course not deviating from what is needed, in ordinary ways. Whatever the case, everyone who sets out to serve and to follow the Lord will need to endure and to persevere.

Let us not become weary in doing good, for at the proper time we will reap a harvest, if we do not give up. (Gal. 6:9)

DON'T GIVE UP

As you know, we consider blessed those who have persevered. You have heard of Job's perseverance and have seen what the Lord finally brought about. (Jas. 5:11)

The temptation is to give up and quit; or to give in to things and actions that we know we should not. There is a harvest to be reaped, a crown of life, a reward waiting for all who continue to stay committed to your faith. The most important thing is to keep your mind and heart fixed upon the Lord and on the blessings that will come as a reward. The Lord kept fixed upon the joy set before Him which enabled Him to endure the cross. (Heb. 1:12) To persevere also implies waiting. We have to wait for the Lord's timing in the relief we are seeking. In Job's life, there was a long and painful process that he had to persevere through and finally received a harvest of blessing. Good things; things that are worthwhile, require perseverance. Do not give up! Dear Lord, help us to endure and to persevere throughout this day moving forward and closer to You . . . Amen

Love always protects, always trust, always hopes, and always perseveres. (1Cor. 13:7)

OVERCOMING DRUDGERY

Arise and shine. (Isa. 60:1)

I was thinking lately about my daily work, all the little things and details that need attention during the course of a day. I was repenting to the Lord for having a bad attitude at times when going through the motions of the ordinary tasks and in feeling frustrated. Frustrated because of the repetition and because time seems to fly and the things that I really want to get to, get crowded out because of other stuff! There are times when we have to pull ourselves up, and just begin to put one foot in front of the other. When our minds are fixed upon the Lord, we find Him meeting us at every simple and repetitive turn. I am comforted when I think about God and His nature; how He continually causes the seasons to come and go in cycles that never cease. God is faithful to bring us every evening and cause the morning light to shine again and again. There are repetitive cycles in all of life that we can observe in our world and universe. We should get into the practice of surrendering over our plans and dreams for Him to hold in the very moment we live; by obeying Him in the littlest things. Our focus should be upon obeying and trusting. In this we can be glad and have a song in our hearts bringing glory to the Lord all the while doing the very most commonplace and ordinary things.

My times are in Your hand. (Ps. 31:15)

May 29

HELPER OF THE OPPRESSED

The Lord who remains faithful forever; He upholds the cause of the oppressed and gives food to the hungry. The Lord sets prisoners free, the Lord gives sight to the blind, the Lord lifts up those who are bowed down, the Lord loves the righteous. The Lord watches over the alien and sustains the fatherless and the widow. (Ps. 146:6-9)

This is a wonderful description of the nature and character of God. He is the great defender of the poor and of the oppressed; full of compassion and mercy, ready to come to the rescue of all those look to Him for deliverance. For the most part, Jesus' ministry was focused upon the poor, outcast, downtrodden, and forsaken. When I see Jesus walking from place to place with His disciples, I can picture Him always reaching out to the widow, the blind, the poor, the sinner and the unlovable ones. The people who were rejected by their society, outcasts in the world, were fully loved and embraced by the Savior. *The Lord works righteousness and justice for all the oppressed.* (Ps. 103:6) As our faith and love for the Lord grows, it follows that our hearts would become more tender and endearing towards those who suffer. Our hearts should ache and cry out for the Lord to work righteousness and justice for all those who are oppressed.

You hear, O Lord, the desire of the afflicted; you encourage them, and you listen to their cry, defending the fatherless and the oppressed. (Ps. 10:17-18)

PRAY FOR THE WEAK

Blessed is he who has regard for the weak; the Lord delivers him in times of trouble. The Lord will protect him and preserve his life; he will bless him in the land. (Ps. 41:1-2)

It may be that you are under the weight of oppression or bondage. Isn't it comforting to know that the Lord is on your side? He is on the side of the one that has everything stacked against him. It is time to begin to pray for all those who are weak and downcast. There are many people around the world today, who are living under oppressive governments; facing extremely hard times and are suffering. The Lord listens to our hearts cry when we lift our voices and begin to pray for them to receive His help and deliverance. The Lord may have blessed you with provision and a measure of health, all the more reason for you to have in mind the poor, the weak, homeless and oppressed; to always be ready to daily pray for them, to encourage and help in whatever way you can. Pray to have a heart like Jesus toward those who are without. Dear Lord, please bring help and relief to all those who are suffering today under the oppression of injustices and are in need of provision or healing; Please bring to them comfort and help in their time of desperation and need. Amen . . .

He defended the cause of the poor and needy, and so all went well. "Is that not what it means to know me?" declares the Lord. (Jer. 22:16)

May 31

MORE FAITH

The Scripture foresaw that God would justify the Gentiles by faith, and announced the gospel in advance to Abraham: All nations will be blessed through you. So those who have faith are blessed along with Abraham, the man of faith. (Gal. 3:8-9)

Our whole Christian lives are centered and dependent upon this one great virtue, our faith. Many people are stepping out in faith and believing in God for the fulfillment and the fruition of their endeavors. It might be a project you have been spending time upon; work related, tied to finances, a health issue, or on a personal nature involving family, friends, or loved ones. In every area of our lives as believers, our faith is tried and is really the heartbeat of everything we say or do. I have been thinking of the fact that what we all need more of is faith. When our moods shift, and our emotions rise up, we can get off track. It causes our thinking to get off course. The Word of God is the strong foundation that we can always depend upon. The more we hear the Word of the Lord, the greater our faith and strength to stand will be in times of emotional strain. Everything good, every blessing, every fulfillment of your deepest hearts desires hinge upon how great or small your faith is. My prayer this morning is for more faith. It is the one thing that will move the Lord's hand in our lives and circumstances, and is the one thing that pleases Him the most. The more I stay in His word, the stronger my faith will grow.

Therefore, since we have been justified through faith, we have peace with God through our Lord Jesus Christ, through whom we have gained access by faith into this grace in which we now stand. (Rom. 5:1)

CONTENTMENT

Let your conversation be without covetousness, and be content with such things as you have, for He has said, "I will never leave you, nor forsake you." (Heb. 13:5)

We are all rich in Christ Jesus and have been given the pearl of great price that abides within our hearts. Don't allow yourselves to be deceived by the wealth of the world that is rapidly passing away. Bring your thoughts captive to the Word of the Lord and resist being swayed by the attentions and distractions that may entice you. There are so many hurting and starving people throughout the whole earth right now. We walk into super markets and see the abundance of food products and yet so many are still going hungry here in our country, and throughout much of the world. Looking around you see the appearance of prosperity, yet this all could vanish in a moment of time. *Submit yourselves then to God, Resist the devil, and he will flee from you. Come near to God and He will come near to you.* (Jas. 4:7-8) We need to resist the inclinations of the old nature; it is easier to go with the flow of things, but that is not what we are being called to do. Today we have an opportunity to make a choice to leave the old ways behind and begin to develop new ways and habits that will lead to life and blessing. God's arms are open and He will help you to do this as you draw yourselves near to Him. By making a determined act of your will, draw near to God; and ask to receive His peace. In this world, you will have tribulation, but the Lord comes to give us His peace and contentment. He brings it to all who seek for it and who are willing with open hearts to receive it.

Godliness with contentment is great gain. (1Tim. 6:6)

PLEASING GOD

By faith Enoch was taken from this life, so that he did not experience death; he could not be found, because God had taken him away; for before he was taken, he was commended as one who pleased God. (Heb. 11:5)

Our main goal in this life as believing men and women is to live our lives in such a way as to please God. The Apostle Paul when speaking to the Thessalonians stated, *"We are not trying to please men but God, who tests our hearts."* (1Thes. 2:4) We should ask ourselves the question, "What is it that pleases God the most? What can I do today that will please God?" We know that according to the Scriptures faith and obedience to do His commands please Him. Before we set out each morning into the day ahead, the first thing that sets the tone for pleasing God is a heart examination: a cleansing and clearing of anything that lies heavy or is creating a blockage from having pure communication with God must be removed. There may have been situations that occurred the previous day which you did not handle correctly, in your words, or things done, or left undone. These are the things that need to be brought before the Lord, repented of and cleared up. By making a habit of doing this, you will have confidence when you begin to pray.

Dear friends, if our hearts do not condemn us, we have confidence before God and receive from Him anything we ask, because we obey His commands and do what pleases Him. (I Jn. 3:21)

ACTIONS THAT PLEASE THE LORD

And do not forget to do good and to share with others, for with such sacrifices God is pleased. (Heb. 13:16)

The Apostle John tells us what it will take to please God. The two main ones that we need to focus upon are; #1. To believe in the name of His Son Jesus Christ, and #2. To love one another. It sounds so simple, yet if we are honest, it is what we struggle with the most every day. Yes it is true we all need more faith to believe in order to please God, and we all need to truly love one another the way that the Lord demonstrated in His life of selfless, humble servitude. Jesus Himself walked in a way that always pleased the Father. (Jn. 8:29) If we can remember to focus upon three things before we begin each day, #1. Have a clean and clear heart before the Lord, #2. Meditate upon His Word in order to build up our faith, *(faith comes by hearing the Word of the Lord* (Rom. 10:17)) and #3. Go out into the day showing love to everyone you see. These are important steps we can take each day, if it is our desire to please God.

Finally, brothers, we instructed you how to live in order to please God, as in fact you are living. Now we ask you and urge you in the Lord Jesus to do this more and more. (1Thess. 4:1)

HOPE WAITS

If we hope for that we see not, then do we with patience wait for it. (Rom. 8:25)

God is slowly transforming you into being spiritually mature men and women in Christ Jesus. It is sometimes hard for us to comprehend it, but that is what is happening in reality as we commit ourselves to Him daily. We see the clock on the wall ticking away and know that we too are winding down physically. It is easy to feel as if we need to really get going, or we will run out of time and all will be lost. This is just not true. As believers in Christ, we are no longer subject to time as the world perceives it to be. God's timing is always perfect. Our job is to get in step with Him and realize that although we cannot see His hand moving very fast, we can be assured that He is moving and changing us into the image that He has in His mind. That image will be a glorious one that will last for eternity. This is the reason we do not need to fret over time. We say, it seems like it's taking too long, it feels like forever! Yes, to us it does, but a life that is committed to the Lord will eventually put all his or her trust in the Word of His Promise and with hope, learn to wait. Hope waits. *There is a time for everything, and a season for every activity under heaven. He has made everything beautiful in its time He has also set eternity in the hearts of men; yet they cannot fathom what God has done from the beginning to end.* (Eccl. 3:1, 11)

One day is with the Lord as a thousand years, and a thousand years as one day. (2 Pet. 3:8)

June 5

THE LORD YOUR KEEPER

The Lord is your keeper: the Lord is your shade upon your right hand.
(Ps. 121: 5)

When we realize that it is the Lord who is our Keeper, there is no longer
any reason to strive and worry over the circumstances that life brings our
way. For in every sunny day and through every storm it is the Lord who is
our keeper. We give our concerns over to Him, and are able to enter into a
state of rest. It is a rest that is not dependent upon any outside thing; one
that is trusting upon His Word, and assures us that the God Almighty, who
is all strength, power and wisdom, will be faithful to carry us through. The
providence of God is like a great wheel turning and moving from day to
day, year after year, season following season, everything being kept and
cared for under His watchful eye. Simultaneously we are traveling forward
into time; each to his own; and all fulfilling a purpose and plan that is
unique and one that only God knows completely. We are being kept by the
Father; He is our keeper and we need not fear. God uses everything,
whether good or bad for reasons that we cannot understand right now, but
will be revealed at a future time. There are many things today, as in all
previous generations that we have absolutely no control over; God's will
be done in and through the negative events and even thought the great
catastrophes that may occur. For now, this day, we can enter into a rest for
the Lord is your keeper. *There remains, then, a Sabbath rest for the people
of God; for anyone who enters God's rest also rests from his own work,
just as God did from His.* (Heb. 4:9)

*You will keep him in perfect peace him whose mind is steadfast,
because he trusts in You.* (Isa. 26:3)

161

PROTECTION: OUR PROMISE

Because you have made the Lord, which is my refuge, even the most High, your habitation; there shall no evil befall you, neither shall any plague come near your dwelling. (Ps. 91:9)

In my work area, I have the <u>Bible Promise Book</u> sitting on a counter top close by. In the table of contents there are different topics that have scripture references bringing to mind the many promises that the Lord has given to His people for all time. This little book has been a great source of comfort and strength over the years. The one above in particular drew my attention this morning. There are many reasons to fear and have anxious thoughts about when we observe the world situations today. This Word of Scripture assures me that I will be protected, shielded and watched over as I make the Lord Himself my refuge and habitation. A habitation is a dwelling place for me and for you. If we make Him our refuge and habitation, then, no evil will befall you nor does any plague come near your dwelling. When we do our part in abiding with the Lord throughout our days, and when we are listening to His Word and doing it, we can have the full assurance that He will preserve us to the end. He will keep us from all evil and our hearts from ever having to fear.

The Lord shall preserve you from all evil: He shall preserve your soul. The Lord shall preserve you going out and your coming in from this time forth and even for ever more. (Ps.121:7-8)

SWEET SLEEP

When you lie down, you shall not be afraid: yes, you shall lie down, and your sleep shall be sweet. (Prov. 3:24)

A good night of sleep is a gift. If we cannot sleep, the next day we are not able to function at our best. We need physical rest and sleep to carry on with our daily work. As we learn to abide (to make our dwelling place in Him) moment by moment, hour by hour and day by day, we gain a sense of well being and protection that comes directly from God. What a relief when we know that we are under the protection of the Most High; therefore we can lie down and have a great night of sleep! There are two things here for us to do in order to receive this promise. 1. Make Him, the Lord, our abiding place, our dwelling place throughout each day: and 2. Hearken *unto Him*. Listen to Him. Hear His Words, read and meditate upon the scriptures and take time to quiet yourself in order to hear what it is He is speaking to you about and then do what He shows you. You shall lie down and have sweet sleep.

But whoever listens to me, will live in safety and be at ease, without any fear of harm. (Prov. 1:33)

June 8

MERCY

O give thanks unto the Lord; for He is good: for His mercy endures forever. (Ps. 136:1)

The Lord's mercies are fresh every morning when we wake up to the new day. His compassion for us never fails. Time and time again we fall short and grieve His Spirit in the course of our day, but His love and forgiveness is a fountain that washes and cleanses us entirely. As we acknowledge our offenses and receive His unending mercies and forgiveness we can experience each morning a fresh start and a new beginning. In many of the psalms, David expresses his gladness and thanksgiving for His unending mercy. It is the cause for unceasing praise and thanksgiving. *Bless the Lord, O my soul, and forget not all His benefits . . . who crown you with loving kindness and tender mercies.* (Ps.136:2) His mercies are infinite and high as the heavens: what a thought! The Lord sees and understands our afflictions and weaknesses; He surrounds us with His loving kindness. We need only to turn to Him, humbly ask for help and He will provide the assurance that will lift up our spirits once again. God's loving arms are always open to receive repentant hearts, *His mercy endures forever . . . . As the heaven is high above the earth, so great is His mercy toward them that fear Him.* (Ps. 136:11)

Thy loving kindness is better than life. (Ps. 63:3)

THE FIRE OF HIS LOVE

He led them forth by the right way. (Ps. 107:7)

We need to allow the wind and the waves of life's storms to mold and shape us into the people that God has in His mind. When the tempests come, or if it is here now, and you are experiencing distress, hold fast to the strong anchor of His great love. It is the fire of His love that burns and brings the pain in order to purify and further equip us for a deeper understanding and work. If we keep these things in mind, God will lead us forth by the right way and we will find ourselves in a peaceful place rejoicing once more. Allow the Lord to take you through the fire of His love today. He is working out a greater purpose that has not been revealed to you yet. Trust Him. *Be strong and take heart, all you who hope in the Lord.* (Ps. 31:24)

Who shall separate us from the love of Christ? Shall trouble or hardship or persecution or famine or nakedness or danger or sword? No, in all these things we are more than conquerors through Him who loved us. (Rom. 8:35 36)

June 10

HIDDEN

Since then, you have been raised with Christ, set your hearts on things above, where Christ is seated at the right hand of God. Set your minds on things above, not on earthly things. For you died, and your life is now hidden with Christ in God. When Christ, who is your life appears, then you also will appear with Him in glory. (Col. 3:1-4)

Our lives, who it is we truly are in our heart of hearts, our deepest desires and inner thoughts and feelings, are in a very real sense, hidden; hidden from the world around us, even from the ones that are closest to us. The outward actions that we do, the words and attitudes we have are a reflection of what lies within, but in reality, the only one who really knows, loves, and understands everything about you is God; it is a fact that is important to realize. As we come into the knowledge of this, we enjoy intimate communion with Him and that love creates in us a longing and a thirst for more. Our real lives are hidden with Christ in God. Our real home is an eternal one that is yet to come.

Do not conform any longer to the pattern of this world, but be transformed by the renewing of your mind, then you will be able to test and approve what God's will is; His good, pleasing and perfect will. (Rom. 12:2)

FIX YOUR ATTENTION UPON JESUS

For we who are alive are always being given over to death for Jesus sake, so that His life may be revealed in our mortal bodies. (2 Cor. 4:11)

One of the reasons why it so important to fill our minds and spirits with God's Word is that it will enable us to test and to approve what the Lord's will is for our lives. If we are living in the way that His Word asks us to do, we will be transformed into a life that will be in accord with His perfect will. There is always an "if" attached. That is because we have free will to decide which way to go. The world in all its temporary glory is rapidly passing away. There is nothing hid from the eyes of the Lord. He knows you in all your weaknesses and shortcomings and yet His love, compassion and mercy for you never fail. If ever there was a time to set your minds and hearts upon heavenly things, it is now. With the death of our old nature, comes a new life springing up in Christ. The hidden life of Christ in us, is a full life that is rich with inner joy, peace and blessing. If you are not experiencing this at the present time; maybe you have been keeping your eyes fixed upon the world and your concerns more than what you should. It is time to re-establish your focus upon what matters. Turn you attention to the Lord today and fix your eyes upon the things above, for your life is hidden and understood fully and completely by Him; and by Him alone. Lord, help us to keep our minds and attention fixed upon You, and upon Your perfect Word.

Here is a trust worthy saying: if we died with Him, we will also live with Him. (2 Tim. 2:11)

June 12

A PROMISE FOR HARD PLACES

Your life will I give unto you for a prey in all places where you go. (Jer. 45:5)

There are various degrees of pressure; sometimes it is very intense and we learn to lean upon the Lord to take us through it. We are all affected when great tragedies come upon the earth. We see the devastation that comes from great earthquakes, tsunamis, hurricanes, etc., and it can shake our faith as we wonder why. How could a loving God allow so many innocent people to perish? The answer is: that we really have no answer. Some things we will never know in our lifetimes. The position we should take is one of waiting and of trusting in God. The Lord has a plan and purpose for everything that happens; He is just and righteous. His justice will eventually be established upon our earth. There will be long trials of our faith but those who persevere to the end shall be saved. The Lord has promised to take us through every storm and pressure that comes, no matter if it is for a day or if it should last for years. We are all called to endure and to trust in the event of such things. God will give us our life, a promise for hard places. Let's all pray for one another and to continue in our faith no matter what happens or comes our way.

As you know, we consider blessed those who have persevered. You have heard of Job's perseverance and have seen what the Lord finally brought about. The Lord is full of compassion and mercy. (Jas. 5:11)

TRIALS OF PURPOSE

So the Lord blessed the latter end of Job more than his beginning. (Job 42:12)

Job's was a most extreme example of suffering. Everyone suffers to some degree, many times we are not aware of what is going on, or what that person is experiencing inside. To the believer, we have the Scripture to read and meditate upon, which gives us strength, courage, and endurance during our times of pain and suffering. Everyone is going through something, and if we can just show compassion towards others with this awareness, we can be a healing balm of comfort to them. We know that God is serving a purpose in and through all trials and sufferings. The very thing that Satan means for harm, God turns into a good thing, and the misfortune into a much greater blessing. Job trusted the Lord and although tried severely, he ended up being more blessed than he had been in the beginning. If we could say, let Your will be done in everything, even in the midst of a major trial, you will receive great peace and comfort from the Lord and have victory in the end. Just hold on to your love and trust in Him, He will fulfill His promises to you and reveal the purpose for the trial you are going through. He is faithful forever! Let His will be done in and through all things.

And the God of all grace, who called you to His eternal glory in Christ, after you have suffered a little while, will Himself restore you and make you strong, firm and steadfast. (1 Pet.5:10)

QUIET TIME

The fruit of righteousness will be peace; the effect of righteousness will be quietness and confidence forever. (Is.32:17)

It is up to us to find the time and get quiet before the Lord. We can do this and practice it, but we have to take the necessary steps and get ourselves away from the business of the day. This is not always the easiest thing to do! Yet, if we are on the lookout for an opportunity to stop for awhile what it is we are doing, even for ten minutes, in order to reflect and quiet ourselves in order to draw near to God, we would gain peaceful rest in the process. If we practice this, these times will become very important and we'll receive the blessings they bring. When and if you are able to place yourselves in a natural environment such as the beach or park, it is even better and easier to gain a greater degree of rest and peace. When you go out of your way to seek the Lord early in the morning, during the course of the day, and at night before bedtime, He rewards you with a peace and a spiritual discernment that will cause you to be strengthened and energized bringing inner joy.

In repentance and rest is your salvation. In quietness and trust is your strength. (Is.30:15)

DEFEAT TURNED TO VICTORY

For every child of God overcomes the world: and the victorious principle which has overcome the world is our faith. (1 Jn.5:4)

At every turn in the road one can find something that will rob him of his victory and peace of mind, if he permits it. Satan has not retired from the business of deluding and ruining God's people if he can. Sometimes a person can, if he will, actually snatch victory from the very jaws of defeat, if he will resolutely put his faith up at just the right moment. Faith can change any situation. No matter how dark it is, no matter what the trouble may be; a quick lifting of the heart to God in a moment of real, actual faith in Him, will alter the situation in a moment. God is still on His throne, and He can turn defeat into victory in a second of time, if we really trust Him in that moment. *Through You we push back our enemies; through Your name we trample our foes.* (Ps. 44:5) These attacks will not cease as long as we are still in this fallen world. But, we have been given all we need through Christ to assure our victory. When we call upon Him, He answers and in a moment's time, can turn the tide from evil back to good. *This is the victory that overcomes the world, even our faith.* (2 Jn. 5:4)

In all these things, we are more than conquerors through Him who loved us. (Rom. 8:37)

VICTORY IN REVERSE

Rejoice not against me, O mine enemy: when I fall, I shall arise; when I sit in darkness, the LORD shall be a light unto me. (Mic.7:8)

There are sacrifices and things that are necessary to give up that every believer is asked to do in order to make room for the Savior. Sometimes we have to choose the Lord over people, places and things because faith bids us to. In the process, we will most likely face difficulty and severe trials and defeats. Nothing we lose, suffer, or give up for Christ's sake is of any importance in the larger scheme of things. When everything gets sifted out in the end, the ones who have been put down and are in the last position will be brought into first place. This is the Lord's doing and it cannot fail. Down equals up and up will come down. Trusting Him to do this is our trial of faith. If you are experiencing a trial or test of faith right now, be glad in that you have been counted worthy to suffer for His name sake, you are blessed and shall be comforted. Defeat will turn to victory and what appears to be a defeat is in reality a victory in reverse. *Thanks be to God, who always causes us to triumph in Christ Jesus.* (2 Cor. 2:14)

Everyone who has left houses or brothers or sisters or father or mother or children or fields or my sake will receive a hundred times as much and will inherit eternal life. but many who are first will be last, and many who are last will be first. (Matt.19:29-30)

ALIVE IN HIM

Let not sin therefore reign in your mortal body, that you should obey it in the lusts thereof. Neither yield your members as instruments of unrighteousness unto sin: but yield yourselves unto God as those that are alive from the dead, and your members as instruments of righteousness unto God. (Rom. 6:12-13)

The whole reason Jesus came was to take away the sins of the world; to die and take upon Himself all the pain and punishment we deserved. Now that it is finished and all is atoned for, He asks us to live for Him and take upon ourselves His righteousness. He offers life, renewed and empowered by His Spirit, enabling us to resist sin and all of the old nature. As we daily present ourselves unto God, at the same time learn to acknowledge our death to sin, we become alive in Him and in the new resurrected life. We are His and He is ours. The scripture Galatians 2:20 is a great scripture to repeat and to say out loud, "*I have been crucified with Christ and I no longer live; but Christ lives in me. The life I now live in the body, I live by faith in the Son of God, who loved me and gave Himself for me.*" We have been made to be truly alive with Him and in Him. *Here is a trustworthy saying, if we died with Him, we will also live with Him.* (2 Tim. 2:1)

He Himself bore our sins in His body on the tree so that we might die to sins and live for righteousness: by His wounds you have been healed. (1 Pet. 2:24) *For you died and your life is now hidden with Christ in God.* (Col. 2:2)

June 18

THE PRAYER OF RELINQUISHMENT

He who does the will of God abides forever. (1 Jn. 2:1)

Not only do we know not what to pray for as we ought, when we do pray, we do not have a guarantee that we will get what it is we are praying for. If we are relinquishing our will over to His, in the end we will receive something far better and the answer will become clear even if it is not what we originally prayed. If we sincerely desire God's will to be fulfilled in our lives, then we must give up our interpretation of what the outcome should be. In the immediate moment, it may not seem that we are getting the results we hoped and prayed for. Yet by relinquishing our own ideas and will to a loving Father who knows exactly what is needed in order to bring about a greater benefit in the end; and saying to Him "let Your will be done," is what we should do. The Lord is always working in us towards a result that we may know little or nothing about. So praying, trusting, and submitting to His will, is central and of great importance. This is showing faith that will bring you peace and assurance when facing difficult and impossible situations. Accepting whatever the Father sends is a good thing to practice whenever we pray. We know that in the end, all will be reconciled and every injustice will be corrected. *And we know that in all things God works for the good of those who love Him, who have been called according to His purpose.* (Rom 8:28)

For our light affliction and momentary troubles are achieving for us an eternal glory that far outweighs them all. (2 Cor. 4:17)

GROWING DOWNWARD IN HUMILITY

Grow in grace and in the knowledge of our Lord and Savior Jesus Christ. (2 Pet. 3:18)

The thought of growing downward in humility is something that all who desire to know Christ more should consider carefully. The Lord gives more grace to the humble. What is grace? Unmerited favor, blessing that is not deserved, given because of love. *For this is what the high and lofty One says—He who lives forever, whose name is Holy: "I live in a high and holy place, but also with him who is contrite and lowly in spirit, to revive the spirit of the lowly and revive the heart of the contrite."* (Isa.57:15) I feel that growing downward in humility is especially important in understanding the heart of God and in knowing His loving Presence and grace. He has told us that He lives with those of a contrite (humble) spirit. He has also promised to revive our hearts and spirits when we show humility and lowliness. Jesus was lowly in heart. This is a great quality that is beautiful in His eyes. When we take this attitude of heart, we receive ever increasing blessings and grace. *God opposes the proud, but give more grace to the humble.* (Jas. 4:6)

And God raised us up with Christ and seated us with Him in the heavenly realms in Christ Jesus, in order that in the coming ages, He might show the incomparable riches of His grace, expressed in His kindness towards us in Christ Jesus. (Ephes. 2:6-7)

ABIDING GRACE AND PEACE

Let us then approach the throne of grace with confidence, so that we may receive mercy and find grace to help us in our time of need. (Heb. 4:16)

What I like so much about the classic Christian authors, is that what was written so long ago is still fresh and new for us today. The truths spoken long ago, apply in our day as it did in theirs. Jesus, the Word of God, is the same yesterday, today and forever. The Holy Spirit anoints the Scripture and words and makes them fresh every time! It helps me to know that the things we struggle with today were the same things the Christians from all generations did also. Abiding grace is what is needed to understand and to believe. If we are lacking in peace today, return at once to the Lord and obtain this free gift that God is so willing to give. The free gift of God is His love that brings this abiding grace into our lives. When we make mistakes, His arms are always open to receive us back the moment we return. There are other places we can go to recover our peace, but it will not be a lasting peace. Only when we return to the Lord and to His love can we have abiding grace and peace throughout everything that may come our way. *For the grace of God that brings salvation has appeared to all men.* (Titus 2:11)

So that, having been justified by His grace, we might become heirs having the hope of eternal life. (Titus.3:7)

June 21

FEAR NOT

The Lord has said to me in the strongest terms: Do not think like everyone else does. Do not be afraid that some plan conceived behind closed doors will be the end of you. Do not fear anything except the Lord Almighty. He alone is the Holy One. If you fear Him, you need fear nothing else. He will keep you safe. (Isa. 8:11-14)

God was speaking to Isaiah during the time of a coming invasion by Assyria. All the people of Israel were fearful, and it was God's intention to cause Israel to fall and for many to be captured due to their unfaithfulness and rebellion against Him. The Lord promised Isaiah in the strongest terms not to be fearful about anything and that He would keep Him safe regardless of any plan or attack that would happen. We have this same assurance when observing the circumstances of our day; in dangerous times or when there is a sense eminent disaster on the horizon. Over and over and throughout scripture, the Lord tells us *"fear not."* Everyone who loves, trusts, and who walk in His ways will be safe. The only thing we ever need to fear is the LORD God Almighty Himself.

Though an army besieges me, my heart will not fear; though a war breaks out against me, even then will I be confident. Ps. 46:2 You will not fear the terror of night, nor the arrow that flies by day. (Ps.112:8)

June 22

CONFIDENCE TOWARDS GOD

Dear friends, if our hearts do not condemn us, we have confidence before God. (1Jn. 3:21)

I believe the Lord is sifting, shaking, and moving His people greatly at this time. He wants to do new things within the Church, purifying and bringing His people into a greater degree of light and understanding. We do not need to worry ourselves about the hidden things of darkness; our attention and focus should be upon Him and on Him only. He is the righteous judge and will bring all into accountability at the perfect and appointed time. The Lord is our Shield and Protector; our confidence as long as our attention is fixed upon Him, nothing can harm us. If in our hearts, we are free from condemnation and know the joy that true repentance that forgiveness brings, neither does God condemn us and we have confidence towards God.

The name of the Lord is a strong tower: the righteous run into it, and are safe. (Prov. 18:10) *Surely God is my salvation; I will trust and not be afraid. The LORD, the LORD is my strength and my song He has become my salvation.* (Isa. 12:2)

ALWAYS NEAR

How great is the love the Father has lavished on us, that we should be called children of God! (1 Jn. 3:1)

It was the Father's love that first drew us to Him. He will also keep us every moment in that same great love. Jesus' life on earth showed us the love of the Father. It is an eternal love that has promised to watch over and care for us until the very last moment we live. His desire is to have unbroken fellowship with His people. Always remember that you are loved more than what you can know or understand. Some people did not have a very good example of a father's love, and for them; it is harder to comprehend the Heavenly Father's love which is so great. He Himself is love in its truest and purest form, and this love encompasses us about day and night. We may have had earthly fathers that rejected or deserted us, but our Heavenly Father, will never leave or forsake us. This great love of His is so important to always remember and to know. *The Lord appeared to us in the past, saying; "I have loved you with an everlasting love; I have drawn you with loving-kindness." (Jer. 31:3)*

The LORD bless you and keep you; the LORD make His face shine upon you and be gracious to you; the LORD turn His face toward you and give you peace. (Num. 6:24-2)

June 24

ATTRIBUTES OF THE KING

When one rules over men in righteousness, when he rules in the fear of God, he is like the light of morning at sunrise on a cloudless morning: like the brightness after rain that brings the grass from the earth. (2 Sam. 23:4)

These were the last words of King David as recorded in this scripture. The Lord Jesus will one day come to rule and reign upon the earth; to establish His Kingdom and to sit upon the throne in direct lineage to King David. It is interesting the way David describes what a righteous king will look like, *the light of morning at sunrise, like the brightness after the rain that brings the grass from the earth.* King David knew the Messiah would one day come to rule and reign from his throne for God established it forever, (Lk. 1:32) and in his very last words he gives us a picture of the righteous king. I can see Jesus shining forth in all His glory and righteousness reigning from this throne; like the light of morning at sunrise on a cloudless morning, is a beautiful picture of what the Lord will appear to look like when we see Him. Love, justice and mercy are the attributes of our great King Jesus. The Bible tells us that we (His Church) have been made as kings and priests to rule and reign with Him in this new Kingdom that is coming. (Rev. 1:6) Now is the time of preparation, to prepare the way for the Lord and His Kingdom.

Love and faithfulness keeps a king safe, through love, his throne is made secure. (Prov. 20:28)

A KINGDOM GIVEN

By justice a king gives a country stability. (Prov. 29:4)

Christians have been given a restored Kingdom that lives and rules in our hearts today: in this present moment. Let us strive to establish it now upon these principals of love faithfulness, justice and mercy. Let Jesus sit as King upon the throne of our hearts and give Him full reign. Let His palace, (our hearts) be a glorious place. Many times when we first come to Christ, He enters our heart to live and the place is a mess! As we allow Him to occupy and renovate, slowly this Kingdom that the Lord is establishing within us begins to get more stabilized and clean; and at long last glorious! Proverbs has many things to say about the reign of kings: *If a king judges the poor with fairness, his throne will always be secure.* (Prov. 29:4) Dear Lord, help us to fix our attention upon You so that we will not need to fear; to know and experience Your loving Presence here within us and all around us throughout our day, let Your glorious Kingdom be established within our hearts and lives . . . Amen

Surely God is my salvation; I will trust and not be afraid. The LORD, the LORD is my strength and my song He has become my salvation. (Isa.12:2)

THE WELCOME RAIN

As surely as the sun rises, He will appear. He will come to us like the winter rains; like the spring rains that water the earth. (Hos.6:3)

Rain is a welcome sight when we see the earth receiving showers that bring new plant life and all creation is renewed by the fresh rain that falls. This is a description of what the coming of the Lord will be like to His waiting people. Jesus will come as a sunrise and as a welcome spring or winter shower. Jesus will come surely as the sun rises, He will appear . . . We are assured that the sun will rise, and rise again to the end of time; it will never stop, nor will the seasons ever cease. From the very beginning mankind has always observed nature, its seasons and cycles, the stars and the whole of creation; to discern and to have understanding of its movement, time, and position in the skies. The Lord draws our attention in order for us to know those things, but also to see and acknowledge His hand working and moving throughout all the earth and universe. When watching a colorful sunset, an amazing animal, or a scenic view of nature, we get a glimpse into the heart and character of God who is all perfect and beautiful throughout all of His creation and universe.

As long as the earth endures, seedtime and harvest, cold and heat, summer and winter, day and night will never cease. (Gen. 8:22)

SOW RIGHTEOUSNESS

Sow for yourselves righteousness, reap the fruit of unfailing love and break up your unplowed ground, for it is time to seek the Lord, until He comes and showers righteousness on you. (Hos. 10:12)

This is an admonition for us to seek the Lord while He may be found; to break up the hardness of our hearts so we will be able to receive the refreshing spiritual showers that the Lord will shower upon us when He comes. Live righteously, gather the fruit and blessings that come along in awareness of His unfailing love. Many times we may not feel righteous, but His Word tells us that we have been made to be His righteousness. It is time to believe and receive this righteousness that comes from the Lord for there will be a day when He will come and will pour it out, overflow us with spiritual showers that will never cease.

Jesus Christ, who has become for us wisdom from God—that is, our righteousness, holiness, and redemption. (1Cor. 1:30)

June 28

JESUS RESCUES

Grace and peace to you from God our Father and the Lord Jesus Christ, who gave Himself for our sins to rescue us from the present evil age, according to the will of God and Father to whom be glory forever and ever. Amen . . . (Gal. 1:2-5)

The act of a rescue is an act that is associated with courage, bravery, and self-sacrifice. It implies there is imminent danger and distress. Paul tells us that Christ gave Himself through His death upon the cross in order to rescue us from the present evil age. The age that was in Paul's time was no less evil than what we know of in our world today. Jesus came and snatched us away from the jaws of death, hell and destruction, and brought us to a place of safety and rest. Jesus Christ is in a very real sense of the word our hero. The Bible tells us that He single-handedly purged away the sins of the whole world.

Who being the brightness of His glory, and the express image of His person, and upholding all things by the Word of His power, when He had by Himself, purged our sins, sat down on the right hand of the Majesty of High. (Heb.1:3)

DOING THE IMPOSSIBLE

All things are possible to Him that believes. (Mk.9:23)

Sometimes we might be called to do something that seems impossible. With Christ in our hearts, we can rise to the occasion and single-handedly do things we never thought we would, or could do. It is supernatural strength and wisdom that we receive from God as our faith grows. Serving the Lord becomes more exciting and interesting as we begin to see the part that God has given us to do individually, and collectively. We are (the body of Christ) one in spirit, in trials, in joy, and in pain. No matter what you maybe going through today, Jesus has already rescued you from the ultimate, which is death and eternal separation from Himself. Can we trust Him together to deliver us from this present evil age and show Him our courage by stepping up in response to His love and guidance? Yes, we can do all things through Him who strengthens us. Let us say this morning with Paul:

"I have learned the secret of being content in any and every situation, whether living in plenty or in want. I can do everything through Him who gives me strength." (Phil 4:12-13)

BE BLESSED AND KNOW LOVE

You are heirs of the prophets and of the covenant God made with our fathers. He said to Abraham, "Through your offspring all peoples on earth will be blessed." When God raised up His servant (Jesus) He sent Him first to bless you, by turning each of you from your wicked ways. (Ac. 3:25)

In the process of spiritual growth, we learn more of God's character, our desires are changed and we become more like Him. He causes us to want to turn from our previous wicked ways and enables us to receive blessings. In living a righteous life, we will be blessed, and know blessings. The reason Jesus came was to bless us by turning each one away from sinful behavior, setting us free to receive untold blessings. It is His goodness that leads us to the point of repentance. (Rom.2:4) It is through the knowledge of the forgiveness of our sins, His unsearchable sacrifice for us, that our hearts become filled with love for God. As time goes by this love grows stronger and stronger for Jesus our Savior. Compassion and mercy towards all people begin to fill our hearts us as we gain the understanding of the pain and sorrows of others; we share in their joys and successes too.

Praise be to the God and Father of our Lord Jesus Christ, who has blessed us in the heavenly realm with every spiritual blessing in Christ. (Ephes. 1:3)

THE UNFINISHED CANVAS

*Dear Friends, we are children of God and what we will be has not yet been
made known. But we know that when He appears,
we shall be like Him for we shall see Him as He is . . . 1 John 3:2*

The waves of the ocean
Carve the rocks on the shore.
The winds of the tempest
Form the mountains of lore.

The winds of the storm
And the pounding of the waves,
Slowly shaping nature's display;
Ever moving and ever changing,
On an unfinished canvas
In the brightness of day.

Let the winds and waves of Your love
Rush through my soul.
Slowly transforming, breaking, and creating,
Painting a picture that only You can know;
On the unfinished canvas of my soul.

There's a picture unfinished
By an artist's unseen hand,
That only His eyes can see and understand.
He's molding and shaping our hearts and desires,
Coloring and painting the unfinished canvas of our lives.

Let the winds and the waves of Your love,
Rush through my soul.
Slowly transforming, breaking and creating
Painting a picture that only You can know,
On the unfinished canvas of my soul.

July 1

BROKEN CISTERNS

My people have committed two sins: they have forsaken me, the Spring of Living Water, and have dug their own cisterns, broken cisterns, that cannot hold water. (Jer. 2:13)

Jeremiah was just a young man when the Lord called him to stand against the whole land, the kings of Judah, its officials, priests and all the people. (Jer.2:18) *"They will fight against you, but will not overcome you, for I am with you and will rescue you." declares the Lord.* (Jer. 1:19) These were not a foreign people, they were the chosen ones that the Lord had led through the desert, fed with heavenly manna and had brought into the land of promise where fruit and prosperity abounded. It seems that over all the ages and generations, God's people, as the Scripture records seem to commit these same two sins. One, they forsake the Spring of Living Water, the one and only true source of life and goodness; and second, they do things apart from their Creator building their own houses as if the Lord were not in it. Its foundation will be like the sand; when the storms come, it will fall. Today God is still warning the Church not to forsake the Spring of Living Water; to renew our devotion and love for the Living Water who is Jesus daily and to cease trying to do things our own way; for they will fail. Insisting to do it on our own, apart from God, will only produce broken cisterns that will not hold water or last.

Therefore everyone who hears these words of mine and puts them into practice is like a wise man who built his house on the rock. The rain came down, the streams rose, and the winds blew and beat against that house; yet it did not fall, because it had its foundation on the rock. But everyone who hears these words of mine and does not put them into practice is like a foolish man who built his house on sand. The rain came down, the streams rose, and the winds blew and beat against that house, and it fell with a great crash. (Matt.7:24-2)

July 2

LET THE LORD BUILD YOUR HOUSE

Unless the LORD builds the house, its builders labor in vain. (Ps. 127:1)

If we submit to God's will and allow Him to build our houses, not only will we be able to withstand all the storms and trials of life, but we will receive a great inheritance, a double portion in our land and have everlasting joy. *They will be called oaks of righteousness, a planting of the Lord for the display of His splendor.* (His glory will be seen in His people) *and so they will inherit a double portion in their land, and everlasting joy will be theirs.* (Is.61:3, 7) The Lord always gives us a choice each day. Will we choose to allow the Lord to direct our steps today? God's way is the sure and safe way to go. The foundation is unshakable. Jesus is the rock upon which we stand and from which we build. The great master builder is God. He has the floor plans for your home. It is custom built just for you. Yield to the Lord's will for your life on a daily basis and watch in amazement what the Lord will create!

I know, O Lord, that a man's life is not his own, it is not for man to direct his steps. (Jer.10:23)

July 3

CAPTIVES GO FREE

The Spirit of the Sovereign Lord is on me, because the Lord has anointed me to preach good news to the poor. He has sent me to bind up the brokenhearted, to proclaim freedom for the captive and release for the prisoners. (Is. 61:1)

We were being held captives, prisoners, bound up and chained by the lies and illusions of the world, false religions, physical or emotional addictions. There are many other things we can become a prisoner to which can even appear to be good things such as education, family, prestige, title, wealth and fame. Then there are the more subtle things such as watching too much television, over eating, or sleeping too much. Any one of these can become idols in our lives if we over do or allow them to take precedence over our relationship with God. It is the Lord who gave us everything, made everything, and wills that we choose not to be in bondage to anything, or to place other things before Him so that we might enter into the glorious freedom of a loving relationship with our Creator. God has given us everything that is good to enjoy, but we should use moderation and balance. Allow the Lord to have the priority in your life and enjoy the good things He has given. Let us celebrate this liberation!

For the creation was subjected to frustration, not by its own choice, but by the will of the One who subjected it, in hope that the creation itself will be liberated from its bondage to decay and brought into the glorious freedom of the children of God. (Rom.8:20)

July 4

THE SON SETS US FREE

If the Son sets you free, you shall be free indeed. (Jn. 8:36)

In America, the Fourth of July is a celebration of our independence when we became a free nation from England; a time to show our love and appreciation for all the men and women who sacrificed their lives and who are presently serving to help keep our country free. *To the Jews who had believed him, Jesus said, "If you hold to my teaching, you are really my disciples. Then you will know the truth, and the truth will set you free."* (Jn. 8:31) There is another freedom that we can celebrate on this day and that is the freedom we have from the slavery of our old sinful nature because of the Lord's willingness to sacrifice His life for all of us. This is true freedom and liberty that is not only here and now, but will last throughout all eternity. The Scripture tells us that it is the *truth that sets us free;* the truth of God's everlasting and unchangeable Word. The very first scripture Jesus said in a public place was found in Isaiah. *"He has sent me to bind up the brokenhearted, to proclaim freedom for the captive and release for the prisoners."* (Is. 61:1)

Now the Lord is the Spirit, and where the Spirit of the Lord is, there is freedom. (2 Cor. 3:18)

July 5

UNWAVERING TRUSTFULNESS

Beyond all question, the mystery of godliness is great. (1 Tim. 3:16)

It is for this reason: "the mystery of godliness," that steady and unwavering trust, play such an important role in our Christian walk with the Lord. We truly do not know what the day will bring. It is the Lord in which providence moves and creates everything that is happening around us. Living out our faith in life is a great mystery! Keeping this in mind, we establish an atmosphere in which our trust can grow and be pleasing to Him. In many previous experiences, we have come to understand that it is faith that pleases God. Having faith is also very similar to having trust; we place our confidence in what we do not yet know for certain, or have become a reality as yet. It is placing our future and everything we have at the foot of His great throne of grace and mercy for Him to hold. We learn to wait upon the Lord with our eyes and heart fixed upon Him, and completely trusting God to work it out with unwavering trustfulness.

He shall not be afraid of evil tidings; his heart is fixed, trusting in the Lord. (Ps. 112:7)

July 6

COMPREHENDING HIS LOVE

Paul prayed this prayer for us: *And I pray that you, being rooted and established in love, may have power, together will all the saints, to grasp how wide and long and high and deep is the love of Christ, and to know this love that surpasses knowledge—that you may be filled to the measure of all the fullness of God.* (Ephes. 3:17-19)

In spite of all of our differences, complexities, ways of life, and our thoughts and opinions, eventually we'll become one perfectly joined body in complete love and unity with the Father, Son, and Holy Spirit. This relationship of unity and love for God and for one another is a central part, in our Christian life. It is His desire that we comprehend this love and live it out in our day by day experiences. Regardless of Christian denomination, race, language, or country, there is one body of believers, one heart of love for God, and one Holy Spirit that unites them all. Many people within the Church have different interpretations of Scripture. We cannot allow this to divide and separate or cause strife. Our main commission from the Lord is that we love them in spite of the differences. By doing this, we will come to comprehend more of His great love for us.

Though you have not seen Him you love Him, and even though you do not see Him now, you believe in Him and are filled with an inexpressible and glorious joy, for you are receiving the goal of your faith, the salvation of your souls. (1 Pet. 1:8)

July 7

YIELD, SURRENDER, AND REPENT

This is how God showed His love among us: He sent His one and only Son into the world that we might live through Him. This is love: not that we loved God, but that He loved us and sent His Son as an atoning sacrifice for our sins. (1 Jn.4:9-10)

When we surrender our wills and bodies to God, it is an act of obedience that is offered out of love and gratitude for Jesus our Savior. We do this every day as the realization of His sacrifice and love for us begins to grow. Our hearts are drawn to understand the greatness of His suffering, His humble life of a servant through His living example. He has revealed to us the Father's heart of love, compassion and mercy for lost humanity. It is this life of love we come to know; that shines Holy light upon our darkness and brings true repentance. It is because of His forgiveness of our sins that we begin to experience great peace and inner joy. Yielding, surrendering and repenting are needed to be renewed daily as we grow ever more aware and dependent upon His unending grace and love.

The Lord appeared to us in the past, saying: "I have loved you with an everlasting love; I have drawn you with loving kindness. (Jer. 31:3)

July 8

THE KINGDOM WITHIN

I desire to do Your will, O my God. Your law is within my heart. (Ps. 40:8)

This is the life we are called into; we love Him, and in surrender we find a glorious joy. For some this surrender may have happened in an instant, for others, it may have taken a lifetime, but we do know that the Lord is patiently waiting even now for us who have begun, and for others who are still on the way, to let His will be done, and to let His Kingdom come into our heart and lives. We need to be patient also and continue to pray for the ones we love who have not yet given themselves to God. I have seen firsthand the patience and perseverance of God in a personal prayer request for my father's salvation. It took over 25 years of consistent prayer for him, and at last before he passed away, he received the Lord into his heart and is now with Jesus in heaven. One day I will be reunited with him! For some, it is in an instant, for others it may take a life time. What we do know and understand is that God has perfect timing and will do it if we do not give up asking.

Be patient, then until the Lord's coming. See how the farmer waits for the land to yield its valuable crop and how patient He is for the autumn and spring rains. You too be patient and stand firm, because the Lord's coming is near. (Jas.5:7-8)

COMMIT AND TRUST

Trust in the Lord and do good; dwell in the land and enjoy safe pasture, delight yourself in the Lord and He will give you the desires of your heart. Commit your way to the Lord: trust in Him and He will do this: He will make your righteousness shine like the dawn, the justice of your case like the noonday sun. (Ps. 37: 3-5)

When we commit ourselves to the Lord and trust Him with our lives and circumstances, He is faithful to fulfill the promises He made for all who do this. There is joy in our serving and in living. *Delight* the Webster's Dictionary defines it as: *great pleasure, gratification, joy is something that gives pleasure and enjoyment.* The Lord never meant our serving Him to be burdensome or grievous. There was a time when our desires were not in line with His desires for us; we thought we wanted something that would have in the end proved to be wrong and damaging. It is when we begin to trust and commit our ways to Him that things slowly begin to change. Those wants and desires we were praying for become the very thing that He was wanting for us all along! Our realization of God's love for us is what transforms our wills and desires to be in alignment with His own. There will come a point in time when God begins to grant us the very things that we have been praying for.

Trust in the LORD with all your heart and lean not to your own understanding. (Prov. 3:5)

July 10

VINDICATION

He will make your righteousness shine like the dawn, the justice of your cause, like the noon day. (Ps. 37:6)

God brings vindication; our righteousness will shine forth like the dawn and the justice of your cause as the noonday sun. All the things that others may have misunderstood about you, your actions, motives, wrong perceptions; the times when you were judged wrongly or even falsely accused, will be cleared up and others will see and know that the things you were doing were done in and through The Lord.

He will receive blessing from the Lord and vindication from God his Savior. Such is the generation of those who seek Him. (Ps. 24:5-6) This is a great promise to know that all things will be brought into the light and the justification of all of your actions will be vindicated. The Lord's loving presence abiding in our hearts and lives will fill us up with every spiritual blessing and joy. These are the true riches of heaven. brought to earth and into our life experience. We have so many promises that become ours as we seek Him and commit everything over to Him.

Who have I in heaven but You? And being with You, I desire nothing on earth. (Ps. 73:25) *He will call upon me, and I will answer him; I will be with him in trouble, I will deliver him and honor him.* (Ps.91:15)

July 11

FORGIVE, RELEASE, AND LET GO

I do not consider myself yet to have taken hold of it, But one thing I do: forgetting what is behind and straining toward what is ahead, I press on toward the goal to win the prize for which God has called me heavenward in Christ Jesus. (Phil. 3:13-14)

There are times when we are drawn to remember past experiences. I can look back and think; I wish I knew then what I know now and maybe this or that would not have had to of happened. On second thought, it was those very experiences that brought an understanding of my need for God. The Lord uses our past to remind us of where we have been, and also to show us how far we have come; but the danger is in getting stuck in thinking too much about it. It is in the complete forgiveness of the ones that may have hurt you in the past or in the present that brings peace to our souls. Everyone can relate to finding it hard to do this at times. If this is not possible for you to forgive, ask God to help you. Ask for a willing heart to forgive. We cannot grow and move forward without it. What a bright and free feeling it is when we get to that place of true forgiveness. Forgiveness of knowing our sins have been washed away and any bitterness towards others who have wronged us is at last been done away with! Finally comes the full releasing and the letting go! There is an amazing freedom that comes from the act of letting go, and in the releasing of forgiveness towards others.

Be kind and compassionate to one another, forgiving each other, just as in Christ, God forgave you. (Ephes. 4:32)

BELIEVE AND RECEIVE

"Everything is possible for him who believes." (Mk. 9:23)

These are the words of Jesus. We must believe, and have faith in the God in whom nothing is impossible. Believing and receiving go hand in hand. In order to receive answer to our prayers; we must pray prayers of faith, and then wait with thankful hearts and with a hopeful expectation for the answer. We know the Father is good and desires to bless us when we respond to His love, and in faith ask for His provision, help and blessing. Asking with faith filled prayer is the way the Lord enables us to receive. Jesus spoke many times of the power that faith has in releasing the blessings that God desires to pour out. Loving relationship is always the center of and the key to the Father's heart. It becomes a question of our love for, and obedience to what the Lord is trying to fulfill in your life according to His purposes. Jesus tells us to *"ask."*

So I say to you: "ask and it will be given to you; seek and you will find; knock and the door will be opened to you." (Lk.11:9)

July 13

OUR FAITHFUL GOD

Know therefore that the LORD your God is God: He is the faithful God, keeping His covenant of love to a thousand generations of those who love Him and keep His commands. (Dt. 7-9)

There are so many accounts of the Lord emphasizing this: "*If you have faith as a grain of the mustard seed.*" (Lk. 17:6) The question comes to my mind, what are we to have faith in? The answer is in *His faithfulness* to fulfill the Word of promise to us. That is why the study and meditation on His Word is so important in this principal of receiving. Think of all the times in your life that God showed His faithfulness to you. Our faith will grow in proportion to the love and belief we place in Him, His Word, and in His faithfulness. *Faithful to a thousand generations*, this includes us! Notice that this fulfillment is based upon His love for us and to those who love and keep His commands. If we desire the answer to our prayers, let us pray in faith, love, and in accordance with His Word. God will be faithful to His covenant of love that He has made with us. Then believe you receive and allow the Lord to show you His goodness and faithfulness. He is our faithful God.

If you remain in me and my words remain in you, ask whatever you wish, and it will be given you. (1Jn. 5:7)

July 14

BEING FILLED UP TO GIVE AWAY

Freely you have received, now freely give. (Matt. 10:8)

The healthy life of a Christian is really like a natural spring of fresh water. We drink the Living Water of His Word and Presence, get filled up to overflow, and like a natural spring we become vessels of light and blessings to the world and to one another. This is a continuous and daily process. Everything that we have here on this earth is a gift from the Father. Freely we have received and continue to receive daily benefits and provision. These things have been given to us to share, in both the physical realms and in the spiritual ones too. When we have an opportunity to give, do it freely and joyfully and you will always be well watered and cared for. There are so many references about giving in Scripture. In the context of Matt.10:8, Jesus was speaking to the disciples about the sharing of the spiritual gifts of healing and deliverance they had received. Everyone receives spiritual gifts from the Lord. The more we learn to wait upon the Lord and to be quiet before Him, the more we will find out what our spiritual gifts are. As we fill ourselves daily with Him through the meditation of His Word and in prayer, we will be filled up and able to give away the blessings to others.

Each man should give what he has decided to give in his heart to give, not with reluctance or under compulsion. For God loves a cheerful giver. (2Cor. 9:7)

July 15

USING THE GIFTS

There are different kinds of gifts, but the same Spirit. There are different kinds of service, but the same Lord. There are different kinds of working, but the same God works all of them in all men. Now to each one the manifestation of the Spirit is given for the common good. (1 Cor. 12:4-7)

Sometimes we can see the gifts of the Spirit operating in others but wonder what is it that I have to give? As I draw near to the Lord each day these gifts will become more apparent. There are spiritual gifts from the Lord that we can share with others in different ways and times. Always and in everything, we should have an attitude of thanksgiving in the fact that we have something to give. No matter whether your gift is large or small, physical, financial, or spiritual, when given with love and gladness you will receive blessings. The more we study and meditate upon God's Word and practice it, we will become *like trees planted by streams of water, which yields its fruit in season and whose leaf does not wither. Whatever he does prospers.*(Ps. 1:3) It is in the practicing of His Word that instills in us the desire to give, for we are becoming more and more like Him who gives unceasingly to all creation. It is in the giving away that we are able to receive. The more we fill up on God's Presence and on His Word, the more we will understand how to use the various gifts that we have received from the Lord.

For God loves a cheerful giver. (2 Cor. 9:7)

July 16

PURPOSEFUL TRIALS

Beloved, do not think it strange concerning the fiery trial which is to try you, as though some strange thing happened to you; but rejoice to the extent that you partake of Christ's sufferings; that when His glory is revealed, you may also be glad with exceeding joy. (1 Pet. 4:12-14)

You may be going through a trial that has lasted many years, or it may be a more recent one that you are facing today. Whatever the case, God sees, knows, and has compassion upon you. No matter how long or great the trial or pain, it is still only a momentary affliction in the light of eternity. *For our light and momentary troubles are achieving for us an eternal glory that far outweighs them all.* (2 Cor. 4:17) These trials and sufferings are a part of life for Christians. It is to be expected and recognized as something that the Lord is using to build and purify our characters, and to bring us and our faith to greater maturity. *No discipline seems pleasant at the time, but painful. Later on it produces a harvest of righteousness and peace for those who have been trained by it.* (Heb. 12:11) Purposeful trials are the ones that God allows to come into our lives in order to humble us, try our faith, and to test us: to know what is really in our hearts and whether or not you will keep His commandments.

Know then in your heart that as a man disciplines his son, so the Lord your God disciplines you. (Dt.8:5)

July 17

UNHINDERED INNER JOY

My son, do not make light of the Lord's discipline, and do not lose heart when He rebukes you, because the Lord disciplines those He loves, and He punishes everyone He accepts as a son. (Heb. 12:6)

The Lord tests and tries every son or daughter He loves and accepts. He does not keep us from trial and pain, but takes us through because He wants us to grow up and not keep going back to old ways and habits that are destructive. Another reason is that thorough pain and suffering we learn to have compassion for others and are able to help them because we have the understanding that would not have been there otherwise. When it is all over with; if we are steadfast in our faith and trust Him as we go through these trials, we will come forth as gold. We are victorious through Him in all these things, not in spite of them, but as we are going through them. The Apostle Paul says: *"I am exceedingly joyful in all our tribulation."*(2 Cor.7:4) *"In all these things, we are more than conquerors through Him who loved us."* (Rom. 8:37). We can obtain unhindered inner joy while we are going through hardship and trial. It is not built on anything perishable, but on the love of God that nothing can alter or change.

These have come so that your faith—of greater worth than gold which perishes even though refined by fire—may be proved genuine and may result in praise, glory and honor when Jesus Christ is revealed. (1 Pet. 1:7)

CONTENTMENT IN ALL SITUATIONS

And I in righteousness, I will see Your face; when I awake, I will be satisfied with seeing Your likeness. (Ps. 17:15)

The Lord is in the process of transforming us to His image more and more every day that goes by. During this refining process, we learn to be satisfied with the provision He gives, knowing that a greater purpose and plan is being fulfilled in the process. When we awake each new day, He will satisfy the longing of our hearts as we become more aware of the deep work He is doing in our lives. *For He satisfies the thirsty and fills the hungry with good things.* (Ps.107:9) The more we know of the Lord's love and character, the more content we become in whatever state we find ourselves in. Paul the Apostle showed us by his example just exactly what this means when he began singing and praising God in the terrible prison he found himself in. We can praise God in the most extreme states because we know our deliverance is sure and eternal.

The Lord will guide you always; He will satisfy your needs in a sun scorched land and will strengthen your frame. You will be like a well watered garden, like a spring whose waters never fail. (Is. 58:11)

July 19

GOD IS MY PORTION

God is the strength of my heart and my portion forever. (Ps. 73:26)

Every morning and night, when we reflect upon our day, there are things we can find to thank God for. While living in the United States, we enjoy relative peace with minimal violence in the streets. Our country is holding on to some stability, though it may seem shaky at times. We can go outside and walk about freely without the fear of being arrested or attacked because of our faith. Most everyone has enough food and water and has mobility. All of these things are daily provisional gifts from the Father to us. As the days go by, let's try to slow down and appreciate the beauty that surrounds us in nature, people, and in all of God's creation. When we make an effort to encourage an attitude of thankfulness unto God for everything, we will find contentment in knowing that He Himself is your portion forever.

Better is a little with the fear of the Lord than great wealth with turmoil. (Prov. 15:16)

Godliness with contentment is great gain (1 Tim. 6:6)

July 20

DWELL AND ABIDE IN HIS LOVE

As the Father has loved me, so have I loved you, now remain in my love. (Jn. 15:9-16)

Why is this remaining (abiding) so important and central to our Christian faith? What Jesus emphasizes here is not just the dwelling and abiding alone, but that we are dwelling and abiding in His love. Where there is love, there is peace and inner joy. Love covers all, protects and nourishes, guides and sustains us in every situation at all times. Jesus is our true Vine that provides everything we need to have life in the fullest extent. It is this love of the Lord for us that gives us the sure and strong foundation of our faith in relationship with Him. *As the Father has loved me, so have I loved you* We must always remember the love that the Lord has shown and continues to demonstrate each and every day. For even in our imperfect and uncertain lives, we can always depend upon the great and sustaining love the Lord has for us and His everlasting mercies, as we choose to remain in His love and Presence every moment. The reason Jesus emphasized the abiding in Him as being so central in our Christian lives is so that we could experience joy; His own joy, and that our joy might be full.

These things have I spoken unto you that my joy might remain in you and that your joy might be full. (Jn. 15:11)

July 21

FRUIT BEARING BRANCHES

I am the true vine, and my Father is the husbandman. Abide in me and I in you. As the branch cannot bear fruit of itself, except it abide in the vine, no more can you except you abide in me. Herein is my Father glorified that you bear much fruit, so shall you be my disciples. (Jn. 15:1, 4, 7, 8)

It is the will of God that we might become fruit bearing branches abiding in Jesus our true vine. This is what brings glory to the Father and to the Son. *The fruit of righteousness is a tree of life.* (Prov. 11:30) It is God's intention that we all bear fruit and to flourish; to know what real life is in its fullest extent: to be ever green and flourishing. During the process of being changed and transformed more and more into His likeness, just like a plant or flower, the fruits of righteousness will appear in our lives. It will occur effortlessly as we choose to daily abide in His great love. *The fruits of the Spirit are: love, joy, peace, patience, kindness, goodness, faithfulness, gentleness, and self control.* (Gal. 5:22) The Apostle Paul's prayer to the Colossians *"That you may live a life worthy of the Lord and may please Him in every way: bearing fruit in every good work, growing in the knowledge of the Lord."* (Col. 1:10) So we see that there are fruits of the Spirit and fruits of righteousness, and fruits of our works. As we abide in Jesus our true vine, over time, these fruits will begin to appear

The righteous will flourish like a palm tree, they will grow like a cedar of Lebanon; planted in the house of the Lord, they will flourish in the courts of our God. They will still bear fruit in old age; they will stay fresh and green. (Ps. 92:12-15)

July 22

NEVER GO OUT AGAIN

I give them eternal life, and they shall never perish; no one can snatch them out of my hand. My Father, who has given them to me, is greater than all; no one can snatch them out of my Father's hand. I and the Father are one. (Jn. 10:28-30)

There will be a point in time when we will no longer be tempted or drawn away from the Lord, by the world or the physical temptations of this life. In the meantime, we take comfort from the Scriptures that tell us many times over that nothing can separate us from the love of God in Christ Jesus, and nothing can snatch us away from God's hand. We have a hope that speaks of a place prepared where the life that we've come to know in Christ will no longer be subject to the negative changes and experiences that we have on earth. Life will be swallowed up by life and we will never have to go out into the world as we know it again. Sin, sorrow, pain and death will be put away forever. We will know at last the fullness of uninterrupted and everlasting joy. We will be able to comprehend God's love to a much greater extent. It will take all of eternity to be able to grasp the height and depth of His love! We have this eternal and incorruptible house built by God that we shall one day enter into and never have to go out again!

Now we know that if the earthly tent we live in is destroyed we have a building from God, an eternal house in heaven, not built by human hands. Meanwhile we groan, longing to be clothed with our heavenly dwelling, because we do not wish to be unclothed but to be clothed with our heavenly dwelling, so that what is mortal may be swallowed up by life. (2 Cor. 5:1-4)

July 23

FOREVER WITH THE KING

"Do not let your hearts be troubled. Trust in God; trust also in me. In my Father's house are many rooms, if it were not so, I would have told you. I am going to prepare a place for you; I will come back and take you to be with me that you also may be where I am." (John 14:1-2)

It is time for us to enter in where His love and life can bless us. Sometimes we may hesitate and stand outside, not fully going in. If a King would like to invite you into His palace and sit you down to serve you the best meal you ever could dream of, would you stand in the entry way and choose not to go inside? It would be foolish to stand outside in the cold and not go into the beautiful palace and eat the meal that was specially prepared for you. The Lord has prepared this place for each one of us who will come and enter in. It is the most welcoming and warm place you could ever imagine, made specifically for you. Come in and dwell with the King forever! What a hope and what a promise!

You have made known to me the path of life; You will fill me with joy in Your Presence, with eternal pleasures at Your right hand. (Ps.16:11)

July 24

WORSHIP THE LORD

You are worthy, our Lord and God, to receive glory, honor and power, for you created all things, and for Your pleasure they were created and have their being. (Rev. 4:11)

The LORD our God is the only being in the entire universe that is worthy of our worship and adoration. We were created to worship Him and there's a need inside of us to show love in this way. When hearts are drawn away from God and enticed into the fleeting pleasures of this world, false idols are created to worship instead; they are worshipping the creation instead of the Creator. (Rom.1:25) We see so many examples of this everyday and all around us, lives that have gone after and have become addicted to the allurements of the world. Their hearts appear to have become hard and cold towards God and man. *Yet a time is coming and has now come when the true worshipers will worship the Father in Spirit and truth, for they are the kind of worshipers the Father seeks. God is Spirit and His worshipers must worship in Spirit and in truth.* (Jn. 4:23-24) The Webster's Dictionary defines *worship—The reverent love and allegiance accorded a deity, ardent, humble adoring devotion: To venerate, love or pursue devotedly.* Love always flows from the heart; Jesus has captured our hearts and it is from the deepest place of our hearts that the desire to worship Him comes from. This is the true Spirit of worship that the Father desires. It is natural and right to worship the One who made us and who has created us and all things for His good pleasure.

Love the LORD your God with all your heart and with all your soul and with all your strength. (Dt. 6:4)

July 25

WORSHIP AND REST

Come to me, all you who are weary and burdened, and I will give you rest. Take my yoke upon you and learn from me, for I am gentle and humble in heart, and you will find rest for your souls. For my yoke is easy and my burden is light. (Matt. 11:28)

As worshippers of the Lord, the people of God enter into a rest. We rest from our own works, our burdens, worries, and cares are lifted off from us. Jesus carries these concerns for us and gives us rest. Worship brings to us a sense of peace and of contentment. Worship acknowledges and opens our eyes to see the beauty of the Lord. It was the reality of this beauty that prompted Timothy the Apostle to say: "*I know Whom I have believed, and I am persuaded that He is able to keep the things I've committed to Him until the day of His glorious return!*" (2 Tim. 1:12) The Christian life is a life of worship and loving adoration for the Lord; a heart to heart love relationship that will continue to grow deeper and on into eternity. This is the abiding place: the resting place that Jesus has prepared for you and me to enjoy today and forever. *Come, let us bow down in worship, let us kneel before the LORD our Maker.* (Ps. 95:6)

Ascribe to the LORD the glory due His Name. Bring an offering and come before Him. Worship the LORD in the splendor of His holiness. (1 Ch. 16:29)

July 26

COMMUNION IN SLEEP

Likewise the Spirit also helps our infirmities: for we know not what we should pray for as we ought: but the Spirit itself makes intercession for us with groaning which cannot be uttered. And He who searches our hearts knows the mind of the Spirit, because the Spirit intercedes for the saints in accordance with God's will. (Rom. 8:26-27)

In sleep there's a release; a letting go of our conscious minds; during this time we are most receptive to the Spirit's work in us. He is able to meet us at the point of our deepest subconscious needs. He (the Holy Spirit) searches our hearts and does this in order to help fulfill the will and purposes of God. The Lord wants to produce spiritual fruit in us while we are awake, and during our sleep. It is an opportune time for the Lord to be at work in us. I never thought of Romans 8:26-27 in this light before; but it makes perfect sense. I know that through my own experience, after a good night's sleep, things that seemed overwhelming or confusing the night before, upon awakening, appear to be bearable; suddenly, I have clarity of mind. God's Spirit in us does not sleep; He uses every opportunity in our waking and in our sleeping to fulfill His great plan, design, and purpose. We are slowly being transformed into His own image through the working of His Spirit by day and night. The Lord is ever watching over us, ever performing and perfecting His will in us. Praise God!

Therefore my heart is glad, and my tongue rejoices: my flesh also shall rest in hope. (Ps 16:9)

July 27

PRAYER BEFORE SLEEP

I will lie down and sleep in peace, for You alone, O Lord, make me dwell in safety. (Ps. 4:8)

I remember as a child my mom taught me the prayer, "Now I lay me down to sleep, I pray the Lord my soul to keep. If I should die before I wake, I pray the Lord my soul to take." Amen . . . It is such a simple prayer, so childlike and to the point; yet it is these small heartfelt prayer offerings the Lord hears, accepts, and works for us. It is on those subconscious levels in our minds that the Lord is able to work unhindered by our conscious thoughts. If we sleep on average of say 5 to 8 hours each night that is a good amount of time. Before we enter into sleep, let's remind ourselves to offer up to God a prayer of love, worship and thanksgiving for the day and also for protection through the night. We should also remember our friends, loved ones and family that we know are in need of help from the Lord. The Lord will answer and intercede because of your faithfulness to pray. He will work in their lives even as they sleep. It is a small thing for us; but I believe that praying before bedtime is an important thing to do. We are safe in God's providential care. To Him be praise and thanksgiving in our waking and in our sleeping!

At this I awoke and looked around. My sleep had been pleasant to me. (Jer. 31:26)

July 28

RIGHT PERCEPTION

He is the image of the invisible God, the firstborn over all creation. For by Him all things were created: things in heaven and on earth, visible and invisible, whether thrones or powers or rulers or authorities: all things were created by Him and for Him. He is before all things and in Him all things hold together. (Col. 1:15-1)

Seeing and understanding who we are in Christ and how God sees us and others is an important practice. It is challenging because we know within ourselves that we fall so short of that perfection on a daily basis, not to mention the poor behavior we observe in others at times. That is why we need to rely so strongly upon the grace of God that continues to cover, protect, and heal; bringing forgiveness with peace of mind. It is so important to grasp in our hearts and minds the right perception of The Lord; His glory and His power. King David understood this great perception of the LORD in His mighty power and majesty. He expressed it so beautifully in many of the psalms. It is the right perception that everyone should have when considering the Lord God Almighty.

The Mighty One, God the LORD speaks and summons the earth from the rising of the sun to the place where it sets. From Zion, perfect in beauty, God shines forth. (Ps. 50:1-2)

July 29

DARKNESS FLEES FROM GOD'S LIGHT

The ransomed of the LORD shall return, and come to Zion with songs and everlasting joy upon their heads: they shall obtain joy and gladness, and sorrow and sighing shall flee away. (Isa. 35:10)

There will be a glorious day that is coming when all darkness, sorrow, and sighing will flee away and we will have eternal joy and gladness! By keeping our hearts and eyes looking to and pondering upon the Lord's beauty, power and light; the negative influences of Satan and his attempts to bring fear and temptation suddenly come into the correct perspective. Faith that is focused on the beauty, power, and light of God will enable us to see the darkness for what it is: nothing! It will give us the joy and peace of being untroubled by it. The more we see who God is, the more we realize that the devil is under His control forever and always! We do not have to do heavy spiritual warfare to defeat the devil. We just need to look to the One who has already done it for us; gaze into His beauty, power, and glory. The darkness will flee away for it cannot exist where there is light.

The Son is the radiance of God's glory and the exact representation of His being, sustaining all things by His powerful Word. (Heb. 1:3)

July 30

INTIMATE AUTHORITY

You prepare a table before me in the presence of my enemies. You anoint my head with oil; my cup overflows. (Ps. 23:5)

Intimate authority is what we have in Jesus the more we learn of Him and know Him. He desires to fill our cups to overflow and to prepare our tables in the presence of our enemies so we will see and understand the power of His love for us. In the past, there have been many times when I felt I had to work myself up into a frenzy doing spiritual warfare against the devil. I felt I had to conquer the evil principalities and strongholds in order for God to hear and answer. Everyone encounters spiritual battles; but why not approach God from a more intimate place of trust and calmness in knowing that he hears, cares, and desires to help. Jesus already defeated the enemy of our souls. God wants us to come to Him; as loving sons and daughters; a family with confident trust and in humbleness. As we learn to share with Him openly and honestly, to speak confidently and with love, we will know and have the assurance that He hears, cares, and is ready to join with us in the battle. Our fight is the Lord's, and He has already attained the victory!

How great is Your goodness, which You have stored up for those who fear you, which You bestow in the sight of men on those who take refuge in You. (Ps. 31:19)

July 31

REMAIN CALM

Therefore, prepare your minds for action; be self-controlled, set your hope fully on the grace to be given you when Jesus Christ is revealed. (1Pet. 1:13)

It is easy to panic when things start getting out of our control. We should resist this feeling and learn to stand strong; taking the authority we have been given in Christ. Just speak to the rock, calmly; you don't need to start hammering it. Moses hit the rock so hard that it displeased God and because of that he never entered into the Promised Land. Satan wants us to get intimidated and fearful; it is a tactic he uses that will soon disappear once we learn to stand in assurance and take the authority that we have and is established upon love and trust in the One who is all power and authority. This will cause you to remain unmovable in faith, standing firm and unshakeable in the presence of your enemies. Satan knows exactly what it takes to cause you to waver and stumble. The Lord is greater than anything the devil and his army of demons can throw at you. Overtime it will become more apparent when these attacks start to come and you will be able to ward off the initial panic as your faith and trust grow in God and in the authority you have in Christ and in His Word. Remain calm. *We are more than conquerors through Christ who loved us.* (Rom.8:37)

It is for freedom that Christ has set us free. Stand firm, then, and do not let yourselves be burdened again by a yoke of slavery. (Gal. 5:1)

August 1

THE POWER OF PERSEVERING PRAYER

Men ought always to pray and not to faint. (Lk.18:1)

Keep on praying for your family and friends who are serving the Lord and especially the ones who are not. Keep on and on, never give up and don't think that God has not heard, or that He will not fulfill your requests. It often takes a long time; wait, and pray His Word of promise; persevere with continuous prayers of faith, and you will finally see the fulfillment. *Against all hope, Abraham in hope believed and so became the father of many nations, just as it had been said to him, "So shall your offspring be." Without weakening in his faith, he faced the fact that his body was as good as dead— since he was about a hundred years old—and that Sarah's womb was also dead. Yet he did not waver through unbelief regarding the promise of God, but was strengthened in his faith and gave glory to God being fully persuaded that God had power to do what He had promised.* (Rom.4:18-21) Believe in the promises of the Lord, persevere in prayer and do not give up. *Surely the arm of the Lord is not too short to save.* (Isa.59:1)

Because Jesus lives forever, He has a permanent priesthood. Therefore He is able to save completely those who come to God through Him, because He always lives to make intercession for them. (Heb. 7:25)

August 2

PROMISE FOR PROVISION

Though the fi g tree does not bud and there are no grapes on the vines, though the olive crops fail and the fields produce no food, though there are no sheep in the pen and no cattle in the stalls, yet I will rejoice in the LORD I will be joyful in God my Savior, the Sovereign LORD is my strength; He makes my feet like the feet of a deer, He enables me to go on the heights. (Hab. 3:17-19)

There will be times that we face economic hardship. It affects us individually and as a nation. It is in those times when we need to cut back, even on some of the necessities just in order to keep our households together and running. What is comforting to hear and to understand in the Word of Scripture; is that even in our weakest and most vulnerable times, our God will show Himself strong on behalf of all those who are putting their trust in Him. He will continue to provide what is needed to pull us up to even much greater heights as we look to Him for our needs and necessities. We have, and can experience great spiritual blessing and joy even in those lean and adverse times. Over and over He proves His Word true to all those who in faith place their lives in His care. The Words of Jesus:

"Therefore I tell you; do not worry about your life what you will eat or drink; or about you body, what you will wear. Is not life more important than food and the body more important than clothes?" (Matt. 6:25)

GREATER HEIGHTS

And if the Spirit of Him who raised Jesus from the dead is living in you, He who raised Christ from the dead will also give life to your mortal bodies through His Spirit, who lives in you. (Rom. 8:11)

Although our physical bodies may feel weak and our spirits downcast, when we call out to the Lord He lifts us up and strengthens us. I think of King David in his many highs and lows. God was faithful to bring him out every time. Always remember that the Lord is fulfilling a greater plan that takes time, and our part is to keep the greater purpose in the forefront of our minds. He has a good future planned for you, better than what you could think or dream of. He will give you the strength and provision that you need every time and in all things. God wants to lift us up higher in the Spirit and bless us with every spiritual blessing. Open your hearts to receive, look to the Lord you will find that the journey you are on is an upward one, going up to greater heights. *And God raised us up with Christ and seated us with Him in the heavenly realms in Christ Jesus, in order that in the coming ages He might show the incomparable riches of His grace, expressed in His kindness to us in Christ Jesus.* (Ephes. 2:6)

The LORD gives strength to His people; the LORD blesses His people with peace. (Ps. 29:11)

August 4

UNSHAKABLE

Once more I will shake not only the earth but also the heavens. Therefore, since we are receiving a Kingdom that cannot be shaken, let us be thankful, and so worship God acceptably with reverence and awe for our God is a consuming fi re. (Heb. 12:26-28)

The words *once more* indicate the removing of what can be shaken: that is, created things; so that what cannot be shaken may remain. Our faith is what causes us to stand firm when all is shaking and moving around us; the earth and even heaven itself will be shaken. *Shaken: defined in the Strongs concordance (Greek): To agitate, rock, topple destroy; to disturb, incite, move, and shake together.* There is an old song that comes to my mind, it goes: "I shall not be, I shall not be moved, I shall not be, I shall not be moved. Just like a tree that's planted by the waters, I shall not be moved." The testing of our faith today is no different than what it has been for all ages. How we react to the shaking will determine whether or not we will stand firm to the end, or fall.

Those who trust in the LORD are like Mount Zion, which cannot be shaken but endures forever. (Ps.125:1)

STANDING FIRM

Therefore put on the full armor of God, so that when the day of evil comes, you may be able to stand your ground, and after you have done everything to stand, stand firm then. Ephes. (6:13-14)

We have been given everything we need to stand and to stand firm no matter what comes. It is the Lord Himself that enables us to stand. *And he will stand, for the LORD is able to make him stand.* (Rom.14:4) It is our belief in God's promise to give us strength, and in His faithfulness that enables us to keep us standing firm to the end. In Isaiah it speaks about a *lookout* (someone who watches): he cries, *Day after day, my Lord, I stand on the watchtower; every night I stay at my post.* (Isa.21:8) We are all being called to *watch,* and to *stay at our post.* Stand: and after having done all to stand, keep on standing. We have been assured that we have received a Kingdom that cannot be shaken. Paul tells us to *be thankful and to worship.* This is one of the greatest defenses that we can have to use when the shaking begins. The Lord has given us everything that we need to stand victorious in Him in the midst and through every storm and trial that we will face. Our part is to take a hold of what we have been given and stand firm until the end.

He will stand, for the Lord is able to make him stand. (Rom. 14:4)

August 6

GOD IS ON OUR SIDE

If the LORD had not been on our side, the flood would have engulfed us, the torrent would have swept over us, and the raging waters would have swept us away. We have escaped like a bird out of the fowler's snare; the snare has been broken, and we have escaped. Our help is in the name of the LORD the Maker of heaven and earth. (Ps. 124:1 4-7 & 8)

This Psalm of King David was written after one of the many escapes he had made. David was a man who fought a lot of battles, both physical and spiritual ones. The LORD delivered him along with his people out of the enemies hand every time. He had confidence that God would because of the loving relationship he had with his Creator, *the Maker of heaven and earth.* He could, with God's help win every battle and escape the fowler's snare. The Lord is on our side and in Him we will always be victorious. Things may appear to be bleak and circumstances beyond our control, but with God on our side, we will get through it and come out triumphantly, for we have the LORD, the maker of heaven and earth who is our help. If the Lord was not on our side, our enemies would sweep over us and bring us down to the depths with no remedy. But God, in His mercy and grace stands with us and for us. He is on our side.

The gates of hell shall not prevail against His Church. (Matt 16:18)

SOME THINGS NEVER CHANGE

I lift my eyes to the hills where does my help come from? My help comes from the LORD the Maker of heaven and earth. He will not let your foot to slip— He who watches over you will not slumber. The LORD watches over you— the LORD is your shade at your right hand; the sun will not harm you by day or the moon by night. The LORD will keep you from all harm He will watch over your life; the LORD will watch over your coming and going both now and forevermore. (Ps.121:1-8)

Things have changed greatly from David's time to ours today. But some things never change: the character of God's goodness, love, and mercy towards those who love and trust in Him, and the truth of His Word remains unchanged and lives on eternally. Another thing that does not change is the character of the devil; he is a murderer, a thief, a liar and an accuser of the believers; his evil nature will never change either. His sole ambition and passion is to wage war against what God loves the most, which are His people. The lies of the enemy, the deceptive tactics he uses against Christians does not change from age to age. We are over comers in all things because Jesus overcame and has all authority both in heaven and in earth. Jesus is the same yesterday, today and forever and does not change but remains the same. He is continually making intercession for you and me as our great High Priest. With God watching over us, we need not ever fear evil for The Lord has said:

"Never will I leave you; never will I forsake you. So we say with confidence, *The LORD is my helper; I will not be afraid."* (Heb. 13:6)

August 8

HUMILITY

Oh LORD, our LORD how majestic is your name in all the earth! When I consider your heavens, the work of your fingers, the moon and the stars, which you have set in place, what is man that you are mindful of him, the son of man that you care for him? (Ps.8:1-3)

King David in this psalm helps us to understand the humility of Jesus during His incarnation and on through His resurrection and glory. It is a picture also of the gift God purchased for mankind and our restored position as the Church, the Bride of Christ. We know that the reason Jesus came to earth was to redeem us, to restore, heal, and bring deliverance as He stated in Isaiah 61. He came to set the captives free: (you and me who were held captive by Satan with our selfishness and pride that was our old nature.) He points out so clearly that the example of Jesus' humility and His willingness to come as one, who serves, is an example to us of the single most effective way of winning the hearts of men and women. He came as a servant among us, there by showing us the path we all must take in order to win the lost of this world back to Christ. If we are prideful, no one will listen or be drawn to know the Lord. Winning and praying for the lost must be a work of love with humbleness; this is the way that God has shown us through the Lord's example.

For this is what the high and lofty One says, I live in a high and holy place, but also with him who is contrite and lowly in spirit, to revive the spirit of the lowly, and to revive the spirit of the contrite. (Is.57:15)

TEACH ME TO DO YOUR WILL

Teach me to do Your will, for You are my God, may Your good Spirit lead me on level ground. (Ps. 143:10)

All of us need to show the same servitude and willingness to think of others more highly than ourselves. Allow God to develop this virtue in the daily act of surrendering your will up, in order to have His will be done. Without His Spirit working this quality in you, it cannot be done. The encouraging part is that you do not have to stress or strain for it. As we lean and depend upon Him more and more, it will occur effortlessly as our faith grows. God is glorified through humble hearts. *Teach me to do your will for You are my God; may Your good Spirit lead me on level ground.* (Ps. 143:10) The Lord will instruct and teach us every step of the way. When trying to do things on our own, we run into uneven and rocky ground. He will light our path and make a clear highway for us to travel on, if we are determined to allow His will to be done. Finally, we'll get to the place where we quit fighting against the wind of His Spirit. His good and great Holy Spirit will lead and guide us all the way. The older we get, and the longer we are reading and meditating upon His Word, it will become a part of us. There will come a time when we will gain the full assurance of knowing that His will is being done in our lives on earth, as it is in heaven.

I desire to do Your will, O my God; Your law is within my heart. (Ps.40:8)

August 10

HUMILITY AND GLORY

Has not God chosen those who are poor in the eyes of the world to be rich in faith and to inherit the kingdom He promised those who love Him? (Jas. 2:5)

Being lifted up and exalted is what God desires to do for everyone who is willing to be brought low and made to be humble in heart. Can we live our lives in such a way that will bring glory to God, while at the same time our spirits are being lifted up and are experiencing the Kingdom of God within? I believe the answer is yes. The Lord desires to show us the true meaning of glory through the humbling of ourselves: the way up is to go down. *Blessed are the poor in spirit, for theirs is the Kingdom of heaven.* (Matt. 5:3) *The Kingdom of God is within you.* (Lk.17:21) In these scriptures we see the correlation between humility and the glory of heaven. *Humble yourselves before the Lord and He shall lift you up. (Jas. 4:10)* In Jesus' own words He says:

"For whoever exalts himself will be humbled, and whoever humbles himself will be exalted." (Matt. 23:12)

GLORY AND SUFFERING

In bringing many sons to glory, it was fitting that God, for whom and through whom everything exists, should make the author of their salvation perfect through suffering. (Heb. 2:10)

The correlation between glory and suffering can be clearly seen; for trials and sufferings are the doorway that leads and allows us to enter into glory and into the state of heavenly bliss. Looking to Jesus the Captain of our Salvation who was made perfect through the things He suffered, was later glorified and received up into heaven returning to His original glorified state and even now so much more having brought many sons and daughters into their glory with Him. We have this hope that sustains us during our times of trials and sufferings. When we are made aware of the Lord's sustaining presence, we can experience an unexplainable inner joy and peace knowing that what is happening is for our greatest good; that there really will be an end and also a new beginning. Times of trial are meant to bring needed changes and growth. Welcome the Lord's pruning shears; you will become a very fruitful branch if you allow His Spirit to take control of the situation.

We rejoice in the hope of the glory of God. Not only so, but we also rejoice in our sufferings, because we know that suffering produces perseverance: perseverance, character; and character, hope. And hope does not disappoint us, because God has poured out His love into our hearts by the Holy Spirit, whom He has given us. (Rom.5:2-5)

August 12

ENTERING INTO GLORY

Let him who glories, glory in the Lord. (1 Cor. 1:31)

The word glory as defined in the Webster's Dictionary: *Exalted honor, praise, or a highly praiseworthy asset, adoration, thanksgiving, majestic beauty and splendor; resplendence; the splendor and bliss of heaven; a state of perfect happiness. To rejoice triumphantly, exult . . .* The glory we receive is from the Lord and by the Lord when we have fulfilled all that He has asked of us and we hear Him say "*Well done thou good and faithful servant.*" The thought that it is through a loving relationship we develop with God that makes us known and understood by God; to know and to be known of God is the highest glory! The hints of glory we feel now in the experience of a beautiful piece of music or art, the magnificence of nature, all of these things do fade away in a moment and leave us with a sense of approaching it, so close, yet still being left outside as the vision disappears. The beauty of the sunset, the feeling we get when watching a spring rain, the ocean and its changing tides, all the moments of beauty we want to hold on to, will one day be upon us and will not end or fade away, but will with increasing brightness and glory continue on and on with greater and greater magnitudes into eternity. We will see it, enter into, and become one with it at last . . . It is the Lord . . . . we shall know Him and be known of Him with ever increasing revelations of His glory throughout eternity.

Christ in you, the hope of glory. (Col. 1:27)

THE ARMOR OF LIGHT

The sun will no more be your light by day, nor will the brightness of the moon shine on you, for the LORD will be your everlasting light, and your God will be your glory. Your sun will never set again, and your moon will wane no more; The LORD will be your everlasting light, and your days of sorrow will end. (Isa. 60:19-20)

In chapter 60 of Isaiah, he speaks of the time right after the coming of the Lord. God fills His people with His light and we will shine light into this dark world that we live in. The light of God's love in you will overcome all darkness. It is an armor of light that we have received and will preserve and protect us to the end. *The night is nearly over; the day is almost here. So let us put aside the deeds of darkness and put on the armor of light.* (Rom.13:1) Now is the time to shine God's love and light into the darkness that surrounds us in this world. The light of His love as it shines ever brighter will overcome all the darkness, and be an armor of protection and defense. Many will see and believe.

Arise, shine, for your light has come, and the glory of the LORD rises upon you. See darkness covers the earth and thick darkness is over the peoples. But the Lord rises upon you and His glory appears over you. (Is. 60:1-2)

GLORY AND THE MORNING STAR

To him who overcomes and does my will to the end, I will give authority over the nations. I will also give him the Morning Star. (Rev. 2:26, 28)

Sometimes when I get up early in the morning and look up at the sky, I can see a morning star. It seems more beautiful than the evening stars that were there the night before; ones that I barely noticed. This promise from the Lord makes me want to really do the Lord's will to the end, and be a victorious over-comer; to receive from the Lord the morning star! I don't know how that it will come about, but it sounds amazing! There will come the time when the mortal will put on immortality, we will leave all the struggles and pain behind forever. Seeing the beauty of the stars and of nature that God has made, is just a foretaste, a dim shadow of what we will come to know in the realms of heavenly goodness and beauty. There is so much more we have to look forward to living for Christ and with the hope of seeing His glory. *Christ in us, the hope of glory! And we, who with unveiled faces all reflect the Lord's glory, are being transformed into His likeness with ever-increasing glory, which comes from the Lord, who is the Spirit.* (2 Cor. 3:18)

And we have the Word of the prophets made more certain, and you will do well to pay attention to it, as to a light shining in a dark place, until the day dawns and the Morning Star rises in your hearts. (2 Pet. 1:19)

THE WEIGHT OF GLORY

For our light and momentary troubles are achieving for us an eternal weight of glory that far outweighs them all. (2 Cor. 4:17)

The weight of glory that we bear in a sense can also be seen as a responsibility we have towards one another and to God. As time goes by, we become more aware and awakened to a reality that is hidden beyond the veil of our physical limitations: which is the Presence of God and of His power. He is in the process of transforming people into glorious beings or horrifying ones. C.S. Lewis explains this so well in his book The Weight of Glory. It is a sobering thought to realize that our actions and attitudes either help or hinder the work of the Spirit in our lives and in other people's lives as well. The Lord has set His heart and sights upon us. We are His treasure and delight. What awaits us beyond that door is the unspeakable gift of God Himself, in the knowing, and in the being known and accepted by the God of the entire universe! Somehow in our smallness and insufficiencies, the God of all Glory has invited us in to share this indescribable existence with Him! This is a true weight upon everyone who has received the heart and mind to understand. In the daily interactions with our neighbors, co-workers, and family members, we can learn with all humility, to see them as Christ sees them; to love them as Christ loves them and wants to love them through us. It is through prayer and the work of God's Spirit that they will come to find the hidden Christ within themselves. For now, although I cannot wait for the Son to appear, it is still only another Monday morning.

You guide me with your counsel, and afterward you will take me into glory. (Ps. 73:24)

PRAISE HIM IN EVERYTHING

For God has said, "Never will I leave you, never will I forsake you."
(Heb. 13:5)

It may feel as though you are walking across a desert, dry and barren. It is important for you to know that you are not alone. You have a Heavenly Father that loves you and the Lord Jesus who is continually leading and guiding you by His Spirit making your way safe and sure across that desert. Give Him thanks and praise for the fact that He is with you. Show your love and appreciation for the present day and moment, if only for the gift of being alive if you are in that dry and barren place. On the other hand, perhaps you are experiencing abundance of blessings; do not forget the One who brought you to that place. Praise, love, and show Him the appreciation He deserves in whatever state you find yourself to be in, whether in the good or in the bad, praise Him in everything.

Bless the LORD O my soul; all my inmost being, praise His Holy Name. Praise the LORD, O my soul, and forget not all His benefits. He forgives all my sons and heals all my diseases; He redeems my life from the pit and crowns me with love and compassion. He satisfies my desires with good things, so that my youth is renewed like the eagles. The LORD works righteousness and justice for all the oppressed. Bless the LORD O my soul . . . (Ps. 103:1-6)

August 17

ALL THINGS WERE MADE BY HIM

All things were made by Him, and without Him was not anything made that was made. (Jn. 1:3)

Back before the beginning of time itself, and previous to the creation, there must have been nothing. In Job the Lord tells us that: *He spreads out the northern skies over empty space; He suspends the earth over nothing.* (Job 26:7) The whole earth is suspended over nothing but God Himself! There are many psalms and other books that tell us that God (Jesus) as the Word of God spoke creation into existence. When He said "*Let there be Light,*" light came into being. And so on it went throughout, sustaining all of His creation. When I see the beauty of the universe, all the plant and animal life and the beauty of all the earth itself, it gives me understanding of how very much God loved us when he made all of these good and great things for us to enjoy. The Lord now speaks words of life to us and throughout the course of time, creates something good, beautiful, and alive out of our nothingness. Jesus is holding all of creation together by the Word of His power; you can be assured that He is able to hold and to keep you and bring you into all the fullness of what you were created to be.

The Son is the radiance of God's glory and the exact representation of His being, sustaining all things by His powerful Word. (Heb.1:3)

GOD AT WORK IN US

Now to Him who is able to do immeasurably more than all we ask or imagine, according to His power that is at work within us, to Him be glory in the Church and in Christ Jesus throughout all generations, forever and ever! Amen. (Ephes. 3:20-21)

God's power and His Spirit are continuously at work within the believer's heart and life. As our faith in this truth grows, it is the Lord's pleasure and delight to fulfill our hearts desires and to give us an abundant life. *For it is God who works in you to will and to act according to His good pleasure. (Phil. 2:13)* You are in Christ Jesus. The whole Christian life depends on the clear consciousness of our position in Christ. The Apostle Paul has an additional thought, of almost greater importance; *Of God* are you *in Christ Jesus.* He wants us not only to remember our union to Christ, but especially that it is not our own doing, but the work of God Himself. As the Holy Spirit teaches us to realize this, we will see what a source of assurance and strength it must become to us. *"I know and have believed,"* is a valid testimony. But it is of great consequence that the mind should be led to see that behind our repentance, believing, and accepting of Christ, there was God the Father's Almighty power doing its work, inspiring our will, taking possession of us, and carrying out His own purpose of love in planting us into Christ Jesus. This is the Lord's doing, of God I am in Christ Jesus.

Of God are you in Christ Jesus, who was made unto us wisdom from God, both righteousness and sanctification, and redemption. (1 Cor. 1:30)

August 19

THE LORD HAS DRAWN YOU

The Lord has appeared of old unto me, saying, "Yes, I have loved you with an everlasting love: therefore with loving kindness have I drawn you." (Jer. 31:3)

It was the loving kindness of the Lord that first drew you to Him. It is with that same loving kindness, compassion and mercy that He holds us. It is God the Father who unites me to Christ, in order to perfect His own divine work, to work in me both to will and to do of His good pleasure. *You are God's workmanship, created in Christ Jesus unto good works.* (Ephes. 2:10) Whatever God creates is perfectly suited to its end. He created the sun to give light: how precisely it does its work! He created the eye to see: how beautifully it fulfills its object! He created the new man and woman unto good works: how admirably it is fitted for its purpose. Of God, I am in Christ, created a new, made a branch of the Vine, fitted for fruit bearing as I yield and submit my will unto the Father's. Our Heavenly Father will produce the fruit in our lives as we submit and yield to His will daily. Our part is to abide, His is to do the work in order to fulfill His purpose in us and in all of creation. God the Father oversees our progress as we grow in our faith and love.

And God is able to make all grace abound to you, so that in all things at all times; having all that you need, you will abound in every good work. (2 Cor. 9:8)

August 20

PRESERVATION AND OBEDIENCE

Remember Your Word to your servant; for You have given me hope. My comfort in my suffering is this: Your promise renews my life. I have suffered much; preserve my life O Lord according to Your Word. (Ps. 119:49,50,107)

It is through the pain of affliction that we learn and come to understand the Lord's preservation that He has provided for all who follow in the paths of His righteousness. It is through much suffering, trials, and persecutions that we enter into life everlasting. Without this occurring, we would never come to understand the Lord's suffering and sacrifice. Many times the very act of obedience, leads to trials and sufferings. Obedience to the Lord's commands and in the understanding of His precepts, we find comfort, assurance, and hope. When we take the time to learn and to study the Lord's ways, we learn the ways of righteousness, and through obeying, we can receive what He has promised to fulfill for every believing soul.

It was good for me to be afflicted, so that I might learn of Your decrees. Your hands have made me and formed me; give me understanding to learn Your commands. Preserve my life according to Your love, and I will obey the statues of Your mouth. (Ps. 119:71, 73, 88)

BLESSINGS FOR THOSE WHO OBEY

Although He was a son, He learned obedience from what He suffered and once made perfect, He became the source of eternal salvation for all who obey Him. (Heb. 5:8)

There is also the hope and joy of promised blessing for all those who obey. The Lord has promised to preserve us body, soul, and spirit unto the coming of the Lord. He will preserve, protect, and keep us in the shelter of His love. We can take great comfort in His promise that assures us He will be with us and keep us whole to the very end of our days. It is the Father's desire to give us not only life, but for us to have a blessed life. What earthly father would not want his child to have the best in life? This is so much truer of our heavenly Father! The one thing that is required in order to enter into this blessed life is obedience to Him and to His Word.

Now if you obey me fully and keep my covenant, then out of all nations you will be my treasured possession. (Ex. 19:5) *Oh that their hearts would be inclined to fear me and keep all my commands always, so that it might go well with them and their children forever!* (Dt. 12:28)

GOD'S PRESERVES

Whoever tries to keep his life will lose it, and whoever loses his life will preserve it. (Lk.17:33)

It is the Lord's great desire to bless and preserve us, our children, and our children's children; if we would only allow the Lord to work His works in our lives and give attention to His commandments. They are given to protect and preserve us. God Himself is able to keep us unto our dying day, or to the coming of the Lord. He is faithful and He will do it when we seek to follow in His ways. We can have that assurance and hope to the very end that he will watch over every aspect of our lives and give us everything that we need to live and to be productive. It is the Lord's desire that we become fruitful branches bearing good fruit that will last and last. The older I get, I realize that I am not able to physically do some of the things I used to do and I find that more and more I need to depend upon God's strength to help and to carry me when I cannot go any farther. When I yield to His will and commands, He is so faithful to help and preserve my life in whatever way is needed for the time.

May God Himself, the God of peace, sanctify you through and through. May your whole spirit, soul and body be kept blameless at the coming of our Lord Jesus Christ, The one who calls you is faithful and He will do it. (1Thes. 5:23)

OUR MASTER AND LORD

"You call me Master and Lord and you say well, for so I am." (Jn.13:13)

Our Master is the one who made us, created and formed us. He had us in His heart and mind before we ever came forth to be born. He chose our genetic makeup, decided who our parents should be, the color of our hair, eyes, and skin, our place of birth; in all of this we had nothing to say about; no choice. He, (our Master) willed us into existence. He gave us the breath of life, and then called us to be His very own. When we yield to the Master's plan; to His Holy Spirit and will, we bring to Him honor and glory. Our reward is that we shall enjoy Him for all eternity. To have a master and to be mastered are two different things. A master is one who knows me better than myself and knows the innermost and intimate details of my life. He can solve every perplexity that life presents, and bring with it a sense of complete security and safety. Love is the motivation of the Master. Our Lord and Master never forces obedience. We are His sons and daughters, in the same way that Jesus was God's son. *Though He was a son, yet He learned obedience.* (Hew. 5:8) It is a loving relationship that causes us to want to obey without even being conscious of it. Obedience to the Master becomes just a natural outflow of love.

For you have one Master, who is the Christ. (Matt.23:10)

August 24

LET PEACE RULE AND BE THANKFUL

Let the peace of Christ rule in your hearts, since as members of one body you were called to peace. And be thankful. (Col. 3:15)

As we continue to be grateful and have a thankful heart towards God, the scripture says; *"Let the peace of the Lord rule in your hearts."* This is something we need to do. We were called to have this peace and we can obtain it if we will let the peace of the Lord rule in our hearts. His peace will overtake us and all anxiety will vanish away into joyful song. *Let them sacrifice thank offerings and tell of His works with songs of joy.* (Ps. 107:22) One of the best ways to overcome stress is to sing a song of praise unto the Lord. When you begin to practice this; it is amazing how your spirit is lifted high above the concerns of the hour and peace is restored. It is the Lord's will that we give thanks in all circumstances. Whether in happiness or in sorrow, in plenty or leanness, sickness or health, in all things and in every circumstance; let us learn to give thanks to the Lord for He cares for you and is working all things out in order to bring us a future of hope and of His peace.

Give thanks in all circumstances, for this is God's will for you in Christ Jesus. (1Thess. 5:18)

SPIRITUAL CROWNS

Everyone who competes in the games goes into strict training. They do it to get a crown that will not last; but we do it to get a crown that will last forever. (1 Cor. 9:25)

Life is not a game or a sport, but as we learn to exercise our faith in Christ, there are tests and trials that require us to use discipline and to put into action the things we have been taught. We may not agree with what we see happening or be able to bring about change in an instant, but we know that perseverance and steadfast faith, will in the end produce a crown upon our heads, one that will last forever! *Blessed is the man who perseveres under trial, because when he has stood the test, he will receive the crown of life that God has promised to those who love Him.* (Jas. 1:12) There are many different crowns that the Bible mentions; the presenting of these crowns is a part of the reward we will receive from the Lord if we stay true to the finish. Everyone who serves the Lord faithfully and who yearns for His appearing will receive the crown of righteousness. (2 Ti. 4:8) We all have been made righteous through the Lords atoning sacrifice in the shedding of His blood. Every good thing we receive in life comes from God because of His goodness, mercy, and grace. Whatever reward we receive in the form of crowns, will not even come close to the reward of being welcomed into His Presence and in experiencing the glorious revelation of seeing Him and actually being with Him at last!

The twenty-four elders fall down before Him who sits on the throne, and worship Him who lives for ever and ever. They lay their crowns before the throne . . . (Rev. 4:10)

CROWN OF RIGHTEOUSNESS

Now there is in store for me the crown of righteousness, which the Lord, the Righteous Judge, will award to me on that day—and not only to me, but also to all who have longed for His appearing. (2Tim 4:8)

This is our great hope and longed for conclusion. It is only the Lord who can judge righteously. *And when the Chief Shepherd appears, you will receive the crown of glory that will never fade away.* (1 Pet. 5:4) *I am coming soon. Hold on to what you have, so that no one will take your crown.* (Rev. 3:11) The enemy of our souls, Satan, the liar and accuser wants so badly to take your crown and trample upon it. We must resist the temptation to retaliate; hold on to what we have been given thus far. If we are to be over comers in this life, we fight the darkness with the light, anxiety and fear with our faith, doubt and unbelief with hope, strife and anger with peace. The enemy cannot stand or prevail against these. The ultimate blessing will come when we will at last lay our crowns down before God's throne and forever worship the One who laid down His crown of glory for a crown of thorns in order to purchase for us the crown of everlasting life.

The twenty-four elders fall down before Him who sits on the throne, and worship Him who lives forever and ever. They lay their crowns before the throne. (Rev. 2:10)

SPIRITUAL STONES

That He might gather together in one all things in Christ, both which are in heaven, and which are on earth. (Ephes. 1:10)

We have so much to learn from many Godly men and women who have gone before us. Each has given us a special gift in the sacrifice and in the offering up of their lives so that we who follow after can grasp and have more understanding of the Scripture and of the promises. We are commissioned to carry on what has been already established since the birth of the Church. *You also, as living stones, are built up a spiritual house, to be a holy priesthood, to offer up spiritual sacrifices, acceptable to God through Jesus Christ.* (1Pet.2:5) We are living stones built upon one another Jesus Himself our Chief Cornerstone. God through His Holy Spirit is willing to reveal to us many mysteries concerning creation; our origin and purpose in His Divine Plan. We can gain wisdom from these lives of men and women who paved the way before us; all built together one upon another, from the beginning to the present, one holy spiritual house.

For we are God's fellow workers: you are God's field, God's building. According to the grace of God which was given unto me, as a wise master builder I laid a foundation; and another built thereon. Know you not that you are a temple of God, and that the Spirit of God dwells in you? (1 Cor. 3:9, 10, 16)

NO MORE STRANGERS

So then you are no more strangers and sojourners, but you are fellow-citizens with the saints, and of the household of God, being built upon the foundation of the Apostles and Prophets, Christ Jesus himself being the chief corner stone; in Him the whole building is joined together and rises to become a holy temple in the Lord. And in Him you too are being built together to become a dwelling in which God lives by His Spirit. (Ephes.2:19-22)

There will be a day when all the saints of old will be joined together with us and we will all be made perfect in one. The scriptures speak of us being surrounded by a cloud of witnesses. It is a comforting thing to think of all the people who have journeyed through this life and finished well. They serve as great examples that go on shining throughout the ages leaving books and legacies for us to receive in order for us to gain hope, insight, and wisdom. They are a part of the "great cloud of witnesses" cheering us on to our finish line. This may be the last generation that we are living in. Still the house will go on being built until the very last stone is in place.

And these all, having had witness borne to them through their faith, received not the promise, God having provided some better thing concerning us, that apart from us they should not be made perfect. (Heb.11:39-40) Therefore let us also, seeing we are compassed about with so great a cloud of witnesses, lay aside every weight, and the sin which doth so easily beset us, and let us run with patience the race that is set before us. (Hew. 12:1)

NO SEPARATION

No in all these things we are more than conquerors through Him who loved us, for I am convinced that neither death nor life, neither angels nor demons, neither the present nor the future, nor any powers, neither height nor depth, nor anything else in all creation, will be able to separate us from the love of God that is in Christ Jesus our Lord. (Rom. 8:37-39)

As Christians we have an inseparable relationship with the Lord Jesus. To separate implies pulling apart something that is united together. When Jesus promised to come and to abide in us, and we would abide in Him, that union cannot be severed by any force of nature or spiritual power either. The loving relationship will go on and on throughout all eternity. His very Divine Presence walks with us all during the day, abides continually as we sleep and gradually captivates our every move and thought. As we abide in Him, the glorious light within each believer shines more luminous as the days and years go by. There is a peace and an assurance that comes when we begin to understand and to believe what this scripture implies. We can live our lives in the full confidence of absolutely knowing that our Lord is with us continually and will never leave us or be separated from us.

"I will never leave you or forsake you." (Heb.13:5)

August 30

FIRST LOVE

Yet I hold this against you: You have forsaken your first love. (Rev. 2:4)

Awakening to first love is a mystery, an incomprehensible thing. It can come upon you in an unexpected moment. We recall an unsettling churning within our hearts, then a gentle drawing, almost like the coming home after a long journey. At the same time there is an excitement and anticipation for the next meeting with the special one that has captivated our heart. When first awakened by the love of God, it is similar to a first love; incomprehensible, a sense of a homecoming, of a welcome and warmth that can only be expressed in the language of hearts. It also can be described as an excitement and an anticipation of a new companionship; a desire to get to know and be with the one we now love. This is how the Lord desires us to be and return to, in our relationship with Him. He wants us to remember the love we felt in the beginning when we first believed. All the affection we have felt for people and things in the world, were but small reflections of the greater love we can find in Him. All the beautiful things we love in this world come from Him. He is the creator and source of all that we have loved, love at present, and will love. His is all encompassing and knows no end. The things we now see are only dim reflections of a deeper beauty and love that the Lord desires to reveal. The loves we experience in this world are fleeting and for the most part do not last, but His endures forever! We need to return to our first love in Him and yearn for the one and only true love that is, that was, and will forever more be true.

As the Father has loved me, so have I loved you. Now remain in my love. (Jn.15:9)

READINESS IN AND OUT OF SEASON

Be prepared in season and out of season. (2 Tim. 4:2)

There are always times when we may feel we are out of season, maybe not up for the job that is being requested of us, or that may be our responsibility to carry out. Sometimes it appears as if we are walking in a fog, just mechanically going through the motions of everyday ordinary things. We feel out of touch with what is going on in our lives and begin to question the Lord because we cannot understand why we are here or His purpose in all of it. The Word of God tells us that we are to walk by faith not by sight. Because of the circumstances surrounding us, and by every common sense standpoint, we feel we have a right to feel that way. This is when we need to resist thinking those negative thoughts and call upon Him in faith. To be prepared when out of season is to basically will ourselves to see with spirit eyes and hear with spiritual understanding the voice of the Lord saying to us *"I am with you and I will walk along side you. You are not alone. I will never leave you."* Being ready or being in readiness is really being in right relationship with God. Then no matter what we are asked to do, small or great, we do it with an attitude of readiness, and soon our spirits will be lifted up and we shall mount up with wings like the eagles.

Be strengthened with all power according to His glorious might so that you may have great endurance and patience. (Col. 1:11)

HOPE FOR THE MISSION

But as for me, I will always have hope; I will praise You more and more. Since my youth, O God, You have taught me, and to this day I declare your marvelous deeds. Even when I am old and gray, do not forsake me, O God, till I declare Your power to the next generation, Your might to all who are to come. (Ps 71:14, 17, 18)

King David was given a mission to fulfill, a purpose for his life. He knew that it was God's will and intention for him to declare God's power and might to all, and to all that would come in future generations. In spite of David's many adversaries, trials and sufferings, he always had hope. He fought many battles within and without. Still he was able to praise the Lord throughout his life, from his youth to his old age and maintain his hope. He had learned to put his confidence in the Lord and in Him alone, in doing this, he always found refuge and renewed strength. Although life for him was many times tumultuous and uncertain, he knew he was on a mission. Its course had been set, its purpose revealed: it was to declare God's power to the next generation, His might to all who would come after.

For everything that was written in the past, was written to teach us, so that through endurance and encouragement of the Scriptures, we might have hope. (Rom. 15:4)

DECLARING GOD'S POWER

For we are God's workmanship, created in Christ Jesus to do good works, which God prepared in advance for us to do. (Ephes. 2:10)

To declare God's power in such a way that will last and effect future generations, is a mission that the Church, God's people continue to carry out today. It is a mission every believer in Jesus has been called to do. In whatever way or method you have been given individually by the Lord to fulfill, it is God Himself who will be faithful to perform and perfect His work in you until the day of Jesus Christ. *Being confident of this, that He who began a good work in you will carry it on to completion until the day of Christ Jesus.* (Phil 1:6) It is through our daily submission and surrender to His will that allows God to perform the good work in you. It is in Him alone that we have this great hope. Knowing that is God Himself who is performing the work, we do not need to fret or worry about the outcome. As long as we are surrendered to His will, He will do the work that is needed. The results will declare His power to the world and our lives will bring Him glory.

Now to Him who is able to do immeasurably more than all we ask or imagine, according to His power that is at work within us, to Him be glory in the Church and in Christ Jesus throughout all generations, forever and ever! Amen . . . . (Ephes. 3:20)

September 3

JOY IN THE WAITING

Yet the Lord longs to be gracious to you. He rises to show you compassion:
For the Lord is a God of justice. Blessed are all who wait for Him. (Isa. 30:18)

There is joy and a privilege in the waiting; and blessed are all who wait for Him. May our hearts really feel and know the great honor and joy of waiting and in the privilege of continuing to intercede for others. As we wait unceasingly for the blessings that the Lord delights and desires to give, you can begin to feel the prospect and the great expectation of long awaited answers to prayer. This is our faith put into action: believing for, not giving up, always in continuous intercession for the things and circumstances that are not presently manifested. Let joy and thanksgiving fill our hearts today as we wait for our desired answered prayers. The Lord longs to be gracious and compassionate to you. Blessed are all those who wait for Him.

O LORD, be gracious to us; we long for You. Be our strength every
morning, our salvation in time of distress. (Isa. 33:2)

THE GIFT OF HELPS

In the Church, God has appointed first of all apostles, second prophets, third teachers, then workers of miracles, also those having gifts of healing, those able to help others, those with gifts of administration, and those speaking in different kind of tongues. (1 Cor. 12:28)

God appoints each one of His people to function in many varied ways. As individuals we do not perform alike nor have all the gifts operating in our lives. There are high offices within the Church that also bear great responsibility along with it. In this Scripture, the one gift listed that stood out to me was *those able to help others.* This is something I know I am able to do when I look for opportunities, or when one presents itself to me. If I help others, I will have fulfilled an appointed office. In small ways, and in big ways, let us look for chances where we can bring assistance to others today. When we have compassion for the poor and needy, it is the Spirit of the LORD that is pressing upon our heart to help. This was a main concern that Jesus had and his followers who were always mindful of the hungry and poor. When we give, God blesses us beyond what can be measured. If we are not able to give materially, we can help through our praying for them. Paul the Apostle was always mindful of how important and needed were the prayers for the work of ministry.

She opens her arms to the poor and extends her hands to the needy. (Prov. 31:20)

MOVING FORWARD TO JESUS

Let us then approach the throne of grace with confidence, so that we may receive mercy and grace to help us in our time of need. (Heb.4:16)

We need to re-position ourselves in a forward manner. The unfair and unjust things that happen to us and to our loved ones are things we struggle with our whole lifetimes. These are things that the Lord has allowed for reasons only He may know. The suffering we feel help shape and form who we are. Sometimes we have the tendency to look back and re-live past sufferings, this helps in order to learn valuable lessons which can bring relief to someone going through similar things; although, we should not dwell there too long. It is important to keep our focus moving forward to the things that the Lord is calling us to do in the future. This brings to us new hope, for Jesus will justify and put everything back into perfect order in His time. We may never know the reasons why. It is important to realize that some things we just have no answer for, they remain a mystery. Let's move forward looking to Jesus our hope. He is the one who will re-establish everlasting righteousness and justice.

One thing I do, forgetting what is behind, and straining toward what is ahead. (Phil. 3:13)

HELPING THE NEEDY

On Him we have set our hope that He will continue to deliver us, as you help us by your prayers. Then many will give thanks on our behalf for the gracious favor granted us in answer to the prayers of many. (2 Cor. 1:11)

It is easy to overlook or ignore someone who is in need and just continue on your way. It might not be convenient, you may have to go out of your way or take some extra time. But if you do an act of kindness to help someone not expecting a reward or even to be noticed, you will have reward in heaven. Jesus will speak of this at the end of the age. Everyone can do little things to help. Prayer is a big way to help; when no one sees or pays attention, the Lord always does, and is pleased when we show compassion. Jesus continuously stopped and took time to help the ones who were poor, sick, and weak. If you have nothing to give, you can say a prayer for the person or maybe have a word of encouragement to offer. The Lord is always concerned about the attitude of our hearts when it comes to helping others. If you find yourself lacking compassion for people who are in need, pray that God will give it to you along with a willingness to help in whatever way you are able to.

"Come, you blessed by my Father; take your inheritance, the Kingdom prepared for you since the creation of the world. For I was hungry and you gave me something to eat, I was thirsty and gave me something to drink, I was a stranger and you invited me in, I needed clothes and you clothed me, I was sick and you looked after me, I was in prison and you came to visit me." (Matt. 25:34-36)

September 7

ETERNAL PURPOSE

God, who has saved us and called us to a holy life not because of anything we have done, but because of His own purpose and grace; this grace was given us in Christ Jesus before the beginning of time. (2 Tim. 1:9)

It is important to keep an eternal perspective in mind. It is God's own purpose that is being fulfilled in you and in me. This is the way God has planned it when He gave us our original birth, before there was time. I know it is hard to imagine but it is what Scripture tells us; we were perfected in His mind before there was time. If we look at life from that standpoint, our problems do not seem quite so large. It is because we have been given this grace, this gift in Christ, and His Word of promise that we are able to rise above the circumstances of life and have an optimistic attitude. God created time. We live between the bookends of birth and death. Our whole lifetimes are really just a very small dot on the timeline of the universe, and then we vanish away like a vapor. How can we make the very most of the time we are given here on earth? God through the sacrifice of Jesus has shown His great love for us; we are His treasure and joy. When we give our hearts and love to Him, we can know and experience our eternal purpose here and now today. In Him we have eternal life now, there is no death for the ones believing, loving, and trusting in Jesus Christ. Our eternal purpose is found in loving Him.

To those who by persistence in doing good seek glory, honor and immortality He will give eternal life. (Rom. 2:7)

ETERNAL INHERITANCE

For the perishable must cloth itself with the imperishable and the mortal with immortality. (1 Cor. 15:53)

We have been given an eternal inheritance that is waiting for us in heaven. If we are persistent in doing well; if we seek to love, honor, and glorify God, we will obtain this inheritance that the Lord is preparing for us. Everything around us including our physical bodies are in a state of deterioration, and we are dying. All the treasures found on the earth are corruptible and will perish. What is there that we can take with us when death arrives at our door? Nothing, just as we entered this world at birth, so will we leave it. The Lord has made a way to receive eternal life and an eternal inheritance as sons and daughters, heirs of God, joint heirs with Jesus. The Lord tells us to redeem the time; use it in a worthy and wise manner. Our treasure is in heaven not on this earth. Serving Him and taking the time to know Him is what is what really matters in our lives. Jesus Himself is our eternal inheritance.

Now if we are children, then we are heirs, heirs of God and co-heirs with Christ. (Rom. 8:17)

THE MOST EXCELLENT WAY

And now I will show you the most excellent way. (1 Cor. 12:31)

The most excellent way is the way of love. In the scriptures before 1 Cor. 12:31, Paul is talking about the gifts of the Spirit. The greatest gift of the Spirit is love. The Lord is slowly transforming our old natures into one where love is made perfect in Him. Every day we are learning new things; improving upon our ways, using our minds to create easier and more efficient methods to accomplish everything from simple tasks to complex problems. The Lord gives us wisdom and creative ideas that make living more efficient and our time more productive. When I step out into a new project or in an unfamiliar area; although I may fail to reach the desired result or goal, I find that in the process of doing it, the Lord is showing me a more excellent way. His ways are not our own, but He is always desiring to show and teach us the most excellent way; to do all things with love.

God is love. Whoever lives in love lives in God, and God in Him. Love is made complete among us . . . (1 Jn. 4:16)

LOVE PERFECTED

To prepare God's people for works of service, so that the body of Christ may be built up until we all reach unity in the faith and in the knowledge of the Son of God, and become mature, attaining to the whole measure of the fullness of Christ. (Ephes. 4:12-13)

This is the work of the Spirit, as we submit and commit everything over to Him the pressure is off of us and He Himself perfects His love within the church. It is through love that we can find out God's most desired way. There is success, even in the face of apparent failure, when we seek His will and guidance first. Becoming mature and growing up in love is what the Lord is aiming for. The way of God is the way of love; in all we do, say, or think; our love for one another and our love for God should be the motivation that puts us into action and empowers us in all we do. It is His will that this love be perfected in the church. Paul the Apostle prayed this prayer:

And I pray that you, being rooted and established in love, may have power, together with all the saints, to grasp how wide and long and high and deep is the love of Christ, and to know this love that surpasses knowledge; that you may be filled to the measure of all the fullness of God. (Ephes. 3: 17-19)

THE MEANING OF SUCCESS

Do not let this Book of the Law depart from your mouth; meditate on it day and night, so that you may be careful to do everything written in it. Then you will be prosperous and successful. (Jos.1:8)

When Jesus came and established the New Covenant, the old was done away with but the Word of the Lord stands forever and just like in the days of Joshua, meditation upon the Scriptures is central in our Christian lives. If you delight and take joy in the reading and meditation of God's Word, you will be like a tree planted by streams of water, bearing fruit with leaves that will not wither and whatever you put your hands to will prosper. (Ps. 1:3) The true meaning of success is having the approval of God. Meditating upon His Word is what builds our faith, which in turn produces works that God will bless. The Lord has planned a good future and has given us hope for a life that is abundant and full. It is when we take to heart His Words of promise, and of caution, that true success can be found. To hear the words of the Lord saying, "Well *done my good and faithful servant!*" (Matt. 25:21) Success in life is being found faithful to hear and to do God's Word. The Lord is forever faithful to His Covenant of love for us and it was demonstrated through Jesus' life and death. How will we respond today? Be faithful to read and do His Word and you will know the true meaning of success.

Dear friend, I pray that you may enjoy good health and that all will go well for you, even as your soul is getting along well. (3 Jn. :2)

September 12

PURPOSEFUL DIFFICULTY

May the LORD answer you when you are in distress. May He give you the desires of your heart and make all your plans succeed. May we shout for joy over your victory and lift up our banners in the name of our God. May the LORD grant all your requests. Some trust in chariots and some in horses, but we trust in the name of the LORD our God. (Ps. 20:1, 2, 5, 7)

There is a purpose in the difficulty you are in right now. God is using those circumstances in ways you may not understand just yet. What are we going to place our trust in? In King David's time, the people thought that if they had fast chariots and horses that would save them from their enemies. I'm sure they trusted also in their material wealth, position, or status in family etc. over God's providence and care. Many people today are trusting in their money, position of power or family name etc. over God as well. Every day, Christians, are making decisions either based upon the world and its wisdom, or trusting in a loving God who has given His Word of promise that will sustain them and guide them through every trial and difficulty. Daily we must make a conscious decision to allow the Lord direct our path in His way, and trust fully in Him to carry us through. When you finally get past this purposeful difficulty, others will take note and God will be glorified through your victory.

In this you greatly rejoice, though now for a little while you may have had to suffer grief in all kinds of trials. These have come so that your faith, of greater worth than gold, which perishes even though refined by fire, may be proved genuine and may result in praise, glory and honor when Jesus Christ is revealed. (1 Pet. 1:6-7)

September 13

WISDOM AND UNDERSTANDING

By wisdom a house is built, and through understanding it is established. (Prov. 4:7)

Wisdom is supreme; therefore get wisdom. Though it cost all you have, get understanding. (Prov. 9:1)

Understanding in the Webster Dictionary is defined: *The quality of condition of one who understands; comprehension; discernment; interpretation; a reconciliation of differences; an agreement; compassionate and sympathetic.* Having wisdom is one thing, understanding is another. They go hand in hand. We may have great wisdom regarding a matter, but lack understanding. To know the difference, is something that is worth seeking after. Discernment in a matter of importance, the right interpretation of a situation is crucial. *For the LORD gives wisdom, and from his mouth come knowledge and understanding.* (Prov. 2:6) *Blessed is the man who finds wisdom, the man who gains understanding.*(Prov. 3:1) Wisdom and understanding were two separate functions working together in perfect harmony at the start of all creation. If we have a concern or a problem that needs to be solved, the first thing we should always learn to do is to go to the Lord right away, and ask of Him to give us understanding and wisdom into the particular situation.

For by wisdom the Lord laid the earth's foundations, by understanding He set the heavens in place. (Jer.10:12) *To God belong wisdom and power; counsel and understanding are His.* (Job 12:13)

FRUIT IS THE EVIDENCE

The fruit of the Spirit is love, joy, peace, longsuffering, gentleness, goodness, and faith. (Gal. 5:22)

The fruit of the Spirit is evident when you find these attributes in someone. It is pleasant to be around someone who is peaceful, loving, patient and kind. It is encouraging and uplifting to be around someone who is joyful. This is the evidence of the new nature of God living in them. These are the fruits we need and should desire to have operating in our lives. It is what reflects the Lord's image to others who are in need of your kindness, patience, love and joy. If we allow the Spirit of God to develop these attributes, the heavenly spiritual fruit will become more and more apparent in your life and relationships. We must not give up or get discouraged. If we persevere in our faith and not lose heart, His Kingdom will surely come to us here and now, and His will be done, on earth as it is right now in Heaven. The fruit of the Holy Spirit will be the evidence of our faith put into action.

And be not conformed to this world, but be transformed by the renewing of your mind that you may prove what is that good and acceptable, and perfect will of God. (Rom. 12:2)

September 15

STRIVE TO BE PEACEMAKERS

I appeal to you, brothers, in the name of our Lord Jesus Christ, that all of you agree with one another so that there may be no divisions among you and that you may be perfectly united in mind and thought. (1 Cor. 1:10)

Paul addressed this situation with the Corinthian church when he said *"You are still worldly. For since there is jealously and quarreling among you, are you not worldly? Are you not acting like mere men?"* (1 Cor. 3:3) We are all made so uniquely different from one another that the contrasts of likes and dislikes, life styles, appearances and habits, can cause friction and disagreements; especially when we have to interact with people every day who are opposite from us. Many times it is members of your own family; it is no accident that these people are placed there. The Lord uses trying situations with others to help us learn to love the ones and the things that are contrary to us. Jesus loved everyone; we need to love and show patience for each other in that same way. It is a supernatural kind of love that strives for peace, and peace is a great thing to possess. It is a gift from the Lord. Let us be peacemakers.

Make every effort to keep the unity of the Spirit through the bond of peace. (Ephes. 4:3)

SEEKING, KNOWING, AND TRUSTING HIM

Those who know Your name will trust in You, for You Lord, have never forsaken those who seek You. (Ps. 9:10)

We can say that to *know His name,* is to know Him. The more we become increasingly familiar and close to Him, we begin to understand that God's nature is one of love, mercy, justice, compassion and grace. We come to know His character by *seeking* relationship with Him and the more we do this, the more our trust in Him grows. We can with confidence and assurance, rest our whole life and our concerns fully into His loving care. In this verse of the psalm, David goes on to say in the same sentence, *"You Lord, have never forsaken those who seek You."* In order to truly *know* Him, it follows that we need to earnestly *seek* Him. King David knew that he needed to seek the Lord and yearned for Him in a land where he felt tired and the environment seemed spiritually barren and dry. *"O God, You are my God, earnestly I seek you: my body longs for You, in a dry and weary land where there is no water."* (Ps. 63:1) This is a feeling that we can relate to at times when we come before the Lord and our spirits are dry and barren. We begin to seek Him with our hearts and He starts to fill and refresh us with the living waters of His Presence and Spirit once again; for the Lord has *never forsaken those who seek Him.*

"Never will I leave you, never will I forsake you." (Heb.13:5)

September 17

GRACE: THE ANTIDOTE FOR PAIN

Naked I came from my mother's womb, and naked I will depart. The Lord gave and the Lord has taken away; may the name of the Lord be praised. (Job 1:21)

This was Job's initial reaction after hearing the reports that his flocks, herds, household and children were wiped out. Seeing how Job was a righteous man, *the greatest man among all the people of the East* (1:3); none of what happened to Job made any sense! We think that this is not something a loving God would allow to happen to one of his most beloved servants. It is not fair or justified. This is the way most people react when reading the account of Job's life. This world in which we live is fallen, where bad things happen to good people all the time. It is just as disheartening to see bad people prosper and continue to flourish. Because we live in a sinful world, things are not operating and functioning the way God had originally intended. Everything appears to be distorted and upside down in a sense, many things that occur are unjust. What Jesus Christ had accomplished for us upon the cross is like a great equalizer; all who will to come, can come to Christ and be forgiven and receive salvation. Grace is the antidote for pain and suffering. It is because of grace that we do not get what we deserve when we sin against God and others, grace covers and forgives.

The grace of our Lord was poured out on me abundantly, along with the faith and love that are in Christ Jesus. (Titus 3:6-7)

September 18

WHERE ARE THE NINE?

Jesus asked, "Were not all ten cleansed? Where are the other nine? Was there no one found to return and give praise to God except this foreigner?" (Lk.17:17)

Jesus asked, *"Where are the other nine that were healed, only one returned to give thanks?"* Can you picture the ten lepers walking along and as they continue, their leprosy sores start to disappear, the color and feel of healthy flesh is suddenly restored to their bodies and all ten lepers together receive this amazing miracle from God! As they continue to walk, they rip off the dirty rags and bandages that covered them up with great joy! Gazing into each other's eyes with disbelief, big smiles appear upon their faces as the reality of this miraculous healing begins to sink in. All but one, who was a Samaritan, kept on going without a thought of returning to give thanks to the one who had done this for them. As I look back over my life, I can see where there have been times I have been guilty of this. The Lord answers a prayer and though I knew it was from Him, I neglected to give Him the thanks He deserved, I was too busy getting on with life; forgetting, not considering the wondrous power of God's goodness. When God does something great and you know that it was His hand that did it, always return to give thanks to the Lord and show your appreciation to Him.

For although they knew God, they neither glorified Him as God nor gave thanks to Him, but their thinking became futile and their foolish hearts were darkened. (Rom. 1:21)

FINAL CONCLUSION

Here is my final conclusion: fear God and obey His commands, for this is the duty of every person. God will judge us for everything we do, including every secret thing, whether good or bad. (Eccl. 12:13)

King Solomon at the very end of his life wrote the book of Ecclesiastes. In it he describes the many vanities of life; how meaningless everything seems to be. It has been said that King Solomon was the wisest, wealthiest, and most powerful man in history; the author of the Book of Proverbs speaks to us in this last verse of Ecclesiastes, that the conclusion of the whole matter is to fear God, (show Him reverence, respect and love), keep His commandments, for this is the whole duty of man. Jesus at His appearing said, *"Love the Lord your God with all your heart and with all your soul and with your entire mind. This is the first and greatest commandment. And the second is like it; Love your neighbor as yourself. All the Law and the Prophets hang on these two commandments."*(Matt. 22:37-38) We may gain the whole world and everything along with it, we could become like Solomon, but if we do not have love, our lives we would be empty, desolate, lonely and without hope. All would be meaningless without love, for everything you have on earth, all your riches and possessions will be left behind.

For the sun rises with scorching heat and withers the plant; its blossoms fall and its beauty is destroyed. In the same way, the rich man will fade away even while he goes about his business. (Jas. 1:10-11)

LOVE AND OBEDIENCE EQUALS LIFE

If anyone loves me, he will obey my teaching. My Father will love him, and we will come to him and make our home with him. (Jn.15:10)

The Apostle John wrote more about love than any of the others. This is the common theme and the main point throughout the whole Bible that we obey His commands: love the Lord your God, and love one another. *Love is the fulfillment of the law.* (Rom. 13:10) The children of Israel rebelled time and time again throughout history. *They refused to keep my laws and follow my instructions, even though obeying them would have given them life.* (Ezek. 20:13,21) The reward for obedience is life; and life most full and blessed. The reason we obey is because we love Him, and in doing so we have life, God's life living in us for He is life itself.

Blessed is the man whose delight is in the law of the Lord, he is like a tree planted by the streams of water, which yields its fruit in season and whose leaf does not wither, whatever he does prospers. (Ps. 1:2-3)

OBSERVING THE WIND

He who observes the wind will not sow, and he who regards the clouds will not reap. (Eccl. 11:4)

The NLT interprets this scripture: *Farmers who wait for perfect weather never plant. If they watch every cloud, they never harvest.* This may be true for many people. It seems as though we are waiting for just the right conditions before we begin to do something. There will always be unfavorable circumstances to contend with. If we're focusing upon the clouds, our attention will be drawn away from the sun. It is an exercise of faith when we begin to move and act, plant and sow, in spite of the obstacles and resistance; this is what pleases God. What are we sowing in our world today? Are we planting seeds of faith, love, righteousness and peace? Or are we waiting for the perfect conditions before we step out and do something?

Sow for yourselves righteousness, reap the fruit of unfailing love, and break up your unplowed ground; for it is time to seek the Lord until He comes and showers righteousness on you. (Hos. 10:12)

PLANT IN THE MORNING

Plant your seed in the morning and keep busy all afternoon, for you don't know if profit will come from one activity or another, or maybe both. (Eccl. 11:6)

In the world we observe the wind, the clouds of darkness and the terrible results of sin. The Bible tells us that hearts become cold and hardened because of it. In knowing the truth of God's Word, we have been given the armor of defense and assured of a victory that has already been won for us. We can sow the seeds of righteousness in the softened ground of our hearts and bear the fruit of unfailing love. Keep on planting good seeds of righteousness every day in every activity, through wind, rain, and clouds. We cannot see exactly what God is doing with your labors of love, but your reward will come in its fullness when Jesus returns. Keep on sowing the seeds of love and of righteousness, don't give up even if times are hard and your heart is saddened. *Those who sow in tears will reap with songs of joy. He who goes out weeping, carrying seed to sow, will return with songs of joy, carrying sheaves with him.* (Ps. 126:4-6)

Let us not become weary in doing well, for at the proper time we will reap a harvest if we do not give up. Therefore, as we have opportunity, let us do good to all people, especially those who belong to the family of believers. (Gal. 6:9-10)

FORBEARANCE

For many years you were patient with them. By Your Spirit you admonished them through your prophets. Yet they paid no attention, but in your great mercy you did not put an end to them nor abandon them, for you are a gracious and merciful God. In all that has happened to us, You have been just; You have acted faithfully, while we did wrong. (Ne. 9:30-33)

The Israelites were always in rebellion and in disobedience, not so different than people today. Many times we turn a deaf ear to the Lord and pay no attention to His will and commands; yet He shows us great compassion and forbearance. He does not abandon or give up on us, but shows great mercy, and longsuffering towards us. He is slow to anger even when we willfully disobey and choose not to listen; but because we are His children, eventually He gets our attention and we turn around, and begin to do the right thing once again. In light of the way the Lord shows forbearance with us, forgiving us our trespasses, and is merciful and kind even though we make mistakes, how much more should we show kindness and compassion towards those who may offend or treat us unkindly? Longsuffering with those who are not easy to love is a great virtue.

The Lord is not slow in keeping His promise and some understand slowness. He is longsuffering with you, not wanting any to perish, but everyone to come to repentance. (1 Pet.3:9)

September 24

WISDOM AND TIME

Those who are wise will find a time and a way to do what is right. Yes, there is a time and a way for everything, even as people's troubles lie heavily upon them. (Eccl. 8:5-6)

The older I get, the more I am beginning to realize the importance of using my time wisely. In this scripture from Ecclesiastes it tells us that there is time and a way out if we are wise even when troubles weigh us down. It has been said of Solomon that he was the wisest man who ever lived. I think there is something to the saying: "if there's a will there's a way." Time management for me has always been a great challenge and a discipline that does not come easy. Time seems to be moving fast, it seems before you can turn around another year has gone by! Jesus was never in a rush, He always walked everywhere He went, and He did not run! It is important to walk carefully, not rushing around but taking the time to seek the understanding of the Lord's will and of His wisdom in the opportunities we are given.

See then that you walk circumspectly, not as fools, but as wise, redeeming the time, because the days are evil. Wherefore be not unwise, but understanding what the will of the Lord is. (Ephes. 5:15-17)

September 25

GOD GIVES WISDOM

Turn your ear to wisdom and apply your heart to understanding; if you look for it as for silver and search for it as for hidden treasure, then you will understand the fear of the Lord and find the knowledge of God. For the Lord gives wisdom, and from His mouth comes knowledge and understanding. He holds victory in store for the upright, and then you will understand what is right and just and fair, every good path. For wisdom will enter your heart; discretion will protect you and understanding will guard you. (Prov. 2:4, 7, 9, 11)

The Lord wants us to know His will and to walk in it. He has provided the time and the means; everything we need to do it. Distractions are everywhere! We only have a specific amount of time that is given to each one of us. Now is the time, today is the day, to apply our hearts to gain the understanding and wisdom of the Lord regarding His will and in the use of our time. We can see how wisdom and understanding creates good management of our time, and that it is God's wisdom we need to live and to overcome our trials as we seek and search for it. Dear Lord, Help me to use the time that you give me carefully and wisely, and that I may seek You who is all wisdom to know and do Your will today. Amen . . .

Teach us to number our days aright, that we may gain a heart of wisdom. (Ps. 90:12)

September 26

DIVINE INTERVENTIONS

To another miraculous powers: all these are the work of one and the same Spirit, and He gives them to each one, just as He determines. (1 Cor. 12:10-11)

If you read the whole chapter of 1 Corinthians Chapter 12, you will find that the Lord gives many spiritual gifts to men and women. Have you ever thought, it's going to take a miracle in order for this or that to happen! Have you ever prayed for a divine intervention in a particular situation? The whole Bible is a book of miracles and divine interventions; recording times, places, and events. God reveals supernatural truth throughout history and confirms it to us through recorded accurate evidence. The purpose of miracles is that men might know the power of the Lord and believe. It is our faith that God uses as a channel for miracles and divine interventions. Jesus is the same yesterday, today and forever. His miraculous power is here for us today although we do not see very many miracles happen very often. If we stop and think, I'm sure we can recall a time when God showed to us His divine intervention in various situations. We can say that it was miraculous! Our faith was increased by it, and we ascended to new heights. As time goes by we find ourselves back in the valley with only faint recollections. I think it's time to start believing, remembering, and praying for new miracles to happen: divine interventions.

Jesus of Nazareth was a man accredited by God to you by miracles, wonders and signs, which God did among you through Him, as you yourselves know. (Ac. 2:22)

ANGELIC INTERVENTIONS

Are not all angels ministering spirits sent to serve those who will inherit salvation? (Heb. 1:14)

Angels perform divine interventions for us all the time although we might not be aware of their presence. Let's start praying that the Lord would open the eyes of our understanding as to how the angelic hosts work in our lives To guard and go before us to observe our comings and goings. They have a supernatural power that is used to help all the heirs of salvation. They can do the miraculous in our lives. When we put our faith in Jesus, we not only have a new life that is filled with blessings, but we receive divine angelic interventions that follow us throughout our whole lives, from the time of our birth unto death.

For He will command His angels concerning you to guard you in all your ways. (Ps. 91:11)

JOY OF BENEVOLENCE

You have loved righteousness and hated lawlessness, therefore God, Your God, has anointed You with the oil of gladness more than your fellow companions. (Heb. 1:9)

Although Jesus was a man of sorrows and acquainted with grief, He was at the same time the most joyful man of all His fellow companions. The joy that Jesus had in His heart empowered Him to endure the cross. The word benevolence: defined by the Webster's Dictionary: *An inclination or tendency to perform charitable acts; good will, a kindly act, concern with charity.* Jesus' life was to us the greatest example of benevolence that this world has ever seen. We can begin to understand the correlation between benevolence and joy when we think upon the Lord and all the ways He showed His generous and giving heart throughout His ministry on earth. He gave us of Himself, the Bread of Life, the Living Water of His Word, rest and peace, and the ultimate gift of His life's blood, the Holy Spirit, a new heart and eternal life. It was because He gave so much, and continues to give so much that He is the most joyful in all of creation.

Freely you have received, freely give. (Matt. 10:8)

ASK AND RECEIVE

Ask and you will receive, and your joy will be complete. (Jn. 16:24)

The Lord was speaking to His disciples here before He sent them out to spread the Gospel. He's saying the same thing to us today; freely give to others what you have received weather it's physically or spiritually and you will have joy to overflow. He will always give to us the things that we need. It is His nature to always give. In the same way it is in the asking that we receive. The Lord blesses us with His joy. We may be going through some great trial or testing, but the moment we ask for His help and take our eyes from off ourselves and circumstances and on to the need of another, we find relief. It is in the asking that we receive and when we do receive, it is in the giving away that we receive back. What sacrifices are we being asked to do that may cause others to misunderstand or even condemn you because of your faith in Christ? These are hard questions; ones to meditate upon when we think about the gift of salvation and what it cost our Blessed Redeemer. Ultimately, regardless of the sacrifices you may make, joy will be your reward for your obedience in giving.

At His right hand there is pleasure and joy forevermore. (Ps. 16:11)

THE STATE OF WAIT

How many are Your works O Lord. In wisdom You made them all. The earth is full of your creatures. These all look to You to give them their food at the proper time. When You give it to them they gather it up; when You open Your hand they are satisfied with good things. (Ps. 104:24-27)

In this psalm we can see that there is a *proper time* that the Lord gives provision for our bodies, both of human beings and all the creatures of the earth. We need physical food and spiritual food to live and grow. We receive it all from the Lord. The older I get, every day that goes by I realize a growing dependency upon Him alone to supply my every need. It seems as though I am continually in a state of wait. All of creation in reality is in a state of wait; a state or condition of waiting upon the Lord. So far, as I look back upon my life, I can see many things that the Lord has done already. I can receive what I need today, but there are so many prayers that I am still waiting for God to answer. Daily life never seems perfect. There always is a longing for a better circumstance and a better world. Everybody, in all of creation is in a state of wait until the Lord comes and brings His perfection into the earth and into our bodies making it a reality. Paul's prayer for the Corinthians:

"That you do not lack any spiritual gifts as you eagerly wait for our Lord Jesus Christ to be revealed." (1 Cor. 1:7) *Those who wait upon the Lord will renew their strength.* (Isa. 40:31)

GLOWING THROUGH THE DARK

For God, who said, "Let light shine out of darkness,"
made His light shine in our hearts; to give us the light of the knowledge of
the glory of God in the face of Christ . . . 2 Cor. 4:6

When the sun goes down
And there's no strength left to be found;
Pain and discouragement is all around.
God's Light goes on glowing through the dark.
When candlelight s dim and disappear in a cloud,
The sorrows of this world envelope as a shroud.
As I close my eyes in surrender to the night,
I remember the Lord who is eternally light.
The light of Your Presence that lives in my heart,
Awakens the hope and goes on forever,
Glowing through the dark.
Awaken the hope that lies sleeping within,
Let Your light in my heart blaze brightly again.
Lord sweep the sorrow away like the tide;
Bring Your love, hope and faith with the sunrise.
Lord you are forever glowing in my heart,
Even when all appears to be dark.
Your glistening light shines like stars
Against the blackness of night;
Awakens hope that seems so far out of sight,
And then I realize:
You were there all the while though I could not see,
For the darkness was surrounding me.
Your light sweeps away all my sorrow like the tide;
Faith, love, and hope, comes with a new sunrise,
And I realize, the light of Your Presence
The light of Your love in my heart,
Awakens the hope that goes on forever
Glowing through the dark . . .

GOD IS OUR PORTION:
SO WE WAIT WITH HOPE

The Lord is my portion; therefore I will wait for Him. The Lord is good to those whose hope is in Him, to the one who seeks Him. It is good to wait quietly for the salvation of the Lord. (Lam. 3:24-2)

This scripture speaks about three important thoughts: the importance of realizing that it is God who is your portion in every aspect of living: putting your hope in Him for the answers to your prayers: seeking the Lord and waiting quietly for Him. God is your portion now and forever, nothing else can take His place. His Presence is with you throughout each minute and hour of the day and night therefore your hope is in Him. As we learn to wait for the fulfillment of our prayers and desires, the Lord fills us with His life giving Spirit and gives us the strength to persevere. And so we continue to wait for the answers to our longing prayers. We wait quietly and patiently for the Lord to come and help. The more we do this, the more hope, anticipation, and expectation we will have. *In that day they will say, "Surely this is our God we have waited for Him; let us rejoice and be glad in His salvation."* (Isa. 25:9)

We know that the whole creation has been groaning as in the pains of childbirth right up to the present time. If we hope for what we do not yet have, we wait for it patiently. (Rom. 8:22, 25)

October 2

FAITH AND ENDURANCE

Whenever trouble comes your way, let it be an opportunity for joy. For when your faith is tested, your endurance has a chance to grow. So let it grow, for when your endurance is fully developed, you will be strong in character and ready for anything. (Jas.1:2-4)

Although we may be experiencing various trials and sufferings, God is doing a hidden work in us. If we hold on strong to our faith in Him through it all to the end, the trials and sufferings will turn into blessings. One thing that I am learning daily is that he is faithful to perform His Word. He shows Himself to be true every day as I put all my concerns into His hands. In the first letter of Peter to the early Church, he reminds us that there will be a good outcome and a lot to be gained through experiencing trials. It is because of our faith in Jesus and in His resurrection that we are being shielded, protected, and preserved until Jesus will be revealed at last. As believers, it is our faith that is being tried and in the end will be proven genuine and will bring glory to the Lord if we endure until the end.

We have been given a new birth and a living hope through the resurrection of Jesus Christ from the dead: and an inheritance that can never perish, spoil or fade—kept in heaven for you, who through faith are shielded by God's power until the coming of the salvation that is ready to be revealed in the last time. In this you greatly rejoice, though now for a little while you may have had to suffer grief in all kinds of trials. These have come so that your faith—of greater worth than gold, which perishes even though refined by fire—maybe proved genuine and may result in praise, glory and honor when Jesus Christ is revealed. (1 Pet. 1:3-7)

October 3

LOVE PRODUCES PERSEVERANCE

Blessed is the man who perseveres under trial, because when he has stood the test, he will receive the Crown of Life that God has promised to those who love him. (Jas. 1:12)

It is the love of God that causes a man or woman to persevere under great trial of pain and suffering; and because He loves us, He allows us to go through these things so that in the end His love will be perfected in us and we will receive the Crown of Life as one of our rewards. We need to decide that no matter what is happening around us, we are determined to serve God and to hold firm to His promises by faith. This is what is pleasing to the Lord; to keep doing the things that are motivated by your love for Him and by your faith. No work that is done for God is in vain or unprofitable. *Therefore, stand firm. Let nothing move you. Always give yourselves fully to the work of the Lord, because you know that your labor in the Lord is not in vain.* (1 Cor. 15:58) There is a reward for our perseverance and faith. When motivated by love, it is not really work; it becomes a pleasure to serve.

You need to persevere so that when you have done the will of God, you will receive what He has promised. For in just a very little while, He who is coming will come and will not delay. But my righteous ones will live by faith. (Heb.10:36-38)

GOD'S JUSTICE

The LORD reigns forever. He has established His throne for judgment. He will judge the world in righteousness. He will govern the people with justice. (Ps. 9:7-8)

When a wrong has been committed against us, we want to retaliate and lash out and get back at the one who did it. This is a part of the old nature that seemed like the right thing to do, we even felt justified in reciprocating. The problem is that none of us can really know all the reasons behind the offence; this makes it impossible for us to sit as judge over others. The Scriptures are clear in these matters admonishing us to love our enemies and pray for those who use us despitefully. Once again we see that life is not always fair and often cannot be rationalized. In this psalm of David, the Scripture makes it clear that there is a right way and a wrong way that has been established by the Lord who is over all and the only righteous and just judge. His very Throne is established for this purpose of justice. Let it go, God will bring justification to all who put their faith in His truth, kindness and justice.

"I am the Lord, who exercises kindness, justice, and righteousness on earth, for in these I delight" declares the Lord. (Jer. 31:34)

ENCOURAGEMENT IN THE DARK

When the uproar had ended, Paul sent for the disciples and, after encouraging them, said good-bye and set out for Macedonia. Along the way, he encouraged the believers in all the towns he passed through. (Ac. 20:1-2)

In those days life was so different in regard to lifestyle, custom and environment, but the darkness of sin, man's cruelty and inhumanity to man was present; and it is just as prevalent in the world we live in today. The struggle for survival and for righteous living has always been an uphill battle for everyone everywhere. It was for this reason that the news of the Gospel of Jesus Christ was so encouraging. It brought light and hope for new life and eternal life. When Jesus walked upon the earth He brought this true light of God into ancient darkness. *The people living in darkness have seen a great light; on those living in the land of the shadow of death a light has dawned.* (Matt. 4:16) When He ascended into heaven, He did not leave us to stumble and fall back into the darkness; He gave us the gift of His Holy Spirit to dwell within every believer, the Word of Life found in Scripture, and one another to bring encouragement and strength for the battles against the remaining darkness. Encourage someone today who may be going through dark times.

For everything that was written in the past was written to teach us, so that through endurance and encouragement of the Scriptures we might have hope. May the God who gives endurance and encouragement give you a spirit of unity among yourselves as you follow Christ Jesus. (Rom. 15:4-5)

THE CLOUD OF WITNESSES

Therefore, since we are surrounded by such a great cloud of witnesses, let us throw off everything that hinders and the sin that so easily entangles, and let us run with perseverance the race marked out for us. (Heb. 12:1)

This cloud of witnesses is most likely the angels and possibly our loved ones who have gone into heaven and are cheering us on in heavenly grandstands! I can picture that so clearly in my mind, they are cheering us on all the way to the finish line! Just thinking of that is encouraging to me. Our lives are like an open book. There is nothing that lies hidden from God. We have all of heaven witnessing our struggles, defeats and victories. The holy angels are watching too. There are many more in the spiritual realms that are on our side than the ones who are working against us. Sometimes I think of people who I know are now in heaven. Perhaps they are a part of this great cloud of witnesses. I look forward to the time that I will be reunited with them. This is something that I desire greatly and am looking forward to. The thought of seeing and being together with the ones I have loved and who are now in heaven makes me want to keep my faith, stay in the race, and to finish well!

I have fought the good fight, I have finished the race, I have kept the faith. (2 Tim. 4:7)

THE AGENDA

Like a fluttering sparrow or a darting swallow, an unfair curse will not land on its intended victim. (Prov. 26:2)

It is certain that Satan and his operatives have an agenda that has been carefully planned and is being carried out in America, the entire world, and also concerning you. This agenda has been in force since the beginning of time. We are seeing, witnessing, and experiencing its ill effects on our world every day and in every walk of life. Satan is busy looking for every opportunity to kill, steal and destroy all of God's creation and everything that He loves and cares about: (you and me) and all that stands for goodness and truth. Our faith gives us victory over these satanic forces at work every time. God has an agenda also; His is for our greatest good and promises full abundant life and victory over all of our enemies for every believer. The Bible tells us that all our battles today, and the ones that are yet to come, have already been fought and won for us. In the end, His goodness, truth, justice and divine life will reign eternally and all darkness and evil will be put away forever.

Who is it that overcomes the world? Only he who believes that Jesus Christ is Lord. (1 Jn.5:5)

PRAY FOR THE UNSAVED

The god of this age has blinded the minds of the believers, so that they cannot see the light of the Gospel of the glory of Christ who is the image of God. (2 Cor. 4:4)

There are times when we feel helpless to do anything that will help someone to know the Lord; but there is something we can always do, and that is to pray for them. You may have family, friends, co-workers, neighbors, etc. that are so hard to reach, but God can do what for us would be impossible. Jesus said: *"No one can come unto me unless the Father who sent me draws him."* (Jn. 6:44) He can draw them by His goodness, and send other ministers in their path that may be able to help make a spiritual breakthrough. We know it is the God of this world that has blinded their eyes. Don't get discouraged. Press on to acknowledge Him in all your ways and continue to pray for all of those people you know that need Him but have not realized it yet. It is because of the evil that is in the world that hearts become hardened. It is God's love that can soften hearts and bring a man or woman to see and acknowledge their sin and repent of it. (Rom. 2:4) Make this a daily prayer: Dear Lord, please pour out Your Spirit upon my friends and family (name the person or persons) and draw them by your goodness and love to their salvation. Please bring them to repentance so that they will know the joy of freedom from sin in having received forgiveness. Help me be sensitive to others and understand when it is the right time to speak Your words of love and encouragement so they might see You in my life. Amen . . .

Good and upright is the Lord, therefore He instructs sinners in His ways. (Ps. 25:8)

IDOL WORSHIP

How you have fallen from heaven, O morning star, son of the dawn! You have been cast down to the earth, you who once laid low the nations! You said in your heart, "I will ascend to heaven, I will raise my throne above the stars, and I will make myself like the Most High." (Isa. 14:12-14)

Satan's idol is himself; he thought himself to be so great, mighty, and beautiful that he desired to be worshipped and lifted higher than his Creator. Since Lucifer's fall from heaven, he has sought to use idolatry as a tool to draw men and women away from true worship of their Creator God. An idol is anything that is loved, worshipped, and given higher priority than the One and only true Living God who is worthy of all worship, praise, and glory. An idol is dead and lifeless; it can be in the form of money, fame, or false religion: it is worshipping the creation above the Creator. This idol worship angers the Lord greatly. The Lord will not tolerate idol worship and anything that takes the place of what rightfully belongs to Him alone. He has demonstrated and proven His displeasure and fury all through the ages upon those who were guilty of such things. Today there are multitudes of idols and idol worshippers of every sort and imagination. Worship the Lord your God, He alone is Holy and worthy of your admiration, praise, and glory. Whatever takes priority over your relationship with God, cut it off and get rid of it. Ask the Lord to purge it out from you and He will do it and accept you, preserving your life until the end.

Ascribe to the Lord the glory due His name. Bring an offering and come before Him; worship the Lord in the splendor of His holiness. (1 Ch. 16:29)

October 10

BEAR WITH EACH OTHER

Therefore, as God's chosen people, dearly loved, clothe yourselves with compassion, kindness, humility, gentleness and patience. Bear with each other and forgive whatever grievances you may have against one another. Forgive as the Lord forgave you. (Col. 3:12-13)

The Lord is also longsuffering towards those who have hurt you and desires to bring them deliverance. In truth we are all waiting to be delivered from this present evil world. That is why it is so important to clothe ourselves with compassion and gentleness, bearing with each other and forgiving as Christ has forgiven you. When you have been betrayed or you find out that someone, or even a trusted friend has spoken falsely against you, it is very hard to forgive and to love your enemies. This is the time to ask God to help you to do this. It is not in ourselves to forgive in that way, we need the divine nature of the Lord to empower us. Let it be an act of our faith to say, "I forgive," In time the meaning of bearing with one another and forgiving one another will become a part of our nature as it is the Lord's towards us.

For if you forgive not men their trespasses, neither will your Father forgive your trespasses. (Matt. 6:14)

October 11

DIVINE PURPOSE: TRANSFORMATION

His intent was that now, through the church, the manifold wisdom of God would be made known according to His eternal purpose which He accomplished in Christ Jesus our Lord. (Ephes. 3:10-11)

Have you ever wondered what God's purpose for your life is? My purpose and yours is that the wisdom of God might be made known in our lives. We are here to bring glory to God through transformed lives so that others will come to believe in the Lord through our example. *By one sacrifice, He has made perfect forever those who are being made holy.* (Heb. 10:14) This is an ongoing work; we are *being made,* not instantly changed and transformed. How can we help in the process? We can remember to put God first, every day and in everything we do. God will do the work needed in me; but do I fully trust Him to complete the work? Am I trusting Him or trusting myself? *Show me Your ways O Lord teach me Your paths, guide me in Your truth and teach me. For You are God and my Savior, my hope is in You all day long.* (Ps. 25:4-5) This should always be our cry and prayer; when we do this, God will show us His divine purpose for our lives. Dear Lord, Let Your will be done, be glorified and let your wisdom and divine purpose be fulfilled in us so that others will see and believe . . . Amen

He made known to us the mystery of His will according to His good pleasure which He purposed in Christ. (Ephes. 1:9)

October 12

LIFE IS NOT FAIR

The Lord is known by His justice; the wicked are ensnared by the work of their hands, but the needy will not always be forgotten, nor the hope of the afflicted ever perish. (Ps. 9:16, 18)

For the most part, we do reap what we sow in life; goodness and blessing for our good deeds, and afflictions and suffering for our bad actions. In Job's case, this was one exception to the rule, which shows us that there are things we just do not know and that God is much bigger that what we can completely understand. Throughout the Bible accounts and through our own observations, we can clearly see the end results and the repercussions of good deeds and of bad ones. The challenge for every believer is to hold fast to what we know to be true according to God's Word, His ways and commands even when suffering comes for no reason that you can understand. Although there are afflictions and trials of sufferings our hope will never perish.

The LORD is a refuge for the oppressed a stronghold in times of trouble. Those who know Your name will trust in You. (Ps. 9: 9-10)

October 13

ENTER THE OPEN DOOR

After this I looked and there before me was a door standing open in Heaven, and the voice I had first heard speaking to me like a trumpet said, "Come up here, and I will show you what must take place after this." (Rev. 4:1)

The Apostle John saw in a vision this open door; a door that led into heaven. Revelations is the only book in the Bible that tells us when we read it, it will bring blessings. (Rev. 1:3) Although it has been interpreted many different ways, when I read this particular scripture about *the open door,* I see it as the entryway for the Church of Christ on earth as we make our ascension into Heaven. *After this:* after what? The Spirits exhortation and proclamation of the promised rewards; and then the voice as of a trumpet saying *"Come up here"* The Apostle John goes on to describe the things that should happen after the Lord's dealings with the Church. The voice that is described as sounding like a trumpet: *On the Lord's Day I was in the Spirit, and I heard behind me a loud voice like a trumpet.* (Rev. 1:10) The door will be opened in heaven and the voice of the Lord will shout out like the sound of a trumpet; we will be changed from mortal to immortal and death will at last be swallowed up in victory! I believe this trumpet sound will be the voice of the Lord calling us to enter the open door to our heavenly home. That door is still being held open today; for everyone who will respond to the call of Jesus to come. For only those who know His voice will hear the trumpet and enter the open door.

For the trumpet will sound, the dead will be raised imperishable, and we will be changed. (I Cor. 15:52)

October 14

THE LORD DELIGHTS IN YOU

Serve the Lord with gladness; come before His Presence with singing: know that the Lord is God. It is He who made us and we are His. (Ps. 100:2-3)

What does this scripture look like in our daily lives? It is God who is doing the work revealing His will and inspiring us to act in ways that are pleasing to Him and in ways that will bring Him pleasure. *It is for His pleasure that we are and were created.* (Rev. 4:11) The Father takes pleasure in His people when we choose to walk in accordance with His will. (Ephes. 1:5) God wanted and desired to have a large family. He created us that we might share in all the joys and experience all the beauty of a life that is full of love for our Creator and for one another. The Lord from the very beginning, chose man and woman to be the crown of everything that was created; to give them all the goodness and joy that life could offer. The Father's nature is reflected in the love we have towards our own sons and daughters. Just like our heavenly Father, we take delight in our own children and want to give them all of the very best things and joys in life. As long as you continue to seek the Lord and His will, He will work in you according to His good pleasure. For He takes great delight in you.

Continue to work out your salvation with fear and trembling, for it is God who works in you to will and to act according to His good pleasure. (Phil. 2:12-13)

HUMBLENESS AND SALVATION

For the Lord takes delight in His people. He crowns the humble with salvation. (Ps. 149:4)

Humbleness is a virtue that goes hand in hand with salvation. It is with fear and trembling, respect and admiration for the Almighty power of God that causes us to have a sense of humility and lowliness before Him. Humility is a key ingredient in the working out our own salvation. Our salvation is acknowledging who God is, and humbling our hearts before Him as we yield to His will; then serving Him with gladness, knowing that it pleases Him. This is the reason we were created. *Therefore, whoever humbles himself like this child is the greatest in the kingdom of heaven.* (Matt.18:4) Jesus was the most humble man who ever lived. It is His example that demonstrates to us the meaning of the word, and also how to understand the way to serve one another. *When you are invited, take the lowest place, so that when your host comes, he will say to you, "friend, move up to a better place."* (Lk. 14:10) You may be the last one in line today and feeling left out and deserted, but God tells us that the last shall be first and the first last. Do not despair because of your lowly estate. The Lord lifts up the humble and dwells with them who are of a contrite spirit.

I live in a high and holy place, but also with him who is contrite and lowly in spirit, to revive the spirit of the lowly and to revive the heart of the contrite. (Isa. 57:15)

October 16

HIS MIGHTY POWER

Finally be strong in the Lord and in His mighty power. Put on the full armor of God. (Ephes. 6:10)

The Lord's power is mighty; He is here in our present moment and circumstances to show Himself strong in our behalf. *O Lord God Almighty, who is like You? You are mighty, O Lord, and Your faithfulness surrounds You. Your arm is endued with power; Your hand is strong, Your right hand exalted.* (Ps. 89:8, 13) When first awakening in the morning, I find that it takes awhile for my mind to come to full consciousness. I leave my dreams behind and slowly become aware of my surroundings and the new day that is before me. Then, as I arise to my feet, I notice that my body still feels tired and aches as I begin to move and my blood starts to circulate. Overall, I feel physically weak and it takes a little effort to get moving. I am reminded of the scripture that Paul prayed: *"I pray that out of His glorious riches He may strengthen you with power through His Spirit in your inner being."* (Ephes. 3:16) As I am learning to place myself before Him at the start of each new day, I find that He is always faithful to renew my strength. This is what I need to do every day. As I am consistent to do this, I can and will receive His strength from the overflowing storehouse of His Mighty Power. He is faithful to empower me today, and for as long as I live.

My grace is sufficient for you, for my power is made perfect in weakness. Therefore I will boast all the more gladly about my weaknesses, so that Christ's power may rest on me. (2 Cor. 12:9)

October 17

NO CONTINUING CITY

For here we do not have an enduring city, but we are looking for the City that is to come. (Heb. 13:14)

I am reminded of a saying; "Hold on to things lightly, with a loose grip, for the things of this world are not made to last forever." We are changing all the time and in order to move with the changes, we might be required to let go of some of those things that we possess. Nothing that we have here on earth is ours to keep. We are caretakers and stewards entrusted with the earth and everything in it. All the things we have come to love and appreciate are ours to enjoy, but not ours to hold on to. The Scriptures in Hebrews goes on to say *Through Jesus, therefore, let us continually offer to God a sacrifice of praise—the fruit of lips that confess His name. And do not forget to do good and to share with others, for with such sacrifices God is pleased.* (Heb. 13:15) This is how we should live knowing that all will be returned back to the Creator; we should offer to Him our praise for all He gives to us, express our faith to others, and share what we have been given with others. Nothing that is of this world will last.

You have made my days a mere handbreadth; the span of my years is nothing before You. Each man's life is but a breath. (Ps.39:5)

October 18

GET READY

The Day of the LORD will come like thief. The heavens will disappear with a roar; the elements will be destroyed by fire, and the earth and everything in it will be laid bare. But in keeping with His promise we are looking forward to a new heaven and new earth, the home of righteousness. (2 Pet.3:10, 13)

Now in our day, more than ever, is the time to make ready for the coming of the Lord. I can recall my mother saying to me when I was young, "Why worry, you can't take it with you!" Our love for God and others will last forever, and continue in heaven, but even in our relationships with others, there is a time to let go and allow the Lord to fulfill His purposes in them as well. Like Abraham we are pilgrims passing through for here we have no continuing city. We look for a Heavenly city that is to come and do not need to be afraid, for the Lord will take us through the temporal conditions of earth and lead us gently into the promised reality of our enduring Heavenly Kingdom. For here we have no continuing city. It is time to get ready for the coming of the Lord.

But you have come to Mount Zion, to the heavenly Jerusalem, the City of the Living God. You have come to thousands upon thousands of angels in joyful assembly. You have come to God, the judge of all men, to the spirits of righteous men made perfect, to Jesus the mediator of a new covenant. Therefore, since we are receiving a Kingdom that cannot be shaken, let us be thankful, and so worship God acceptably with reverence and awe, for our God is a consuming fire. (Heb. 12:22-24, 28)

October 19

DOOR OF HOPE IN DESERT PLACES

Therefore I am going to allure her; I will lead her into the desert and speak tenderly to her. There, I will give her back her vineyards, and will make the valley of anchor, a door of hope. (Hos. 2:14-15)

Does it seem as though the Lord is drawing you into desert places? It's your attention and affection that He desires and will make you aware of your need to seek Him in quiet places. There may be things that He is asking for you to give up; to allow Him to hold awhile. The times when we withdraw from the attractions and activities in our lives: it is then we are able to hear the Lord speak tenderly and affectionately to us; we can recognize our deepest need and longing for Him; and also hear what He wants to say to you. When we are able to lay down and surrender everything completely to His care in those quiet desert places, there will come a time when He happily gives us back and restores the very things we surrendered in a much greater way. He will open up a door of hope in our desert places.

I assure you that everyone who has given up house or brothers or sisters or mother or father or children or property, for my sake and for the Gospel, will receive now in return, a hundred times over, houses, property, with persecutions. And in the world to come they will have eternal life. (Mk. 10:29-30)

JESUS IS ALL THAT MATTERS

Christ is all that matters and He lives in all of us. (Col. 3:11)

God has given His Spirit to live in every one of us; the relationships we have and come to know in Christ are meaningful, rich, and fulfilling. The Lord gives to us trusted friendships that are based upon unconditional love and honesty. Relationships that have grown in this way over time and in many instances have required sacrificial giving, but these friendships will last on into eternity. The one relationship we must look to above and beyond all else is to Jesus Himself. If all is taken away and we find ourselves alone, could it be that God has removed these things in order that He Himself may take their place and become the most important focus of our lives? *Christ is all that matters.* This is what we must always come to realize even in the blessings, Jesus Himself is the greatest blessing of all.

Salvation is found in no one else, for there is no other name under heaven given to men by which we must be saved. (Ac. 4:12)

THE BATTLE

May God arise, may His enemies be scattered, and may His foes flee before Him. As smoke is blown away by the wind, may You blow them away. As wax melts before the fi re, may the wicked perish before God. But may the righteous be glad and rejoice before God; may they be happy and joyful. Sing to God, sing praise to His name, extol Him who rides on the clouds His name is the LORD and rejoice before Him. A father to the fatherless, a defender of widows is God in His holy dwelling. God sets the lonely in families, He leads forth the prisoners with singing, but the rebellious live in sun scorched land. (Ps. 68:1-8)

Are you feeling oppressed by your enemies? Leave the burden with your Father, and let Him be your Conqueror. This morning's scripture reading brings to mind not only our personal battles that we encounter daily, but the current battles that go on in many countries throughout the world. The need for us to pray is very great; these are fierce battles that in the end will ultimately win a victory for righteousness and the Lord's justice. *Through our God, we shall do valiantly; it is He who will tread down our enemies."* (Ps. 60:12) Life will triumph over the powers of death and destruction; freedom will win over tyranny and oppression. The Lord, the Great Conqueror will arise and come to heal the broken hearted, to help the fatherless, and the widowed. We have reason to rejoice and to sing even in the midst of everything, whether it is a personal battle or one that the whole world is watching. Hold on to the hope that you have in God, for He will be faithful to do everything He has spoken to us through His Word. Rejoice and be glad in Him today . . .

For the battle is not yours, but God's. (2 Chr. 20:15)

TRUST EQUALS PEACE

You will keep in perfect peace all who trust in You, those whose thoughts are fixed on You. Trust in the Lord always, for the LORD God is the Eternal Rock. (Isa. 26:3-4)

Trust and peace; are two words that go together. We trust someone when we know that we can depend upon them, we can rely upon the fact that they will do what they say, and that what they say they will do. We have peace in knowing that what we have entrusted to them is safe and secure. This describes what our relationship should be like with the Lord for it is the Eternal Rock of His Presence and of His Word that it is based upon. As long as we continuously keep our eyes fixed upon Jesus and upon His Words of promise, we can receive His peace. Not just any ordinary peace but a *perfect peace:* perfectly at peace and rest, secure in knowing that what we have entrusted to the Lord He will keep and perform to completion.

I know in whom I have believed, and am convinced that He is able to guard what I have entrusted to Him for that day. (2 Tim. 1:12)

GOD IS TRUSTWORTHY

How amazing are the deeds of the Lord. All who delight in Him should ponder them. All He does is just and good, and all His commandments are trustworthy. They are forever true, to be obeyed faithfully and with integrity. Reverence for the Lord is the foundation of true wisdom. (Ps. 111:2,7-8, 10)

The rewards of wisdom come to all who obey Him. Praise His name forever! There are two thoughts that come to my mind and are emphasized in these scriptures; one is that all the deeds and actions of God are just, and good; that we should think and meditate upon them. When we hear of the many troubles, heartaches, and problems of others and have personal experience in hardships ourselves, that's when we need to shift our attention upon the goodness and justice of God and all that He has been faithful to do for us. The second thing is that wisdom comes to those who have reverence for God and to those who obey Him. *His commandments are trustworthy, righteous, and true forever.* It is His wisdom we need, man's wisdom will fail, God's wisdom brings life and blessings to all who love and trust Him.

Who is wise? He will realize these things. Who is discerning? He will understand them. The ways of the Lord are right, the righteous walk in them, but the rebellious stumble in them. (Hos. 14:9)

GOOD GIFTS FROM THE FATHER

Which of you, if his son asks for bread, will give him a stone? (Matt. 7:9)

Giving and receiving are the principals that our relationship with the Father, Son, and Holy Spirit are based upon. The Father gives us our very life and breath and is faithful to keep on giving everything necessary to sustain that life. When we have our own children, we desire all that is good for them; we protect and provide everything that is needed for their health and happiness. When we follow in the Lord's ways, we come to understand the Father's generous heart. Our sons and daughters ask when they want or need something, the Father tells us to, *"ask and it will be given to you, seek and you will find."* (Matt. 7:7) Just as the Father desires to give and bless us when we ask, we in return give to others and share with others the things we have received. Giving and receiving should be as easy as breathing in and out. We receive, we give. This is the principal that needs to be lived out as we grow in a loving relationship with each other and with the Father.

Do not be afraid little flock; it is the Father's good pleasure to give you the Kingdom. (Lk. 12:32)

TO OBEY IS TO LOVE

The One who sent me is with me. He has not left me alone, for I always do what pleases Him. (Jn. 8:29)

In God's Word, we learn obedience, in order to experience the fullness of abiding in the Lord's love. A life filled with blessing, or one that is cursed, hinges upon the question of obedience. *If anyone loves me, he will obey my teaching. My Father will love him, and we will come to him and make our home with him.* (Jn. 15:10) We show our love for the Lord when we yield ourselves in submission to His will. The life of obedience to God's laws is a life that is built upon love, trust, faith, hope and wisdom. It is a life that knows abundant living; a life that abides in Christ; Jesus Christ; the same, yesterday, today and forever. His promises of fullness of life and living have always been based upon obedience to His commands. Love is the fulfillment of all the law. When we love God with all of our hearts, it is a joy and privilege to obey and do the things He asks of us.

Greater love has no one that this, that one lay down his life for his friends. You are my friends, if you do what I command. I have called you friends, for everything that I learned from my Father I have made known to you. (Jn. 15:13-15)

MY TIME IS IN HIS HANDS

My times are in Your hand. (Ps.31:15)

God made time itself; time is a created thing. God lives outside of time, in the eternal now. We are creatures living within the confines of time. The earth and all that has been created, lives, breathes, moves, and has it's being all within the structure of time and providence. While observing life, you can see the tangible results of time as it weaves through creation. A baby grows into an adult; a rock or mountain is carved into a shape over time. Any work of art, a masterpiece in music, or a scientific discovery, had a beginning in time and a culmination. Everything is subject to it. Time marches on. God's wheel of providence turns from season to season, decade upon decade, century upon century, and millennium upon millennium. What is a life? Seventy years, maybe an hundred? Such is a very small fraction in the overall picture of time in the universe, and yet the God of all creation oversees every second of the human life and experience. Have we placed the time that God has given us into His hands? Are the hours and minutes we have each day fully surrendered into the hands of God? God is the owner and creator of our time. In some unforeseeable moment, time will end and we will step into eternity. Can we say with the Psalmist David "My times are in Your hands?"

Teach us to number our days aright that we may gain a heart of wisdom. (Ps. 90:12)

OUR WORK IS TO BELIEVE

This is what God wants you to do; believe in the One whom He has sent. (Jn. 6:29)

Faith—belief in the One whom God has sent is our work here upon the earth. Doubt and unbelief are the tools the enemy uses to deceive and to destroy our faith. What is it that we are to believe and to put all of our trust in? If we are to believe in the One whom God has sent, then it is Jesus we are to believe in. Who is Jesus? He is the Living Word of God made flesh. How can we increase our faith? *Faith comes by hearing and hearing the Word of God.* (Rom. 10:17) *Everything is possible for him who believes.* (Mk. 9:23) The more we hear and meditate upon the Word of God and upon His promises, our faith will grow. The more it grows, all things will become possible. God will be true to His Word; we can fully depend and rely upon Him to perform it. More faith is what we all need . . . Dear Lord, help our unbelief and fill our hearts with faith to believe all the goodness and promise of Your Word. Your Word stands forever.

The grass withers, the flower fades, but the Word or our God shall stand forever. (Is. 40:8)

JESUS IS ALWAYS WITH US

"Lo, I am with you always." (Matt. 28:20)

This is a promise we have from Jesus that applies to our daily lives. His Presence can be realized in great degrees, or at times, can be weak and unrecognizable. How great is our desire to experience His Presence in our moments and hours? It depends upon our lives being rightly related to God. Every day and all day long He is with me; this is joy and a treasure experienced in the life that is hidden with Christ in God. We have been given His Holy Spirit that fills us anew each and every morning. (Ephes. 5:18-20) It is the Lord's will that we will be filled with His Spirit; so that His abiding Presence can be revealed to our hearts and minds. The great treasure and riches is in knowing and apprehending His glory within and around us. Invite the Holy Spirit to fill you to overflow each morning; purifying and re-energizing you for the work of the new day. As you practice this, you will experience increasingly the promise of Jesus: *"Lo, I am with you always."*

Christ is our life. (Col. 3:4)

STOP DOING WRONG

See you are well again, stop sinning or something worse may happen to you. (Jn. 5:14)

As men and women of faith in Christ, we know that we have passed from death unto life. We have experienced the joy of forgiveness and the freedom from condemnation. With this new life in Christ, comes an awareness of responsibility; although forgiven, there still remain consequences that happen when we disobey. Much of the pain and suffering we experience as believers in Christ are a result of our willful disobedience, or unconscious disobedience. We are struggling against the sin the flesh and the ways of this world. Yet, to fully overcome problems, many times we revisit past mistakes and bring upon ourselves unnecessary pain. Sadly, there are also times when pain and suffering come through absolutely no fault of our own. It is the results of the fallen world. Here once again, this is where trust and belief must come in and take control. When it is our own fault, we must repent and be restored; our willful sin separates us from God, until we admit and repent. The good news is this can happen in an instant. We no longer have to live under condemnation. We are forgiven today, for things in the past and for potential sins in the future. We are forgiven, but we must stop sinning, (practicing it) or a worse thing could come upon us.

Therefore, do not let sin reign in your mortal body. (Rom.6:12)

October 30

BATTLEFIELD OF THE MIND

Casting down imaginations, and every high thing that exalts itself against the knowledge of God, and bringing into captivity every thought to the obedience of Christ. (2 Cor. 10:5)

It is the Word of God, our Sword of the Spirit that we've been given to fight off the attacks of Satan. Jesus Himself would answer the devil with the words; "It is written:" and then quote a scripture to Him. In the same way we can speak out the victory God has won for us. We know these things well, but there are times when it is necessary to be reminded of the great and complete victory Jesus has won. The second thing we must do is to call upon the Lord for our help. It is *through* God to the pulling down of strongholds, it is *through Christ* that gives us victory. Only in and through God can we become victorious over the battlefield in our minds and over the spiritual attacks that we come up against. As we bring our thoughts into captivity to the Word of God, and call upon Him for help, we will be sure to win a victory over all the spiritual battles we face. The battle is the Lord's and He will fight for us; as we put our lives into His hands and bring our thoughts captive to His Word.

For greater is He that is in us than he that is in the world. (1 John 4:4)
Thanks be unto God who always give us the victory through Christ. (2 Cor. 2:14)

October 31

SPIRITUAL WARFARE

For our struggle is not against flesh and blood, but against the rulers, against the authorities, against the powers of this dark world and against the spiritual forces of evil in the heavenly realms. (Ephes. 6:12)

Jesus calls the devil a liar, the father of all lies and of all that is false. (John 8:44) Many times we will think a thought about a certain person, circumstance or situation that is entirely not true; but the enemy is a master at putting these wonderings, and theories into our heads, bombarding us with suspicions, doubts, and speculations. We must learn to resist these thoughts. The warfare is in our own minds. One of the weapons God has given us is His Word. Through careful strategy and cunning deceit, Satan attempts to set up *strongholds* in our minds. It is an area in which we are held in bondage (in prison) to certain ways of thinking. When we go into prayer, imagine yourself putting on the full armor of God that we may be able to stand against the weapons of our adversary. (Ephes.6:13-17) We have been set free from the devil and all of his lies. Jesus Christ has won our freedom forever! Praise Him!

For the weapons of our warfare are not carnal, but mighty through God to the pulling down of strongholds. (2 Cor. 10:4)

November 1

A THANKFUL SPIRIT

Do not be anxious about anything, but in everything, by prayer and petition with thanksgiving, present your request to God. (Phil 4:6)

Praise and thanksgiving go hand in hand with prayer and prepares us to receive the answer and blessing that God desires to give to us when our hearts are right before Him. In all things let our desire be to glorify Him. God receives glory when we receive blessings in answer to our prayers and petitions; thanking Him in advance for the answer to our prayers, release faith in the acknowledgment of having already received them. *Faith is a substance of things not seen.* (Heb.11:1) We learn to thank Him for things we do not see yet, and praise Him for granting our requests. This is one of the keys to opening up the fountain of blessings that God is holding for us. Let's praise and thank Him with all of our hearts today for all the things that we are standing in faith for, and for all the times He has helped us in the past.

Enter His gates with thanksgiving and His courts with praise: give thanks to Him and praise His name. (Ps. 100:4)

THANKFULNESS OVERFLOWING

So then, just as you received Christ Jesus as Lord, continue to live in Him, rooted and built up in Him, strengthened in the faith as you were taught, and overflowing with thankfulness. (Col. 2:6-7)

We will be celebrating Thanksgiving Day soon; let us be *overflowing with thankfulness.* There is nothing that we have, that we did not receive from God, (1 Cor. 4:7) so let us be thankful for the things we have: however small or great they may be. We do not have to look too far to find something to give thanks to the Lord for. Should we find ourselves in a state of weakness, even in this we can give thanks to God, for in our weakness, His power is perfected in us. *My grace is sufficient for you, for my power is made perfect in weakness. Therefore I will boast all the more gladly about my weaknesses, so that Christ's power may rest on me. That is why, for Christ sake, I delight in weaknesses, in insults, in hardships, in persecutions, in difficulties. For when I am weak, then I am strong.* (2 Cor. 12:9-10) This time of year, we can feel a little overwhelmed with the approaching events; dinners, family reunions etc. Besides all of the activities, the time flies away so quickly it seems that we will never get everything done! It's no wonder we begin to feel stressful and anxious! There will be times during the Holidays that we will need to come away, quiet ourselves, and seek the Lord for patience and wisdom. In everything and in all situations, the Lord will get you through whatever challenge you face during those times as you turn your attention to Him.

Let them sacrifice thank offerings and tell of His works with songs of joy. (Ps. 107:22)

LET PEACE RULE

Let the peace of Christ rule in your hearts, since as members of one body you were called to peace. And be thankful. (Col. 3:15)

As we continue to be grateful and have a thankful heart towards God, the scripture says, *let* the peace of the Lord rule in your hearts; take it in, and receive it. Let peace *rule* and have dominion in your spirit, soul and body. We were called to have this peace and we can obtain it as we *let* the peace of the Lord rule in our hearts. His peace will overtake us and the anxiety of the season will vanish away. One of the best ways to overcome stress is to sing a song of praise unto the Lord, when you begin to do this; it is amazing how your spirit is lifted high, over and above all your problems and concerns. It is the Lord's will that we continue to give thanks in all circumstances. Whether in joy or in sorrow, in plenty or leanness, sickness or health, in all things and in everything let us learn to give thanks to the Lord for He cares for you and is working all things out in order to bring us a future of hope. *"For I know the plans I have for you," declares the Lord, "plans to prosper you and not to harm you, plans to give you a hope and a future."* (Jer. 29:11)

Give thanks in all circumstances, for this is God's will for you in Christ Jesus (1Thess. 5:18)

November 4

BLESSED REST

The Lord replied, "My Presence will go with you, and I will give you rest." (Ex. 33:14)

This was God's promise to Moses when the children of Israel were moving through the desert. It was because Moses had found favor in His sight that this promise was made. This is the busiest time of the year, so we should all the more take the time out to rest. In Hebrews 4:11 it says: *"Let us therefore make every effort to enter that rest."* It sounds a bit contradictory that we should have to make an effort to obtain His rest; but there is something that we must do to obtain it; what it is talking about is making sure we take time out for prayer and in seeking Him even more. If you are hosting a dinner and entertaining friends and family, there is so much that goes into it! There's the shopping, cleaning, decorating and remembering all of the small things that seem so important. We want everything to be perfect so our guests can relax and enjoy the special day. Simplicity is good to remember when you feel overwhelmed. Make every effort to enter into His rest!

Now we who have believed enter that rest, just as God has said. (Heb.4:3)

November 5

HARVEST TIME

The Kingdom of heaven is like a man who sowed good seed in his field. But while everyone was sleeping, his enemy came and sowed weeds among the wheat, and went away. Then the wheat sprouted and formed heads, and then the weeds also appeared. The owner's servants came to him and said, "Sir, didn't you sow good seed in your field? Where then did the weeds come from?" "An enemy did this." he replied. The servant asked him, "Do you want us to go and pull them up?" "No, he answered, because while you are pulling the weeds, you may root up the wheat with them. Let both grow together until the harvest. At that time I will tell the harvesters: First collect the weeds and tie them in bundles to be burned, then gather the wheat and bring it into my barn." (Matt. 13:24-30)

The enemy sows tares; he does this to cause division and strife. He knows the power in bringing division inside the Church; for *a house divided against itself cannot stand.* (Mk.3:25) This is how the enemy gains ground and gets a stronghold within the Body of Christ; He wants to divide and disassemble so that we will become weak and powerless. It is tempting for us to judge others, accuse and take sides against one another. Resist the desire to retaliate like this. There is a way to make your point without giving place to strife and discord. Jesus tells us to speak the truth in love. There are three things we can do in such a situation: 1. Pray and ask for wisdom. 2. Wait for the answer to come. 3. Confront the problem with love and compassion; let us be peacemakers. We will always have battles in this life; the enemy is not going away. Jesus said both would grow together until the harvest. Satan is intensifying his attacks. If we must fight, let's fight the good fight of our faith, with words of truth, love, and compassion.

Fight the good fight of the faith. Take hold of the eternal life to which you were called. (1 Tim. 6:12)

November 6

NOT PERFECT YET BEAUTIFUL

To all perfection, I see a limit; but Your commands are boundless. (Ps. 119:96)

Things do not have to be perfect, what is important is that you do the very best you can with what you have to work with; if you do it with lots of love, all will be beautiful! If you are going somewhere else for Thanksgiving, you know there will be traffic and traveling issues to contend with. There is also the concern of getting along with relatives you will see that you may not be compatible with; this is not too unusual, because in most Families there are incompatibilities. The need to reconcile and the importance of forgiveness may be weighing upon your heart and mind. Besides these things, it is also the loneliest time of the year for single people who may not have family nearby and cannot travel. It is no wonder we feel like fainting! But the Lord reminds us this morning to be still and rest. We can do this even in the midst of activity and emotional strain. The rest comes in knowing the One who is the giver of all rest, and we can get through the busiest times, the loneliness times, in His perfect peace and know His comforting love. For all these reasons mentioned, stop and just take a moment, or an hour if needed, cease from your own doing, lean upon the strong shoulder of the Lord, and be still and know that He is God . . . He has promised that in the midst of the whirlwind of life, He will give you rest; the effort you make, if done with love, may not be perfect but it will be beautiful.

Be at rest once more, O my soul, for the LORD has been good to you. (Ps. 116:7)

THANKSGIVING

When you have eaten and are satisfied, praise the LORD your God for the good land He has given you. (Dt. 8:10)

This Word of the Lord came to the children of Israel right after they entered into the Promised Land. He went on to remind them to follow His commandments pointing out that they should be careful because after they receive such rich abundance there was the danger that their hearts would become proud and that they would forget the Lord their God who delivered them from slavery and brought them through the desert. He was also the one who fed them heavenly manna and with the water that sprung from the Rock. God never changes, He is always desirous of our love and affection. We show our appreciation and thankfulness to Him when we follow His commandments. Many of us have been led out of a desert; some deserts that have been of our own making, and sometimes God places us there because it was in His providence or will for us to be there. Whatever the case, hasn't God been faithful to feed, clothe, and provide for you through those deserts? His covenant of care to us is for a thousand generations. *I will make an everlasting covenant with them: I will never stop doing them good.* (Jer. 32:40)

Let us come before Him with thanksgiving. (Ps. 95:2)

THE TRIAL OF FAITH

Jesus said to him, "If you can believe, all things are possible to him that believes." (Mk. 9:23)

This promise appears to be too good to be true and brings us to consider the trial of our faith. We embrace these words of Jesus with joy and expectation, and then, comes a sense of a great let down when we start to think that such a wonder working faith is way beyond our reach. This is our natural mind that finds this kind of faith so hard to obtain. It lies in the abiding Presence of Christ within us. This faith is only possible to the soul that clings to Christ and places all their trust in Him. *"Lo I am with you always."*(Matt. 28:20) Just as surely as the Lord reveals His abiding Presence moment by moment, day by day, He will lead us into the blessing and power of this divine promise of faith. During those times of struggling with our unbelief, if we consciously place ourselves before Him in His power and love, over time, we will obtain a glorious inheritance and with joy proclaim, "Lord I believe!"

I have come into the world as a light, so that no one who believes in me should stay in darkness. (Jn. 12:46)

November 9

GOD ALWAYS SUPPLIES

He will give you all you need from day to day if you make the Kingdom of God your primary concern. (Matt. 6:33)

As we observe the world today, we can see clearly both the evil and the good at work. When we make God's Kingdom work a priority in our daily lives, we are choosing life and goodness. In doing this, we can have assurance from the Word of the Lord that our needs will be provided for; God shines His light upon our path and upon our hands and feet. It is not for us to see or to know all of His plans for us; we are only asked to trust Him and to commit all our daily concerns, moment by moment. As we practice this, He proves His faithfulness to provide for us, and eventually more of the big picture is revealed. *God is able to make all grace abound to you so that in all times, having all you need, you will abound in every good work.* (2 Cor. 9:8) What is it that we need? We need both physical things and spiritual things. Love is a spiritual gift that we all need. To love and to be loved is our greatest need. Jesus promises to give us all we need if we make His Kingdom's work our priority each day. Look around and you will see good and evil. Choose the good, choose life, enter into the work that Jesus began and has commanded the Church, His people, to finish. He will provide all of your needs on a daily basis.

God is able to make all grace abound to you so that in all times, having all you need, you will abound in every good work. (2 Cor. 9:8)

I LOVE THE LORD

I love the Lord, for He has heard my voice; He heard my cry for mercy, because He turned His ear to me. I will call on Him as long as I live. (Ps. 116:1)

There are many times when we may feel that the Lord is not listening; that He cannot hear us. We cry out in distress and there is just silence, no answer comes. How should we react? David was a man who had a heart that was similar to God's heart. What was it that gave him so much assurance that God heard his prayers? It was because the condition of his heart was right before God. *Who may ascend the hill of the Lord? Who may stand in His holy place? He who has clean hands and a pure heart.* (Ps. 24:3-4) If you want to be assured that God is listening to your prayers, examine your heart and allow the Lord to change it and make it into a heart that is like His. David had a repentant, humble and loving heart towards God. When we draw near to God with that kind of heart, we too can say with David, "He hears my prayers, He is listening, because of this, I love Him and will call on Him as long as I have breath." *David's prayer: Create in me a clean heart O God, and renew a right spirit within me.* (Ps. 51:10)

"I the Lord search the heart and examine the mind." (Jer. 17:10)

PRAYING IN THE NAME OF JESUS

At that time you won't need to ask me anything. The truth is, you can go directly to the Father and ask Him and He will grant your request because you ask in my name. You haven't done this before, ask, using my name, and you will receive, and you will have abundant joy. (Jn.16:23-24)

Prayer is uniting with God; we pray to the Father in the name of His Son Jesus. We can go directly to the Father in His name and experience oneness and loving relationship with our Creator. Jesus made it possible through His sacrificial death and atonement, giving us full access to God Almighty the Maker of the entire universe! It is comforting for us to know that we are dearly loved by the Father Himself and that we can go to Him at any time and have His full attention. Our requests will be answered, yet not always in the way we expect or in the time we desire; because he is good, we know that only good can come from the Father's hand. Sometimes God will use what seems to be unanswered prayer to teach us deep and meaningful lessons. Let us trust Him to bring the ultimate good to us in His perfect time. Keep on going to the Father and continue to ask in the name of Jesus.

Therefore God has exalted Him to the highest place and gave Him a name that is above every other name, that at the name of Jesus every knee should bow, in heaven and in earth. (Phil. 2:9)

HIS FAITHFUL LOVE ENDURES FOREVER

Give thanks to the Lord for He is good His faithful love endures forever. Let all who fear the Lord repeat; "His faithful love endures forever." (Ps. 118:1, 4)

We can be absolutely confident of this one thing; His steadfast, faithful, unending love endures forever. As the days and years go by, the Lord reveals this love and our hearts cannot help but fill up and overflow with thanksgiving and praise. God gives us the victory over all our enemies and causes us to triumph. It may be that we have to wait for it, but that victory will come for His faithful love endures forever! Who can explain love and the reason He loves us to the depths, height, and width, in its full measure? Why such great love? All we can know is that His irresistible great love is constantly being showered upon us through the good and the bad times, always staying faithful and strong in the midst of our trials. His love encompasses us about and brings victory. His faithful love endures forever!

I love the Lord because He heard my voice; He heard my cry for mercy. (Ps. 116:1)

ONLY BY THE SPIRIT

Now we have received, not the spirit of the world, but the Spirit which is of God; that we might know the things that are freely given to us of God. (1 Cor. 2:12)

There are many highly gifted, intelligent men and women in our world today. They can think through and analyze all the multitude of problems, and seem to have the right answers that make perfectly good sense. If you try to explain that Jesus died for them they will say, "I'm alright." It is because they've become self sufficient and have not yet discovered their need for God. *The man or woman without the Spirit does not accept the things that come from the Spirit of God, for they are foolishness to him, and he cannot understand them because they are spiritually discerned.* (1 Cor. 2:14) In those times, you can gently explain why you believe in what the Bible says, and then go on to state the reason for your faith. It's not always easy when you genuinely care for the person and your words seem to fall to the ground. Do not give up. Remember to pray for those individuals for in time they will come to know the love of the Lord, if you are faithful to keep praying for them.

The Spirit of truth, the world cannot accept Him, because it neither sees Him nor knows Him. But you know Him, for He lives with you and will be in you. (Jn. 14:17) *No one can come to me unless the Father who sent me draws Him.* (Jn. 6:44)

November 14

A LOVE PRAYER

The unfailing love of the Lord never ends! His mercies begin afresh each day. The Lord is my inheritance, therefore I will hope in Him. (Lam. 3:22-24)

Dear Lord, You alone are my hope in this life, my inheritance, You have given me Yourself, Your abiding Presence for my inheritance. Your unfailing love will last for all eternity. I will wait silently and patiently for You. There is nothing in this whole world that I desire more than You. Please shine Your beautiful light upon my path and direct my ways, for it is in You that I may move, breathe and have my being. Blessed Lord, hear my prayers and answer from Your throne. Flow down from heaven Your living waters that all may drink and be filled with Your precious Holy Spirit. Jesus help me to see and hear You today, experience You in every moment. Cause me to hope, be my living hope today . . . Amen

And now these three remain: faith, hope, and love. But the greatest of these is love. (1 Cor. 13:13)

ONE WITH HIS LOVE

"And I pray that you being rooted and established in love, may have power together with all the saints, to grasp how wide, and long, and high, and deep is the love of Christ, and to know this love that surpasses knowledge,; that you may be filled to the measure of all the fullness of God." (Ephes. 3:17-19)

It is God's desire that we be made one with Him so that we may *know* of the great love that the Father and Son has for us. All we have is from God and belongs to God, and all that God is and has belongs to us through Jesus. As time goes by, it is Jesus through His Holy Spirit that makes known to us all the treasures we have hidden in Christ. The more transformed our lives become, and the more we are changed into His image from glory to glory; the more we will know the depths of His love for us. We cannot see what the Lord is doing presently, but as we learn to continually place our lives into His hands, trusting and committing ourselves to Him daily; slowly the greatness of the words Jesus will be revealed when He spoke, *"All I have is yours, and all you have is mine."* (Jn.17:10) The greatest of all love exchanges between the Creator and His creation are found here in these words. We can say with our whole hearts, "I'm yours Jesus and You are mine, I am one with Your love!"

They go from strength to strength until each appears before God in Zion. (Ps. 84:7)

WHAT'S IN A MARRIAGE?

For this reason a man will leave his father and mother and be united to his wife, and the two will become one flesh. (Gen. 2:24)

What is the meaning and significance of marriage; in the world and to the Lord? It is a holy union initiated by God Himself. When it is love that brings a couple together in marriage, it is beautiful to see and something to be celebrated. All people everywhere recognize and respect the sacrament of marriage. It is in that commitment to love, honor, serve and respect one another until death do you part that we can understand and sense the union as one both physically and spiritually. The Lord refers to His Church as *His Bride,* and many times in Scripture we find Jesus in reference to *The Bridegroom.* Paul the Apostle spoke of this union between Christ and the Church as *a great mystery.* (Ephes. 5:32) I remember the feeling as a bride before my wedding was to begin; that anticipation, the excitement, the newness of a life that will begin when at last the two will become one. In a very real sense, we, the Church, are that Bride in waiting. We have a Bride groom that is in waiting also. The wedding day between Christ and His Church will be one like no other! We as the body of Christ: His Bride, should be making ourselves ready to meet our Bridegroom!

Hallelujah! For our LORD GOD ALMIGHTY reigns. Let us rejoice and be glad and give Him glory! For the wedding of the Lamb has come, and His bride has made herself ready. (Rev. 19:6-7)

THREADS OF GOODNESS

Surely goodness and mercy shall follow me all the days of my life: and I will dwell in the house of the LORD forever. (Ps. 23:6)

There are threads of goodness that run and weave their way in unexpected places. Should one cross your path, reach out and take a hold of it while you have the chance, for it may soon disappear. Learning to recognize the threads of goodness is not always an easy thing to do, for some are camouflaged and are not what they may appear to be. Still within and under the surface, the substance may appear to be thin and sparse, yet it continues to run true and good. It cannot be anything else but what it has been made to be. Goodness prevails through the lightning, winds and storm. Nothing can stop its unrelenting force that conquers over all. There are threads of goodness that eternally run true and sure here upon the earth and they can be captured in our time. When all seems black and the weight is too much to carry, there is a thread of goodness that can lift the clouds and the weight that binds you; look for it, and when you find it, grab a hold and do not let go.

The Lord is good, a refuge in times of trouble. He cares for those who trust in Him (Ps. 34:8)

THE PEACEMAKERS

Those who are peacemakers will plant seeds of peace and reap a harvest of goodness. (Jas. 3:18)

When we are at peace with God and with man we cannot help but to sow seeds of peace in our surroundings; this is an everlasting peace, one that the world cannot understand. Peace: *tranquility, a sense of wellbeing, security, being held firm and unshakable, calmness, fearlessness.* This defines a peaceful demeanor. It is what the Lord desires for us to have fully in our lives every day. If we open our hearts and ask, we may receive this peace. Those who have peace, sow peace in a world of turmoil and strife and they will reap a harvest of goodness. *Blessed are the peacemakers, for they shall be called the sons of God.* (Matt. 5:9) The life of one who brings peace, lives a life that is blessed by God.

"Peace I give leave with you, my peace I give unto you: not as the world gives, give I unto you." (Jn. 14:27)

THE BRIDE WILL FOLLOW

The Bride will go where the bridegroom is. (Jn. 3:29)

Deep calls unto deep: love is a deep ocean that is full of light, alluring and beautiful. It invites the hearts of men and women to come, to dive into the depths of its wonder and mystery. Marriage is sacred to the Lord. He created man and women to be united in Holy matrimony, sealed it with a vow of love and faithfulness. It is a statement that is made to the world for all to see and to honor. Marriage abides by the laws of God and of man. It is a picture of the complete and sacrificial love of Christ our bridegroom and His Church (we being His beloved bride). *The bride will go where the bridegroom is.* To abide with Jesus Christ our beloved Bridegroom, we will go; we will follow Him where He leads. It is His great love and faithfulness that draws us to Him, nothing else in this world, or any place in this world can satisfy and overflow our hearts with such divine and perfect love as His. Jesus prayed that we might be with Him where He is. Dear Lord, I can't wait to see you and to really be with You where You are. Lead me ever deeper into Your amazing love . . .

Father, I want those you have given me to be with me where I am, and to see my glory you have given me because you loved me before the creation of the world. (Jn. 17:24)

NO MORE THIRST

The water I give them takes away thirst altogether, it becomes a perpetual spring within them giving them eternal life. (Jn. 4:14)

We have this perpetual spring within each of us who believe in Jesus. It is a never ending fountain of life giving water springing up inside of us, day by day, moment by moment, and year by year. The Samaritan woman at the well did not understand what Jesus had meant when He spoke those words. He wanted to take away her thirst forever. Only the water that Jesus gives can do that. It is desire in our human nature that drives us, and we will do anything to fulfill those desires. Once we attain what we think we wanted, it is not too long before we are thirsty again for more, or for other things. They may be good desires; sometimes it's physical, or possibly an emotional one, but the one that Jesus is addressing is a spiritual desire; it is a deep place in our hearts that only God Himself can fill. Nothing will quench it but the love and living water that the Lord offers. When we drink that water we no longer thirst or desire for anything more. He fills us with a perpetual spring of love, joy, hope, life abundant and eternal. Our only desire, once we have experienced this; is for more of Him. We want more and more of His great love and beautiful abiding presence that fills and overflows our deepest desires completely.

To him who is thirsty I will give to drink without cost from the spring of the water of life. (Rev.21:6)

JERUSALEM: GOD'S HOME

For the LORD has chosen Jerusalem. He has desired it for His home. This is my home where I will live forever. (Ps. 132:14)

When the Lord walked upon the earth, His heart and attention was fixed upon Jerusalem. *He came to His own, (the Jewish people) but His own received Him not.* (Jn. 1:1) His death would occur in Jerusalem; throughout His short life, He made many visits and taught in the Jerusalem Temple. This is the city that the Lord will return to at last. It is because He has desired it to be His home forever. We too, His people (Gentile and Jew) will worship Him there and share in His everlasting Kingdom when at last He comes to rule and reign upon His throne that was first promised to King David, which will be in Jerusalem. Part of our reward as over-comers will be to live in the New Jerusalem; that glorious beloved city! The Lord promises us in Revelation:

"Him who overcomes I will make a pillar in the temple of my God. Never again will he leave it. I will write on him the name of my God and the name of the City of my God, the New Jerusalem, which is coming down out of heaven from my God." (Rev. 3:12)

November 22

THE MOUNTAIN AND THE VALLEY

After six days, Jesus took Peter, James, and John with Him and led them up a high mountain, where they were all alone. (Mk. 9:2)

There are times when the Lord will reveal something, some revelation and it will lift us up to a high place; to a spiritual mountain top. If we could, we would remain there, but our life and work is mostly in the valleys: the common places. All life is a gift from God whose design and purpose is to first bring us into relationship with Himself; and to provide for us infinite joy in sharing an eternal family, and a divine destiny that was planned before the beginning of time. Each breath, each ray of sunlight, every drop of water, and all the beauty of nature; our physical bodies themselves; the ability to see, hear, taste, smell, move, feel, walk and run; everything and every experience in life is meant to fulfill this purpose. For the most part our lives are lived in the valley. It involves maintenance and care for things that God entrusts to us as caretakers of this planet. There is an order and clarity that begins to surface out of our chaos as we begin to submit to His will daily. Then, suddenly while doing your ordinary work, the Lord may lift you up to a mountain top where all things at once come into clear focus. These are rare occurrences, but treasured ones to remember and reflect upon when we return to the valley.

And He carried me away in the Spirit to a mountain great and high, and showed me the Holy City, Jerusalem coming down out of heaven from God. (Rev. 21:10)

CLOUD BY DAY: FIRE BY NIGHT

And the LORD went before them by day in a pillar of a cloud, to lead them in the way; and by night in a pillar of fi re, to give them light: to go by day and night. (Ex. 13:21)

A cloud by day and fire by night was there for all to see. You'd think that alone would be enough to keep the children of Israel's full attention upon the ever presence of God. How could anyone become complacent with the majestic cloud of the Living God leading them by day and the awesome pillar of His fire illuminating the darkness of their nights? The people needed to see with their eyes this God that Moses talked about. Life was simple in those days. What more would it take to give them more faith? Yet, they complained and became complacent and ungrateful. They could not see nor understand God's plan to eventually bring them into the Promised Land. So they complained and wandered around stubborn, and unyielding. If only they would have embraced with wonder and majesty of the living cloud by day and the life giving fire by night. They could have walked once again through Eden's gates and have known and received for themselves the love that God longed to give to them. What a shame that they could not embrace the simplicity of Gods cloud by day and His fire by night.

The Lord is my light and my salvation, whom shall I fear? (Ps.27:1)

JESUS HAS ALL AUTHORITY

Father, the time has come, glorify Your Son so He can give glory back to You. For You have given Him authority over everyone in all the earth. (Jn. 17:1-2)

Jesus has authority over everyone in all the earth; we have been invited to take counsel, to come to Him and make known our petitions and desires before Him. He made a way for us to come and approach Him with boldness and confidence. He did this by sacrificing His body for our sins and for the sins of the whole world; making access possible for all who will to come. We never need to fear because the One who has all authority in heaven and in the earth, loves, protects, watches over, and provides for all who love and have placed their trust in Him. Heaven is His throne and the earth is His footstool. King Jesus will come to rule and reign over all the earth and He will sit upon David's throne in the New Jerusalem and His Kingdom will never end.

Then Jesus came to them and said, "All authority in heaven and earth has been given to me." (Mt.28:18)

THE HONOR OF HIS NAME

I will give thanks to Your name for Your unfailing love and faithfulness, because Your promises are backed by all the honor of Your name. When I pray, You answer me, You encourage me by giving me the strength I need. The Lord will work out the plans for my life for Your faithful love O LORD endures forever. (Ps. 138:2-3, 8)

It is good to give thanks to the Lord because of His faithfulness and unfailing love, and because every promise given to us in His Word is backed by all the honor of His name. His name is above everything; there isn't any created thing that is higher or more trustworthy than His name: (Jesus' name) We pray our prayers in this all powerful name; His Holy Word of promise given to us, sealed and confirmed by this glorious name of Jesus. There is no greater surety that the Father God can offer than that of the name of His precious Son Jesus. Every word that God has spoken to us is backed by the honor of His name; we have these great promises given to us and have experienced the faithfulness of God. Reach out and take a hold of what is being offered to you through His Word, for God's name is honored and assures us that He is working out a plan for your life. He has given us the surety of His name that is the ultimate gift and brings us unending hope, power, and encouragement for each new day.

Everyone who calls upon the name of the Lord shall be saved. (Rom.10:13)

November 26

DESIRE WISDOM

Get wisdom, get understanding; do not forget my words or swerve from them. Do not forsake wisdom and she will protect you; love her and she will watch over you. Wisdom is supreme, therefore, get wisdom. (Prov. 4:5-6)

It is good and right to pray for wisdom; I would like to have the skills needed to achieve the most perfect end by the most perfect means. It is the reaching beyond of what I can grasp; if I am trusting in God's divine wisdom and understand that His is perfected, it takes the pressure off of me. *In Him we have redemption through His blood, the forgiveness of sins, in accordance with the riches of His grace, that He lavished on us with all wisdom and understanding and He made known to us the mystery of His will according to His good pleasure.* (Ephes. 1:7-9) By simply asking for His wisdom and His perfect will, I can rest in knowing that it is for His pleasure that I may receive it. Throughout all eternity we will be ever learning, going deeper and deeper into the love, knowledge, and joy of the Lord. It is only through the Holy Spirit that we can have comprehension of things concerning the wisdom of God. He reveals to us as we are able to receive, and in as much as we desire to know. Our will to know Him, our love for Him must surpass our love for the attractions and things of the earth. The Lord wants us, (His Church) to know more and to reveal more to us. It is we who by our stubbornness and unbelief block off the Holy Spirit and our ears become deaf and our eyes blinded. Jesus has prayed *that we may be one with Him and the Father;* being one with Him is definitely knowing Him and attaining wisdom and understanding.

Open my eyes that I may see wonderful things in Your law. (Ps. 119:18)

THE GREATNESS OF GOD'S LOVE

God commended His love toward us, in that while we were yet sinners, Christ died for us. (Rom.5:8)

We should get into the habit of continually thinking about the greatness of God's love for us. While we were yet sinners, Christ died for us the ungodly. When I think of His great love for me, I can't help but to love Him more and more. My eyes become open to the many blessings that He gives to me each day from the smallest things, to the greater; the provision He provides, my friends, and the family He has given me. The list goes on and on of the many ways God demonstrates His love for me. When things go wrong, He assures me of His love and gently leads me back into His peace. It will take all of eternity to comprehend His love for me; we will always be learning and going deeper into His love. God is love and we are being made into His image. *And we, who with unveiled faces all reflect the Lord's glory, are being transformed into His likeness with ever increasing glory which comes from the Lord, who is the Spirit.*(2 Cor. 3:18) We are being made and transformed into having His attributes; love being the main one. Jesus told us the fulfilling of all God's commands was in the love we have for God and for one another. Jesus is coming for a bride that is perfectly joined in the spirit of love; the whole body fit together edifying itself together in love. John the great and beloved disciple, always would come back to the simplicity of little children. He saw the disciples of the Lord as "little children" and so are we in God's eyes

"Love one another, for God is love and everyone who loves knows God and is born of God." (1Jn.4:7)

PROVISION AND TRUST

*For the Lord our God is our light and protector. He gives grace and glory.
No good thing will the Lord withhold from those who do what is right. O Lord
happy are those who trust in You.* (Ps.84:11-12)

When we praise and worship the Lord, it should be the most natural
response from our hearts. It is a return of our love to the Father for all
He has done for us, an act of appreciation and of deep gratitude for His
constant love, provision, and protection. God has promised to provide
and care for us in every way. Happy are those who trust in the Lord.
When we are truly trusting in the Lord, He gives us the power and
wisdom to know how to do the right thing. You have placed yourself
into His hands and in the surrendering of your will over to Him, with
all love and sincerity of heart, that makes God most happy and faithful
to fulfill His part of His promise to us. He will not withhold any good
thing from the ones who have placed their full trust in Him and in the
promise of His Word.

*Praise the Lord, O my soul and all my inmost being, praise His Holy Name.
Praise the Lord, O my soul, and forget not all His benefit. He satisfies my desires
with good things, so that my youth is renewed like the eagles.* (Ps.103:1,5)

THE GIFT OF GOD

By the righteousness of one, the free gift came upon all men unto justification of life. (Rom. 5:18)

When I think about Jesus being the gift of God to us, I need to always come back to the realization that there isn't anything that I have, that I did not receive. When I think about all I have been given in life and in my salvation, it makes me wonder what can I give back to God to show my appreciation and love to Him? The Lord has done all this for us, flowing out of His heart of love for us, and because He Himself desires and receives pleasure from the relationship He has with us. So the answer to this question is that we give Him the gift of ourselves when we show our love for Him through worship, thanksgiving and praise. This is what pleases and gives our Father God His greatest delight, to know that we love and appreciate Him.

Eye has not seen, nor ear heard, neither have entered into the heart of man the things which God has prepared for them that love Him. (1 Cor. 2:9)

ALONE WITH GOD

When they were alone, He expounded all things to His disciples. (Mk. 4:10)

The Lord gives us understanding as we need it; it is a slow work and takes a whole lifetime for a man or woman to really see and understand their purpose. We think we know, but we really do not. We have to get to the end of ourselves, our own interpretations and theories, and allow the Lord to reveal it. When God gets us alone, He shows us the things within us that need changing. We know we are not worthy when we are in His Presence, it takes courage to look into the mirror that God shows us of ourselves. Once we see the problem, it takes time to make the necessary changes. It is especially true when we all want things instantly. The Lord desires to get alone with us so that He can expound to us the things that are needed and necessary for us to know in order to give us wisdom and guidance. Dear Lord, Here I am, please do whatever is needed to fulfill Your purpose and plan. Help me to clear my mind and sensitize my ears that I might hear You when You speak and receive Your wisdom and guidance in my life today. Help me to set aside time together with you each morning that I may build an ever growing and loving relationship with You. Take me into Your inner chambers each day and throughout each day where I may learn of You and of the purpose You have in mind for my life . . . Amen . . .

He who dwells in the secret place of the Most High, shall abide in the shadow of the Almighty. (Ps.91:1)

THE WHITE FUNERAL

We are buried with Him that even so we should also walk in the newness of life. (Rom. 6:4)

Can you remember when you died and were buried with Christ? Those of us who have experienced baptism after being born of the Spirit can recall the new and exciting feeling of being raised from the waters of baptism into the prospect of a life filled and guided by the love of the Lord. It was the death of the old life and nature, giving way to the new resurrected life we now have in Christ! It was a white funeral, one that was joyful and filled with our new found love for the Lord. There is always pain associated with dying, the death of anything brings a temporary pain, but because we know it is necessary for our greatest good and growth; the Lord give us grace and helps us to endure it. After the death comes the feeling of becoming newly invigorated, springs of new life rise up where there was once only desert ground. It still requires the painful peeling away of the old to make way for the new. It is a white funeral.

Do not conform any longer to the pattern of this world, but be transformed by the renewing of your mind. Then you will be able to test and approve what God's will is; His good, pleasing, and perfect will. (Rom. 12:2)

THE LILIES

If God so clothed the grass of the field, shall He not much more cloth you? (Matt. 6:30)

The lilies grow where they are planted. They take no thought or worry, yet when they reach maturity, they have the most wondrous color and beauty. God has set His Church, each one, in a chosen place. As we learn submission to the Spirit in us and are in right relationship to the Lord, we have contentment. It's easy to get our eyes upon what God may be doing in other people's lives. That is not what God wants us to do. In Him is all of our fullness of joy and contentment; He will take care and see to our growth. It is in putting our attention and focusing in upon the Lord that sets our lives in alignment with His will and purpose. As we do this, He does the work that allows for our growth and provision. When seeking Him first: giving Him priority in everything, we have rest and the assurance of His promise to complete and perfect everything that concerns us, today and forever. Our lives will reflect the beauty of the lilies.

Behold the fowls of the air: for they sow not, neither do they reap, nor gather into barns; yet your heavenly Father feeds them. Are you not much better than they? (Matt. 6:26)

WISDOM IN THE FORM OF A BABY

The Lord possessed me at the beginning of His work, before His deeds of old: I was appointed from eternity, from the beginning, before the world began. When there were no oceans, I was given birth, when there were no springs abounding with water; before the mountains were settled in place, before the hills, I was given birth. Before he made the earth or its fields or any of the dust of the world, I was there when He set the heavens in place; when He gave the sea its boundary so the waters would not overstep His command, and when He marked out the foundations of the earth. Then I was the craftsman at his side. I was filled with delight day after day, rejoicing always in his presence. Rejoicing in His whole world and delighting in mankind. (Prov. 8:22-31)

This same Christ, the Son of the father, the power of God incarnate, and the Wisdom of God, was given to us in the form of the babe that was born on that first Christmas morning.

Christ the power of God and the wisdom of God. (1 Cor. 1:24) *Christ Jesus who has become for us wisdom from God.* (1 Cor. 1:30)

December 4

THE FATHER SENT JESUS

I assure you, those who listen to my message and believe in God who sent me have eternal life. (Jn. 5:24)

Throughout the Lord's ministry upon earth, He would always and continually refer and point to "the Father who sent me." Jesus was doing the Fathers will in everything; He was completely obedient walking in the Father's perfect will. From the world's standpoint, they saw Jesus as someone from a town they were familiar with, whose parents and family they knew. So when Jesus spoke of doing His heavenly Father's will and saying "*I am the Son of God* and *The Father and I are one.*" (Jn.5:19) they thought Him to be mad or that he had a demon. However, they could not explain away the miracles and healings that Jesus did, nor could they stop the believing crowds from growing. What a controversial life that He lived! Jesus the Son of God being born, living and walking among us, as one of us! It was God the Father who sent Jesus and He did only those things that pleased the Father, but they loved their darkness more that the light that Jesus showed. They rejected the one whom the Father sent to save, set free, and bring them all into eternal life.

For God did not send His Son into the world to condemn the world, but to save the world through Him. (Jn. 3:17)

THE SILENCE OF GOD

Yet when He heard that Lazarus was sick, He stayed where He was for two more days. (Jn. 11:6)

The family of Lazarus did not understand the Lord's silence and His delay in coming to help after He had received the news of Lazarus' sickness. The Lord had a plan that no one was aware of. Many times when we ask the Lord to come and help, we only get silence and delay. Jesus loved this family, yet did not respond. Eventually He revealed the reason that no one could guess or understand. The raising of Lazarus from the dead showed to the world the undeniable power and authority that Jesus, God's Son had! Lazarus' family finally realized the Lord's purpose in the delay. When God is being silent and unresponsive to our cries for help; He wants you to trust Him and intends to reveal a spiritual truth or revelation. When we learn to quiet ourselves in stillness before Him and wait, over time, the answer will come. If we hear nothing but silence from God; that is the time to absorb it and allow His confidence to grow in you; knowing that He has heard you. God wants us to grow in maturity and learn to appreciate His silences. Everything that He does is for a greater purpose that He has in His mind. Trust Him in silence.

Be silent before the Lord, all mankind, for He has roused Himself from His holy dwelling. (Zec. 2:13)

December 6

VISION FROM GOD

Without a vision, the people perish. (Prov. 29:18)

The Lord gives us a vision: or puts something in our hearts and calls us into action. We in obedience, answer the call and do that thing (whatever it maybe). If we find that in the performing of it, God has not met us there, we have two choices; one, we can get discouraged, disheartened, and withdrawn; or even get angry, feeling misled or ignored by God. On the other hand, we can decide with our eyes of faith, to attempt to see the bigger picture that God has in His mind for us. The vision, the call, may be exactly correct, but your timing may not be in sync with His. As Oswald Chambers once said, "Our efforts and individualism needs to get swallowed up in personal relationship with Jesus Christ." Then God will confirm your work with the power and seal of His Holy Spirit. It is in the surrender of our plans that enable Him to work His plans, which will bring the ultimate fulfillment of the vision to our reality.

For you died and your life is now hidden with Christ in God. (Col. 3:3)

OUR MISSIONARY WORK

All authority is given unto me in heaven and in earth. Go therefore and teach all nations. (Matt. 28:18)

Not everyone is called to go as missionaries to foreign lands. Our foreign land may be our neighborhood. When we share our faith in Christ with others it should be out of our own living experiences. Jesus has all authority in heaven and in earth, when He tells us to go and share our faith in our missionary field, wherever that may be, He gives us authority and in His name we can be His witnesses to the people he places in our lives and that cross our paths. A witness can be with words or many times just in the way we live and act. Action speaks louder than any words we can say! As we grow in relationship with the Lord, His authority and power will be with us in greater and greater degrees. It is His Spirit within us that work to the salvation of souls. Whether in foreign lands or in our own neighborhoods, workplace, or school, we can show Christ to the world by our actions and by the words we say. We know that it is God's will that the world would be saved; everyone is called into the ministry of reconciliation.

He has committed to us the message of reconciliation. We are therefore Christ's ambassadors, as though God were making His appeal through us. (2 Cor.5:19-20)

PRAYER: THE GREATER WORK

Pray you therefore the Lord of the harvest, that He will send forth laborers into His harvest. (Matt. 9:38)

The key to missionary work is prayer, not work. When we pray to the Lord of the harvest, God will engineer the circumstances and send you forth. Many times we get caught up in the doing of various works, (even in the service of the church.) If we busy ourselves with too many things, it can dull our spiritual sensitivities. *Greater works than these shall he do, because I go unto my Father.* (Jn. 14:12) Prayer is the greater work because through strong relationship with the Lord, we receive the power and abilities to do what we could never do on our own. When you labor in prayer for the souls of men and women, and do it faithfully and consistently, results will come. We do not always see the results of our prayers, but when at long last the veil is lifted from our eyes, you will see and know the souls that have been reaped for God simply because you had been in the habit of faithful prayer.

Pray for each other, the prayer of a righteous man is powerful and effective. (Jas. 5:16)

JESUS FULLY GOD: FULLY MAN

That at the name of Jesus, every knee should bow of things in heaven and in things in earth; that every tongue should confess Jesus Christ to the glory of God the Father. (Phil. 2:10-11)

Jesus showed His humbleness as a man and His majesty in His divinity. These two qualities are forever united in Him. To understand the mystery of Jesus being fully God and fully man simultaneously is quite a lot to grasp. When the Holy Spirit comes to us, He enables us to understand a part of this great mystery. We get pictures of Jesus; seeing Him as a babe in a manger with Mary and Joseph as they stand in awe along with the shepherds at the meekness of the Savior of the world just newly born. Then there is Jesus calling His disciples to breakfast along the shores of the Sea of Galilee, once again showing His humbleness and servant's heart. At last we see Jesus as He appears to John on the isle of Patmos full of glory, power and majesty. One day we will see Him in the clouds of glory when He comes for us, then we'll see Him standing before us in meekness as our friend and Bridegroom—forever fully God, and forever fully man.

One generation will commend Your works to another; they will tell of Your mighty acts. They will speak of the glorious splendor of Your majesty. (Ps. 145:4-5)

GOD WITH US

The virgin will be with child and will give birth to a son, and they will call Him Immanuel—which means, God with us. (Matt.1:23)

God is now *with us;* He's with us in the smallest details and in the biggest challenges and trials. He was born on that first Christmas morning to be a living part of our lives and to be born into our hearts eternally. *God with us . . .* The Lord had given signs to the Jewish people through the Word of the Prophets going back to ancient times. Prior to the birth of Jesus, a sign was given through the prophet Isaiah that a virgin would conceive bringing forth the Christ. God chose Mary, out of all the Jewish maidens to give birth to the Messiah; she found favor with God, though she was blessed, she must have suffered greatly being unmarried and being *with child. The Lord Himself will give you a sign: The virgin will be with child and will give birth to a son, and will call him Immanuel.* (Is.7:14) In remembering these things, we cannot help but to be deeply grateful and in awe at the amazing gift of the Christ child to us and to the world. This is the true meaning of our celebration and worship at Christmas time.

Who, being in very nature God, did not consider equality with God something to be grasped, but made Himself nothing, taking the very nature of a servant, being made in human likeness, and being found in appearance as a man, He humbled Himself. (Phil. 2:6-8)

OVERSHADOWED BY THE SPIRIT

The Holy Spirit will come upon you, and the power of the Most High will overshadow you; so the Holy One to be born will be called the Son of God. (Lk.1:35)

When you and I place our faith in Jesus Christ and invite Him to come live within us, the Holy Spirit comes upon us, and the power of God overshadows us, and the life of Jesus is born within us, the spiritual life of Jesus in the Person of the Holy Spirit. It is the indwelling powerful Person of the Holy Spirit who sets me free from the bondages of sin. But the power I possess to live a life that is pleasing to God is directly related to how much I am able to surrender the control of my life to the guidance and direction of the Holy Spirit. My life can be overshadowed by the Holy Spirit in the measure that I give myself to it.

Blessed is she who has believed that what the Lord has said to her will be accomplished! And Mary said: "My soul praises the Lord and my spirit rejoices in God my Savior, for He has been mindful of the humble state of His servant." (Lk.1:45-48)

December 12

I AM THE LORD'S SERVANT

"I am the Lord's servant," Mary answered. "May it be to me as you have said." (Lk. 1:38)

Mary was blessed of all women because she believed God and was found to be lowly and humble in His sight. When she believed the words of Gabriel that the power of God would over shadow her, she humbly submitted and surrendered her whole life to do the will of God. The Lord seeks believing and humble souls to perform His will in great and small ways. Mary had the courage to say, *"May it be done as you have said."* We need courage sometimes to accept by faith and to humbly submit to do God's will. Mary's life was an example of humbleness and servitude. When we submit as the Lord's servant to do His will, His Holy Spirit will overshadow us and come to help us live a life that will be pleasing to God. Let us give the Lord full control so that we may have the power to live the life that pleases Him. Mary lived a life of praise and she rejoiced in her salvation. The Lord Jesus brought great joy to the world at His birth. He came as a humble servant. Let us follow our Lord's example and humbly serve one another. May Your will be done in me today, we will forever praise and find our hope and true joy in Him.

May Your Kingdom come, Your will be done on earth as it is in heaven. (Matt. 6:10)

DIVINE GUIDANCE

For this is our God forever and ever; He will be our guide even to the end. (Ps. 48:14)

We are always in need of guidance from the Lord; and He is forever faithful to lead us all the way until the very end of our days. Looking back over my life, I can see a divine plan and design being lived out through all the events of both happy and sorrowful times. I have found that God is consistent and has set boundaries for His people in order to lead them into divine life. Our consistency forever should be in our devotion to God. We cannot at all times live our lives in set patterns. There should always be room for variations depending upon the circumstances. We experience the freedom of being a child again, unfettered and breathing in newness of life each day as we learn to abandon ourselves to do His will. To find and become one with God's purpose for our lives is something everyone should pursue wholeheartedly. I think of the song The Long and Winding Road, by the Paul McCartney; the road we are traveling leads us back to the Father, our Creator God. So many lessons to be learned! He sees us through, helps and guides us in the process, always faithful, always loving and compassionate towards us. It is a challenge to respond and act right away when the Lord directs, because we tend to over analyze the situation, talk to others and get opinions without seeking His wisdom first. What God is after from us is simple and direct obedience to His leadings just as a child would do, simply trusting in His goodness.

Guide me in Your truth and teach me, for You are God my Savior, and my hope is in You all day long. (Ps. 5:8)

HUMILITY: THE HEART OF JESUS

Set your hearts on things above, where Christ is seated at the right hand of God. Set your minds on things above, not on earthly things; for you died, and your life is now hidden with Christ in God. When Christ, who is your life, appears, then you also will appear with Him in glory. (Col. 3:1-4)

Humility is the heart of Jesus; He opposes the proud, but gives grace to the humble. Our great and humble shepherd cares for you and He is able to hold all your worries and anxieties. Every day we need to cast our cares upon Him and know that He cares for us. Jesus is our Great Shepherd, though humble and meek, He is strong and mighty to protect us from the wolves and the danger of high cliffs. David speaks in the (Ps.23:1) *"The Lord is my shepherd, I shall not want. He leads us to green pastures and leads us besides quiet waters."* Jesus became a meek and mild little baby, taking the form of a humble servant. Let us have humble hearts and serve one another as He showed us to do by His example.

Humble yourselves, therefore, under God's mighty hand, that He may lift you up in due time. Cast all your anxiety on Him because He cares for you. (1 Pet. 5:7)

PROTESTING THE CALL OF GOD

The promise is for you and your children and for all who are far off—for all whom the Lord our God will call. (Ac.2:39)

The Lord calls all men and women with a divine calling, but not everyone responds and some do not hear or understand it at all. It is a unique call that is designed for each one differently, to fulfill a purpose that the Creator has planned for all who will answer. God does not always give us the choice as to where or under what circumstances we will serve Him. Sometimes we protest and do not go voluntarily, Jonah was an example of this; he was literally running from what God had called him to do. He was stubborn, rebellious, and had a very bad attitude; because of his disobedience, he suffered terrible consequences! There are times when we obey God out of fear of the recompense if we do not. *It is a dreadful thing to fall into the hands of the living God.* (Heb.10:3) It is right to fear God, but not in the sense of dread or of being afraid but in contrast, a healthy reverence and respect for Him. The call of God is like being on a mission; we are workers together with Him. There is joy we can find in service to the Lord, always keeping the Gospel of Jesus Christ crucified as the central and motivating factor in all we do. No matter what the enemy does to try to hinder and discourage you, the Lord places His seal on you and confirms His call on your life. As you continue to move forward, His plan and call will be fulfilled even though at times you protest.

Turn to me and be saved, all you ends of the earth, for I am God, and there is no other. (Isa. 45:22)

December 16

UNITED FOREVER

Who shall separate us from the love of Christ? Shall trouble, or hardship, or persecution, or famine, or danger, or nakedness or sword? (Rom.8:35)

When we are faced with trouble, distress, danger, or in the middle of great turmoil, there is an opportunity to lean into the love of God. Those are the times that we might feel that we do not love Him; always remember and bring to your mind His unending, never changing love for us. In the middle of whatever you may be going through, nothing can separate us from His love. We can rise up victorious every time when we call to mind His love and promise that He will never leave us nor forsake us. It does not matter how great the pain or suffering you may be experiencing, He will walk with you through it all and you will come out the other side victorious. When the world and the people around you see this, they wonder and will be able to get a glimpse of God's great power at work through your example. The Lord reminds us in Isaiah that we should not fear, for He has redeemed us and we belong to Him. This is very comforting scripture:

Fear not, for I have redeemed you; I have called you by name. When you walk through the waters I will be with you, and when you pass through the rivers, they shall not pass over you. When you walk through the fi re, you will not be burned; the flames will not set you ablaze. For I am the Lord, your God, the Holy one of Israel, your Savior. (Isa. 43:2-3)

JESUS: OUR HUMBLE SHEPHERD

He tends His flock like a shepherd: He gathers the lambs in His arms and carries them close to His heart; He gently leads those that have young. (Isa. 40:11)

Jesus, our Shepherd, gently cares for His people and watches over all. He is the good Shepherd who holds us close to His heart and will one day gather us all up into His arms. On the night of His birth, the angels appeared to the shepherds and chose them to first proclaim the birth of the Christ child. The shepherds were considered the lowliest in Jewish society. From the very beginning at His birth, Jesus showed His humility in every way. Jesus our humble King, servant of all, born in the lowliest way, in the most humble of circumstances, later exalted to the highest, and we having the promise that one day He will appear again and with us (the Church) along with Him in glory. We will wear a crown of glory that will never fade away. What a promise! And how comforting are those words of Scripture!

When the Chief Shepherd appears, you will receive the crown of glory that will never fade away. Clothe yourselves with humility toward one another, because, God opposes the proud but gives grace to the humble. (I Pet. 5:4-5)

THE LAW IS PERFECT

The law of the Lord is perfect, reviving the soul. The statutes of the Lord are trustworthy, making wise the simple. The precepts of the Lord are right, giving joy to the heart. The commands of the Lord are radiant, giving light to the eyes. (Ps. 19:7-8)

The challenge we face as Christians today; is how to apply these precepts and statues of God's law practically and consistently to our daily lives. We begin to read and meditate upon the Word, and continue for awhile making progress, but then get distracted and drawn away by other activities and attractions. This is a problem that many can relate to; it is a great encouragement to know that the Lord is forever faithful and He never gives up on us. Be patient, there is an appointed time, He will do it in us, trust in the Word of His promise. When we do our part and really prioritize the reading and meditating upon His Word, knowing that every promise is written for you: He is forever faithful to do His part. We are not perfect, life as we know it, is not perfect, but His laws, His Words are absolutely perfect. When we take it seriously, they will bring joy to our hearts and light into our eyes.

The ordinances of the Lord are sure and altogether righteous. They are more precious than gold, than much fi ne gold; they are sweeter than honey, than honey from the comb. By them is your servant warned; in keeping them there is great reward. (Ps.19:9-11)

December 19

LITTLE TOWN OF BETHLEHEM

But you, Bethlehem Ephrathah, though you are small among the clans of Judah, out of you will come for me one who will be ruler over Israel, whose origins are from of old, from ancient times. (Mic. 5:2)

Our Lord came to the earth born in the little town of Bethlehem in the most humble of circumstances. The gentle shepherd king who came seeking the lost, He was filled with humility from His birth and throughout His entire life. He knew that His mission was to be the Lamb of God sacrificed for the sins of the whole world. He accomplished this mission perfectly and completely, fulfilling every prophecy that was long ago foretold. Bethlehem, the city of David, lies five miles south of Jerusalem. Here Jesus Christ was born of the Virgin Mary in a manger: *And she gave birth to her firstborn, a son. She wrapped him in cloths and placed him in a manger, because there was no room for them in the inn.* (Lk. 2:7) I can remember a time when I had no room for Jesus in my life, my heart was unresponsive to the love, grace, and mercy of God. Many times people have to go through much pain and suffering before they are able to make room for the Savior and invite Him into their hearts and lives.

After Jesus was born in Bethlehem in Judea, during the time of King Herod, Magi from the east came to Jerusalem and asked, "Where is the one who has been born king of the Jews? We saw His star in the east and have come to worship Him." (Matt. 2:1-2)

JESUS: THE LION KING

The Lion of the tribe of Judah, the Root of David, has triumphed. (Rev. 5:5)

Our humble Sheppard king will be returning as the triumphant Lion of Judah to reign upon the Throne of David, and of His Righteous Kingdom there will be no end. The coming of the Lord will be a day of vengeance, a year of divine retribution: to uphold, defend, and to justify His Church. *For the Lord has a day of vengeance, a year of retribution to uphold Zion's cause.* (Is. 34:8) The Lion of the tribe of Judah, Jesus the Christ, has triumphed! All who believe and have put their complete trust in Him share in this victory today. We know that every Word of Scripture will be fulfilled. Jesus came as gentle lamb; He will be coming again as a roaring Lion, our conquering King in glory and power. This Christmas as we celebrate His birth and His willingness to become our sacrificed Lamb, let us also contemplate His return as our Great Rescuer, and Conquering King, The Lion from the Tribe of Judah coming to uphold the righteous cause of His Church.

Return to us, O God Almighty. (Ps. 80:14)

GOOD TIDINGS OF GREAT JOY

Behold, I bring you good tidings of great joy, which shall be to all people, for unto you is born this day in the City of David a Savior. (Lk. 2:10-11)

Angels from the Lord brought the news first to the shepherds that were tending the flocks in the fields. They were poor men of low estate, yet the announcement of the Messiahs birth was brought to them first. The angel goes on to say *"Today in the town of David, a Savior has been born to you: He is Christ the Lord."* (Lk.2:11) Christ was born to us. The long awaited Messiah, Savior, and Redeemer had arrived at last and there proclaimed to the meek and humble shepherds *good tidings of great joy.* This Word of peace and goodwill had come to all of mankind at the birth of Jesus. Heaven has sent us infinite joy in the form of a little baby; we may say that it is a lasting joy, a joy that will live forever. It rings all down through all the ages. For when God sent forth the angel in his brightness to say, *"I bring you good tidings of great joy, which shall be to all people,"* He did as much as say, from this time forward, it shall be joy to the sons of men; there shall be goodwill to the human race and peace with men forever and ever, and God's glory will be seen by everyone.

His name shall be called Wonderful, Counselor, the Mighty God, the Everlasting Father, the Prince of Peace. (Isa. 9-6)

UNINTERRUPTED JOY FOREVER

The ransomed of the Lord will return. They will enter Zion with singing; everlasting joy will crown their heads. Gladness and joy will overtake them, and sorrow and sighing will flee away. (Isa. 35:10)

Those redeemed of the Lord are promised everlasting joy and gladness in a future day when all sorrow and sighing will flee away. Uninterrupted Joy is what we are promised and what we have as our future hope. In our world today, we still go through the trials and sorrows but at the same time, we can experience an inner joy in knowing that God has things under control. As we trust Him more and more, He leads us into that everlasting joy that will never end. We also joy in our salvation. *Though you have not seen Him, you love Him; and even though you do not see Him now, you believe in Him and are filled with an inexpressible and glorious joy, for you are receiving the goal of your faith the salvation of your souls.* (1 Pet. 1:8) It is clear that Jesus came to bring us joy, that our joy may be complete in him. May the joy that the shepherds felt that first Christmas evening, be alive in our hearts today as we ponder the advent of the Savior.

"I have told you this so that my joy may be in you and that your joy may be complete." (Jn. 15:11) *"I am coming to you now, but I say these things while I am still in the world, so that they may have the full measure of my joy within them."* (Jn. 17:13)

WORSHIP THE CHRIST

Come, let us bow down in worship, and let us kneel before the Lord our Maker. (Ps. 95:6)

The star that the Magi saw was a star that represented the birth of a king. (The King of Israel) *Magi: A Zoroastrian priestly caste of the Medes and Persians*—they traveled from faraway lands to search for the one who was Christ the Messiah to worship Him. The Magi may have not known the Hebrew Scriptures that spoke of the coming King of Israel that was to be born in Bethlehem or where to find Him, but they followed the star that proclaimed to them that a King, the Christ of God would be born into the world and that the reason for their journey was to come and worship Him. At Christmas time, we now can revisit the Bethlehem that lives in our hearts. The place where Jesus comes to be born and to dwell: and like the Magi and the shepherds, we come to worship the Savior, Messiah.

Ascribe to the Lord the glory due His name. Bring an offering and come before Him: worship the Lord in the splendor of His holiness. (1 Ch. 16:29)

A CHILD IS BORN

For to us a child is born, to us a Son is given, and the government will be on His shoulders. And He will be called Wonderful Counselor, Mighty God, Everlasting Father, and Prince of Peace. Of the increase of His government and peace there will be no end. (Isa. 9:6-7)

Jesus is worthy of all of our worship and adoration as we wonder about the amazing incarnation of the child born in Bethlehem that first Christmas morning. When a woman is about to give birth and goes into labor, it is painful. After the child is born, the pain is also gone and the memory of it soon disappears for the joy of having given birth. It is similar in our Christian lives; before we come into faith and are born of the Spirit, many times we experience pain. Pains from the result of living outside the will of God; the sins that separate us from Him produce pain. Once we have surrendered and given our hearts to the Lord, we forget the pain and rejoice in the fact that we have been forgiven and now have eternal life in Him. Let us go to the Bethlehem that lives in our hearts, and worship the Christ child today.

Suddenly a great company of the heavenly host appeared with the angel, praising God and saying, Glory to God in the highest, and on earth peace to men on whom His favor rests. When the angels had left them and gone into heaven, the shepherds said to one another, "Let's go to Bethlehem and see this thing that has happened, which the Lord has told us about." (Lk. 2:13-15)

THE GIFT OF GOD TO THE WORLD

The Word became flesh and dwelt among us, and we beheld His glory, the glory as of the only begotten of the Father, full of grace and truth. (Jn. 1:14)

To begin to understand the gift of God in sending Jesus to earth as the babe born of Mary and Joseph, we first need to take our minds and imaginations back to a time when there was no time; to the day when the Father begot His only Son. In Psalms we see a picture of this: The Father speaking to the Son saying, *"You are my Son, today, I have become your Father. Ask of me, and I will make the nations your inheritance, the ends of the earth your possession."*(Ps. 2:7-8) Jesus, the Son of God, begotten of the Father. The Hebrew Strong's Concordance definition: *begotten: to bear young, birth, to show lineage, beget, be delivered of child. To be brought forth into being, wrought:* Jesus the Son was born from God the Father. It was the heavens that declared the glory of God to the Magi and spoke of the King that was to be born into the world. It gives us some sense of the great gift and sacrifice made for us in the birth of Jesus. The King of Kings, only begotten Son of the Father: the Wisdom of God became a human baby, the gift of God the Father; His only begotten Son to the world.

Therefore the Lord Himself will give you a sign: the virgin will be with child and will give birth to a son, and will call Him Immanuel. (Isa. 7:14)

Decenber 26

COME UNTO ME

"The Spirit and the Bride say come! All who will may come and drink of the waters of life freely." (Rev.22:17)

Jesus bids us to come. The living water of life is a gift to us and Jesus bids us to drink of it and live. The Lord invites us to join Him, He invites us to come and receive divine life and blessing. By an act of our faith, we drink of the water of life; our part if we *will* is to simply *come*. Why is it that so many people hesitate and hold back from receiving this gift from God? It is because we fear what we do not know or are familiar with. To come to the Lord, our hearts need to be humbled and able to recognize our need and our thirst for the living water. The desires for the things of this world, the cares and riches of the world, blind many people from seeking the true riches that God wants to give. False teaching and religions keep people from understanding the truth of God's Word. *He sent His servants to those who had been invited to the banquet to tell them to come, but they refused to come.* (Mt. 22:3) The door is being held open but one day it will close and there will be those locked outside left in the dark. The invitation stands today; the grace of God covers the earth and everyone in it. Do not neglect so great a salvation. The Lord bids you to *"Come."*

Our salvation is nearer now than when we first believed. The night is nearly over; the day is almost at here. (Rom. 13:11-12)

HOLY IS THE LORD

Who is like You O Lord? Who is like You in majestic holiness, awesome in glory, working wonders? (Ex. 15:11)

We can sense the holiness of God when we come into the awareness of the sin and depravity within our own souls and human nature. The contrast of our existence on this physical plane of life verses the holiness of Almighty God; even when we are at our very best, we should be compelled to fall down upon our knees. When John was on the Isle of Patmos, while in the spirit on the Lord's Day, he heard a voice; he turned and saw Jesus in His majesty. He fell at His feet as though dead. In this world, there is a veil over our eyes, if God were to remove it suddenly, we may fall over dead! In God's mercy and gentleness, He reveals little bits at a time, and no more than what we can bear. When the Lord gives us of Himself and reveals His holy presence, we desire for more and more. It is because He is so glorious! It also makes us more keenly aware of our sins and shortcomings, which in turn causes us to desire holiness. *Just as He who called you is holy, so be holy in all you do, for it is written: be holy, because I am holy.* (1 Pet. 1:15-16) Jesus is purifying His Church, making us a holy people. We shall be like Him, for we shall see Him as He is. We should always remember His holiness when approaching Him; holiness is what and who God is.

Exalt the Lord our God and worship at His holy mountain, for the Lord our God is holy. (Ps. 99:9)

ENCOURAGEMENT

After the readings from the Law and the Prophets, the synagogue rulers sent word to them, saying, "Brothers, if you have a message of encouragement for the people, please speak." (Ac.13:15)

The men of Israel and some of the Gentiles were gathered to hear the words of Paul and Barnabas; they desired words of encouragement. As a result of their sharing the gospel of Jesus, many were converted and they were urged to stay, continuing in the grace of God. They were only obeying what the Lord had commissioned them to do, and by doing it, they were filled with joy and with the Holy Spirit. (Acts 13:52) They experienced this in spite of the jealously and persecution that was stirred up in the process. Paul was asked to speak; many times the Lord is asking us to speak a word or two in a given situation that would serve to bring encouragement to someone. When we obey, the Holy Spirit fills us with the words and with joy. We all have something that God wants us to do; it is designed for you and you alone. Paul and the early disciples had a unique role in the forming of the early church. We all have a unique role as well in this generation. It may be that some people will not agree or understand; we learn to count it as joy, and continue to bring encouraging words, and to be an encouragement to others that need it.

May the God who gives endurance and encouragement give you a spirit of unity among yourself as you follow Christ Jesus. (Rom. 15:5)

December 29

SEEK AND SEARCH

Those who know Your name trust in You. For You O Lord have never abandoned anyone who searches for You. (Ps. 9:10)

The Webster's Dictionary defines: search: *To make a thorough examination of: or look carefully in order to find something: explore in order to find something lost or concealed: to come to know; learn, and probe.* The more we seek and search for the Lord, the more we know about the Lord, the more we know that we can trust Him, and that He is good. We discover His character and ways. Over time we can look back over our lives and see His hand at work making Himself known by His faithfulness. Still at times it seems as though God is hidden away from us and is silent. We know He hears us when we pray but the question I am wondering about is are we really searching and seeking for Him? There is a kingdom that resides in the heart of every believer, as in heaven, so in earth. Seek and search for that hidden kingdom that resides in your heart, where true and everlasting treasure can be found.

The kingdom of heaven is like a treasure hidden in a field. When a man found it, he hid it again, and then in his joy went and sold all he had and bought that field. Again, the kingdom of heaven is like a merchant looking for fi ne pearls. When he found one of great value, he went away and sold everything he had and bought it. (Matt. 13:44-45)

THE ANTIDOTE FOR DEPRESSION

Arise and eat. So he got up and ate and drank. Strengthened by that food, he traveled forty days and forty nights until he reached Horeb, the mountain of God. (1 Kings 19:5-8)

Elijah was at a very low point during this time when he cried to the Lord: *"The Israelites have rejected Your covenant, broken down Your altars, and put your prophets to death with the sword. I am the only one left, and now they are trying to kill me too."* (1 Kings 19:10) He had plenty of reason to feel depressed, but by doing the simplest thing as arising to eat, prompted by the angel of the Lord, he was strengthened to move forward to the mountain where God communicated His plan to Elijah. When we get up and arise to obey even the smallest thing that is at hand, we immediately begin to sense relief and start to move forward to receive further instruction from God. It is initiative that God uses to prompt us into action that lifts the depression. Depression is a part of our human condition in a fallen world that we experience from time to time; but it is through taking the initiative to be obedient to do the task closest at hand, no matter how small, that is an antidote against it.

Let us not become weary in doing good for in the proper time we will reap a harvest if we do not give up. (Gal. 6:9)

LORD OF HEAVEN AND EARTH

Acknowledge and take to heart this day that the Lord is God in heaven above and on the earth below. There is no other. (Dt. 4:39)

God is the Lord over all creation, nothing is out of His control, there is nothing He hasn't foreseen and planned. God reveals His plan to us as we go through time. We receive revelation from God through scripture and through His Holy Spirit that has been given to us. He already sees the end, the finished product; love perfected in us. We on the other hand, see the flaws, and find ourselves struggling to make sense of it all. If only we could learn to trust and believe more in Him and in His wisdom and rely less on our own devises. It is God's joy to bless us with the peace we find in knowing Him; He Himself is our great reward and prize if only we would believe and trust Him. We serve a God with all power and authority; He is wisdom itself and He is good. This is the God we surrender to. He holds all of life itself and every living creature that has breath in His hand, He has purchased us with His own blood and we are His.

Let them know that You, whose name is the Lord, that You alone are Most High over all the earth. (Ps. 83:18)

SUCH LOVE

"Surely, I will be with you always, to the very end of the age." Matthew 28:20

Your arms were made to hold
The joys and sorrows of the world.
The depth of Your love can never be told;
It is mysterious and boundless, infinite, love.

Such love, such great deep love . . .
No words can describe.
The beauty of Your presence,
Here in my heart forever to reside.

Grace and love is what You've shown
Changing the old into the new;
All of the past; like a bird that has flown.
I am moving toward the future that You hold.
You searched for me, rescued me
And gave me a life worth living.
Nothing in this world compares to Your love
That never stops giving.

Now all I want to do is to live for You;
To sing Your praises loud and clear,
Right now, and all my tomorrows
I want to hold You near.

Such love, such great deep love
No words can describe;
The beauty of Your Presence
Here in my heart, forever to reside . . .

ABOUT THE AUTHOR

My devotional reading group, called Hearts in Devotion, began in 2005 when a girlfriend and I would get together every Friday afternoon and read A. W. Tozer. As time went by, more of our friends from our church (North Coast Calvary Chapel in Carlsbad, California) joined our reading group, and in a few years H.I.D. grew to about two hundred members who shared devotionals of the classic and modern Christian authors online via e-mail. The name Hearts in Devotion (H.I.D.) was based upon the scripture: Colossians 3:3-4, that tells us our lives are *hidden* in Christ and that when he appears, we shall also appear with Him in glory.

This book is a compilation of original devotionals that I wrote during that time. My spiritual journey began when I was twenty-one years old. I spent the next ten years searching for the meaning of love, life, and creation through New Age meditation and in the beauty found in nature while traveling and hiking around Northern California and Arizona. I always believed in Jesus as a child, but did not know or understand the Bible until I was invited to attend an evangelical church, where, for the first time, I heard the gospel message. I have never been the same since.

Thirty years have gone by, and the Lord has been so faithful through many ups and downs in my life. Today, I live in Carlsbad, California, with my husband and our Maltese dog, Amore. I continue to work with the Women's Ministries at North Coast Calvary Chapel. I also write lyrics and create oil paintings that are inspired by my faith and by biblical scriptures.